300

FROGS

300

FROGS

Chris Mattison

A Visual Reference to Frogs and Toads from Around the World

FIREFLY BOOKS

A FIREFLY BOOK

Published by Firefly Books Ltd. 2007

First printing

Publisher Cataloging-in-Publication Data (U.S.)

Mattison, Christopher.
    300 frogs : frogs and toads from around the world / Chris Mattison.
[528] p. : col. photos. ; cm.
Includes bibliographical references and index.
Summary: An illustrated account of 300 representative species and forms of frogs and toads from all parts of the world, including fact panels and details of their behavior and other aspects of their natural history.
ISBN-13: 978-1-55407-246-0
ISBN-10: 1-55407-246-8
1. Frogs – Identification.   2. Toads – Identification. I. Three hundred frogs. II. Title.
597.89 dc22   QL668.E2.M388 2007

Library and Archives Canada Cataloguing in Publication

Mattison, Christopher
    300 frogs : frogs and toads from around the world / Chris Mattison.

Includes bibliographical references and index.
ISBN-13: 978-1-55407-246-0
ISBN-10: 1-55407-246-8
    1. Frogs. 2. Toads. I. Title. II. Title: Three hundred frogs.
QL668.E2M33 2006   597.8'9   C2006-904853-3

Published in the United States by
Firefly Books (U.S.) Inc.
P.O. Box 1338, Ellicott Station
Buffalo, New York 14205

Published in Canada by
Firefly Books Ltd.
66 Leek Crescent
Richmond Hill, Ontario L4B 1H1

For The Brown Reference Group plc:
Editorial Director: Lindsey Lowe
Project Editor: Graham Bateman
Editor: Virginia Carter
Design: Steve McCurdy

Page 1: Common Frog *(Rana temporaria)*.
Pages 2–3: Male Painted Reed Frog *(Hyperolius marmorata)*.
Page 5: Green form of Strawberry Poison Dart Frog
    (Dendrobates pumllio).

Cover Photos

Front Cover: Lemur Leaf Frog *(Phyllomedusa lemur)*
    © Michael Fogden.
Spine: Blue Poison Dart Frog *(Dendrobates azureus)*
    © K. L. Kohn/Shutterstock.
Back: Argus Reed Frog *(Hyperolius argus)*
    © EcoPrint/Shutterstock.

Printed in China

Contents

CONTENTS

CONTENTS

Introduction

Frogs and toads are the most abundant and familiar amphibians. They make themselves known to us by croaking or calling, especially in the breeding season. Many have names that describe their voices, such as Bullfrog, Pig Frog, Barking Frog, Spring Peeper, and Blacksmith Frog.

Many species have big bulging eyes and a wide grin, making them appear "friendly," and few people dislike them in the same way that they dislike lizards and snakes, for example. Toads sometimes receive a bad press, however, mainly because of the sinister connotations they acquired during the Middle Ages, when they were associated with witchcraft.

Frogs or Toads?

Strictly speaking, there is no real difference between frogs and toads; all of them are known to scientists as anurans. In plain English, however, we usually reserve the term toad for dry, warty species that run or walk. Many of them belong to the family Bufonidae, but toads are also found in other families. Frogs have smooth damp skins, live near water, and they leap. There are exceptions to this rule, though, and some families contain species that are variously called frogs or toads. It is less confusing to think of *all* the tailless amphibians as frogs and use the word toad for members of certain families such as the Bufonidae.

Frog Diversity

At the latest count there were more than 5,400 species of frogs and toads (order Anura). They account for some 90 percent of amphibians (class Amphibia)— the other groups being about 550 species of newts and salamanders (order Caudata) and 173 species of caecilians (order Gymnophiona).

Frogs and toads are traditionally divided into 29 families, although recent research has indicated that this number is probably too low. Here we have taken a conservative view, while acknowledging that major changes to frog classification are likely to occur over the next few years (see pages 18 to 19). In *300 Frogs* representatives of most families are included.

Some families contain just one species; others have several hundred. Whereas some families are found around the world, others are restricted to very small regions. The Mexican Burrowing Frog *(Rhinophrynus dorsalis)*, for example, is in a family of its own and lives only along the coastal plain that links southern Texas with adjacent parts of northeast Mexico. Several other families contain only two to 10 species—relics of families that were probably more widespread in former times but are now reduced to small populations as other, more efficient species evolved to replace them.

One of the most successful families is the Bufonidae, with more than 400 species. Its members occur on every continent except Antarctica, although there is only one species—the Cane Toad *(Bufo marinus)*—in Australia, and that has been introduced by humans. Another successful family is the tree frogs (Hylidae), with more than 800 species scattered

↪ *A representative of the large family Hylidae is the Clown Tree Frog* (Hyla triangulum). *© Arthur Georges.*

↓ *The Cane Toad* (Bufo marinus) *belongs to another successful family, the Bufonidae.*

throughout most parts of the world but absent from much of the African continent.

Tropical regions are home to the greatest numbers of species. A few acres of tropical forest in South America may contain as many as 80 species—roughly the same number as in the whole of the United States. Other regions with high species diversity include the island of Madagascar, where nearly every species is endemic (restricted to one small region), and West Africa where, in addition to the high numbers already recorded, new species are surely awaiting discovery.

Tropical forests are ideal places for frogs because the conditions are warm and moist and there are plenty of hiding places and plenty of food in the form of insects and other small invertebrates. On the other hand, an abundance of frogs attracts an abundance of predators, so tropical frogs have evolved some ingenious methods of protecting themselves.

With such a large number of species it is no surprise to find that frogs and toads are extremely diverse in shape, size, and color, as well as in lifestyle. The largest species is the Goliath Frog *(Conraua goliath)* from West Africa, which grows to 14.5 inches (36.8 cm) from its snout to the end of its back and can weigh as much as 8 lb (3.66 kg).

There are several contenders for the title of smallest species, but it is often considered to be the

⊕ *The brightly colored Blue Poison Dart Frog* **(Dendrobates azureus)** *is a highly toxic species.*

Cuban Leaf-litter Frog *(Sminthillus limbatus),* which grows to about 0.4 inches (1 cm) in length. There are several other very small species including the rain frogs *(Eleutherodactylus* species). Newly hatched Gardiner's Frogs *(Sooglossus gardineri)* from the Seychelles are about the size of a grain of rice.

Frogs and toads may be colorful or dull. Most are camouflaged, or cryptic, so they are difficult for predators to spot. Depending on where they live, cryptic frogs may be brown, gray, or green. Some, such as the Asian Horned Toad *(Megophrys nasuta),* are even

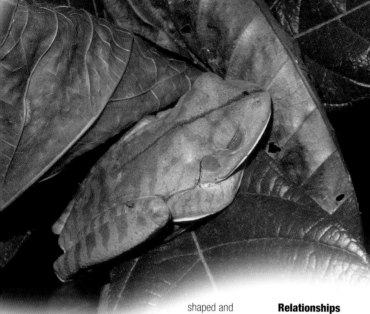

⬅ *A Smith Frog (Hyla faber) mimics a dead leaf.*

⬇ *Warning coloration in the Oriental Fire-bellied Toad (Bombina orientalis).*

shaped and colored to resemble dead leaves; as a result, they are almost invisible when resting on the forest floor.

Others are bright shades of red, orange, yellow, or even blue. These are poisonous species whose colors warn predators that their skin contains toxic substances. The Golden Poison Dart Frog *(Phyllobates terribilis)* is the most poisonous animal known—its skin contains enough poison to kill up to 1,000 humans. Frogs and toads often combine camouflage colors on their upper surface with bright warning colors on their underside—the Oriental Fire-bellied Toad *(Bombina orientalis)* is a good example.

Relationships

Fossils bearing similarities to living frogs are about 150 million years old, although the ancestors of frogs probably first appeared in the Triassic Period more than 250 million years ago. As these animals were exploring new evolutionary pathways, Earth's landmasses were dividing and drifting apart. Some groups that were late arrivals became isolated, while others had already spread to every region and were carried around the world on the new continents. This explains the different distribution patterns of families,

Skin folds on the Lake Titicaca Frog (Telmatobius culeus) *help it absorb oxygen.*

A Small Red-eyed Leaf Frog (Agalychnis saltator) *in a bromeliad plant high in a forest canopy.*

Male Hairy Frogs (Trichobatrachus robustus) *grow "hairs" during the breeding season.*

some of which have small ranges, while others are more widespread. Species that have common ancestors are grouped together in families. The most "primitive" families are lumped together as the Archaeobatrachia, and the more recently evolved families make up a group known as the Neobatrachia (see Table on pages 18 to 19).

Frog Habitats

Frogs and toads have moved into a surprising number of different types of habitats, and many have evolved special adaptations to get around some of the limitations. Because they rely heavily on water to keep their skin moist and for breeding in, frogs and toads are most common around rivers, streams, lakes, ponds, and swamps. Many typically inhabit the water's edge,

feeding and basking within one leap of safety. Others, such as most members of the tongueless frog family, Pipidae and the Lake Titicaca Frog *(Telmatobius coleus)*, are completely aquatic and spend their whole life in the water. These species have heavily webbed hind feet and other adaptations to an aquatic lifestyle.

Other frogs live in fast-flowing streams, torrents, or waterfalls. African ghost frogs *(Heleophryne* species), for example, hide away in rocky crevices behind waterfalls and emerge to feed at night. They have huge

pads on their toes so they can cling to wet and slippery rocks, and their tadpoles have a suckerlike mouth so they are not swept away. In West Africa the Hairy Frog (Trichobatrachus robustus) also breeds in highland streams. Males of this species increase their breathing efficiency during the breeding season by growing long fingers of skin, or "hairs," along the back and thighs.

In the tropics many regions are permanently humid, and frogs do not need to be in or near water to keep their skin moist. That is why these regions have the greatest numbers of species. Rain forest frogs may be found high up in the canopy, in bushes, on the ground, or in burrows. By varying the exact places in which they live many species can coexist in a small area.

The remaining frog habitats include grasslands, mountains, deserts, and urban environments. None of these have very many different species in them, but frogs that live there often have interesting adaptations. Species from habitats that are dry for part of the year often burrow down into the ground and estivate to avoid drying out. Some of them form cocoons in mud, which bakes hard around them, and emerge onto the surface again only when heavy rain moistens the mud and provides them with temporary pools and puddles in which to breed. The Painted-belly Leaf Frog, or Waxy Frog (Phyllomedusa sauvagii), from the dry chaco region of South America does not hide away in the dry season. It remains in the bushes and covers itself with a waxy substance secreted from its skin glands.

Species from high altitudes are often dark in color so that they absorb more heat and at the same time protect themselves from ultraviolet radiation. The

Who's Who Among the Frogs and Toads?

29-FAMILY CLASSIFICATION

Suborder Archaeobatrachia

Ascaphidae: tailed frogs

Leiopelmatidae: New Zealand frogs

Bombinatoridae: fire-bellied toads

Discoglossidae: painted frogs and midwife toads

Megophryidae: Asian horned toads and litter frogs

Pelobatidae: spadefoot toads

Pelodytidae: parsley frogs

Pipidae: clawed and Surinam toads

Rhinophrynidae: Mexican Burrowing Frog

Suborder Neobatrachia

Heleophrynidae: ghost frogs

Limnodynastidae: Australian ground frogs

Myobatrachidae: Australian toadlets and water frogs

Sooglossidae: Seychelles frogs

Leptodactylidae: rain frogs

Bufonidae: true toads and harlequin toads

Brachycephalidae: three-toed toadlets

Dendrobatidae: poison dart frogs

Rhinodermatidae: gastric-brooding frogs

Hylidae: tree frogs, marsupial frogs, and leaf frogs

Pseudidae: paradoxical frogs

Centrolenidae: glass frogs

Allophrynidae: (Ruthen's Frog)

Ranidae: water frogs and pool frogs

Arthroleptidae: bush squeakers

Hemisotidae: shovel-nosed frogs

Hyperoliidae: reed frogs and relatives

Rhacophoridae: Afro-Asian tree frogs

Mantellidae: mantellas and relatives

Microhylidae: narrow-mouthed frogs

44-FAMILY CLASSIFICATION

Archaeobatrachia

Alytidae (11 species, 2 genera)*. Formerly part of Discoglossidae minus species moved to Bombinatoridae (Discoglossidae no longer recognized).

Bombinatoridae (10 species, 2 genera). Formerly part of Discoglossidae, which is no longer recognized.

Leiopelmatidae (6 species, 2 genera). New Zealand frogs plus Ascaphidae, which is no longer recognized.

Mesobatrachia

Megophryidae (134 species, 11 genera). Unchanged.

Pelobatidae (4 species, 1 genera). Now limited to Old World species—7 New World species moved to Scaphopodidae.

Pelodytidae (3 species, 1 genera). Unchanged.

Pipidae (31 species, 5 genera). Unchanged.

Rhinophrynidae (1 species). Unchanged.

Scaphopodidae (7 species, 2 genera)*. Formerly part of Pelobatidae and limited to New World species.

Neobatrachia

Amphignathodontidae (57 species, 2 genera)*. Marsupial frogs, formerly part of Hylidae.

Aromobatidae (88 species, 5 genera)*. Formerly part of Dendrobatidae.

Arthroleptidae (128 species, 8 genera). Unchanged, although once part of Ranidae.

Batrachophrynidae (6 species, 3 genera)*. Formerly part of Leptodactylidae.

Brachycephalidae (793 species, 17 genera). As before, plus *Eleutherodactylus* and related genera that were formerly part of Leptodactylidae.

Brevicipitidae (26 species, 5 genera)*. Formerly part of Microhylidae.

Bufonidae (485 species, 47 or more genera). Unchanged.

Centrolenidae (140 species, 4 genera). As before plus *Allophryne ruthveni* (Allophrynidae no longer recognized).

Ceratobatrachidae (82 species, 6 genera)*. Formerly part of Ranidae.

Ceratophryidae (81 species, 7 genera)*. Formerly part of Leptodactylidae.

Cryptobatrachidae (21 species, 2 genera)*. Formerly part of Hylidae.

Cycloramphidae (96 species, 13 genera)*. Species formerly part of Leptodactylidae plus *Rhinoderma* (Rhinodermatidae no longer recognized).

Dendrobatidae (161 species, 11 genera). As before minus species moved to Aromobatidae.

Dicroglossidae (151 species, 2 genera)* Formerly part of Ranidae.

Heleophrynidae (6 species, 1 genus). Unchanged.

Hemiphractidae (6 species, 1 genus)*. Formerly part of Hylidae.

Hemisotidae (9 species, 1 genus). Unchanged.

Hylidae (814 species, 46 genera). As before minus 57 species moved to Amphignathodontidae plus all species from Pseudidae, which is no longer recognized.

Hylodidae (37 species, 3 genera)*. Formerly part of Leptodactylidae.

Hyperoliidae (198 species, 17 genera). Unchanged.

Leiuperidae (75 species, 7 genera)*. Formerly part of Leptodactylidae.

Leptodactylidae (91 species, 4 genera). As before minus many species moved to new families.

Limnodynastidae (44 species, 8 genera). Unchanged.

Mantellidae (162 species, 5 genera). Unchanged.

Micrixalidae (11 species, 1 genus)*. Formerly part of Ranidae.

Microhylidae (413 species, 43 genera). As before minus 26 species moved to Brevicipitidae.

Myobatrachidae (80 species, 13 genera). Unchanged.

Nyctibatrachidae (13 species, 2 genera)*. Formerly part of Ranidae.

Petropedetidae (26 species, 3 genera)*. Formerly part of Ranidae.

Phrynobatrachidae (72 species, 1 genus)*. Formerly part of Ranidae.

Ptychadenidae (52 species, 3 genera)*. Formerly part of Ranidae.

Pyxicephalidae (59 species, 13 genera)*. Formerly part of Ranidae.

Ranidae (316 species, 18 genera). As before minus many species moved to new families.

Rhacophoridae (272 species, 10 genera). Unchanged.

Sooglossidae (5 species, 2 genera). As before plus *Nasikabatrachus*, recently described from India.

* New family recognized
(Source: American Museum of Natural History)

For ease of use the approach taken to dividing the order Anura into family groups in *300 Frogs* has been the traditional one of 29 families. Recent studies (2006) suggest strongly, however, that the correct number of families is 44. The most notable changes from the 29- to the 44-family system have occurred in the previously large families Leptodactylidae and Ranidae, both of which have seen genera removed to form new families. In addition, five small families have been suppressed: Ascaphidae, Allophrynidae, Discoglossidae, Pseudidae, and Rhinodermatidae.

Summaries of both systems are shown here, and in the species' entries some of the changes and alternative scientific names have been noted.

In the 29-family system, the nine most primitive families are grouped together in the suborder Archaeobatrachia. The more recently evolved families form the suborder Neobatrachia. In the recent system a suborder Mesobatrachia has been added to include families of more evolutionary intermediate frogs.

species that occurs at the highest altitude, however, is the European and Asian Common Toad *(Bufo bufo)*, which has been found at over 26,000 feet (8,000 m) in the Himalayas. Remarkably, this same species has also been found at the lowest altitude: 1,115 feet (340 m) down a coal mine.

Only the most adaptable species can live in urban environments, but most parts of the world have at least one species of "urban frog" living in drains, cisterns, or garden ponds. Some species increase their ranges by stowing away in greenhouse plants and crops, and colonies may be found hundreds of miles away from where they originated.

Frog and Toad Forms

The shapes of frogs and toads have evolved to suit the environments in which they live, and quite a lot can be deduced from a species' appearance. Those that have enormous hind legs are leapers, whereas those with shorter limbs are walkers or hoppers. Species that burrow have powerful limbs that may also have horny bladelike growths on them to help shovel the soil or sand, examples being the spadefoot toads *(Pelobates* and *Scaphiopus* species). A few species burrow head-first and have a pointed snout, but most burrowing species use their hind legs to scoop away the soil as they disappear backward beneath the surface.

⊖ *Swimming frogs, such as the Pool Frog* (Rana lessonae), *have webbed hind feet. Tree frogs like* Hyla boans *(far right) climb using their expanded toe pads.*

The shape of the toes also varies according to the frog's lifestyle. Species that swim strongly, for instance, have webbed hind feet, but those that rarely enter the water do not. Swimmers also have a streamlined body and a pointed snout. Tree and leaf frogs and other climbing species have expanded disks, or pads, on the tips of their toes that act like suckers when they are clambering among branches and leaves.

In extreme cases, tree frogs may also have webbed feet that they use as tiny parachutes to enable them to glide down from tall trees. In these species, such as Wallace's Flying Frog *(Rhacophorus nigropalmatus),* both the hind *and* the front feet are webbed. They live in Central and South America and in Southeast Asia.

Streamlined frogs with a pointed snout are good swimmers and are found around water, but short, rotund frogs have a body shape that has a relatively small surface area. This reduces the amount of water

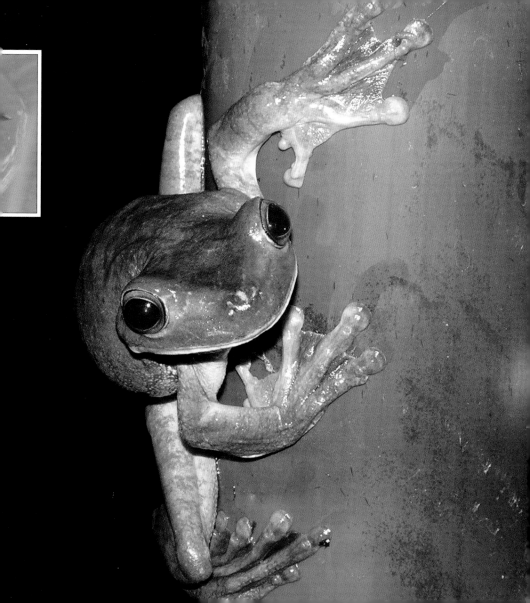

they lose and, sure enough, frogs with a dumpy body are found mostly in areas that have dry climates. They do not swim well.

All frogs and toads have lungs, but they also breathe through their skin. The skin may be smooth, wet, and slimy or rough, dry, and warty. Frogs with damp skin rely more on skin breathing (cutaneous respiration) than those with dry skin, because the skin must be moist to allow gases such as oxygen and carbon dioxide to pass across it. Glands keep the skin moist and, if the conditions become very dry, the frogs may dehydrate.

Frogs and toads that live in deserts and other dry places do not have as many moisture-producing glands in their skin and therefore do not dry up as quickly. On the other hand, they cannot breathe through their skin as efficiently as damp-skinned frogs, so they need larger lungs. Frogs and toads can reduce the amount of water they lose through evaporation by resting in a hunched position with limbs and toes tucked under the body, thereby reducing their exposed surface area.

Food and Feeding

All adult frogs and toads are carnivorous: They eat other animals. Since they are stimulated by movement, their prey is usually alive when they eat it, although some species, such as the Cane Toad, eat carrion. The prey that a species eats will depend largely on size and availability. Frogs cannot break food up into smaller pieces, so they have to swallow it whole. Apart from this limitation, they are not very choosy and will attempt to eat more or less anything they can fit in their mouths. Small species are restricted to invertebrates such as ants, termites, other insects, spiders, slugs, and snails. Large frogs can tackle bigger prey, especially since many of them have a wide mouth. Items include mice and rats, small birds, lizards and snakes, other frogs and toads, and smaller members of their own species.

Some of the more voracious species include the South American horned toads (*Ceratophrys* species)—sometimes known, with good reason, as "pacman" frogs—the American Bullfrog, and the Giant Bullfrog *(Pyxicephalus adspersus)*. Aquatic frogs eat aquatic invertebrates and their larvae and fish, which they swallow underwater. It will come as no surprise to learn that the Crab-eating Frog *(Fejervarya cancrivora)* from Southeast Asia eats crabs.

Finding and catching prey is done in different ways, according to species. The larger-bodied species that tend to eat large prey items rarely go looking for them. These frogs sit and wait for prey to come to them instead. These species are often camouflaged

⟵ *Frogs are preyed on by many animals, including this giant water bug, which has caught a Northern Leopard Frog* (Rana pipiens).

⬇ *A Great Plains Toad* (Bufo cognatus) *devours a large insect.*

23

⊕ *Frogs feed on a wide range of prey. This Northern Leopard Frog* (Rana pipiens) *is swallowing a worm.*

or lie partially concealed in moss or leaf litter. Once something tasty comes within range, the frog leaps from its hiding place and grabs its meal in its mouth, sometimes using its front legs to cram it in.

Smaller species are usually more active and spend many hours searching under leaves and in nooks and crannies in the hope of finding small items. Many of them flick out their tongue to pick up small items. Species that eat ants and termites may be able to stay in one place and eat large numbers as they file past; and some burrowing species simply live with their food in the nests of ants or termites.

In contrast to the adults, most frog and toad larvae (tadpoles) eat vegetable matter, using several rows of rasping teeth to scrape algae and bacteria from leaves, rocks, and underwater debris. Their mouthparts become more powerful as they grow, and they may switch to a diet of higher plants or even meat, feeding on unfortunate invertebrates such as worms that have fallen in the water. In hard times they may eat other tadpoles, including their own brothers and sisters.

Some species have tadpoles that filter particles of food from the water by pumping it over their gills, while others have predatory tadpoles that eat small aquatic invertebrates as well as tadpoles of their own and other species. A few tadpoles eat the eggs of other frogs, and an even smaller number, including several of the poison dart frogs (family Dendrobatidae), eat special eggs that their mother lays for them.

Reproduction and Life Cycles

The evolution of frogs' reproductive systems and life cycles seems to have run riot. People living in the cooler parts of the Northern Hemisphere will be most familiar with the "standard" life cycle, in which males call from a breeding pond during the spring to attract the local females.

All frogs and toads that mate in the water pair up with the male clinging to the back of the female. This

position is known as amplexus, and it is the best position for him to fertilize the eggs as they are laid. But not all species have the same type of amplexus. The males of the more primitive families (those that evolved early on) grasp the females in front of their hind limbs in a position known as inguinal amplexus. Males of the more advanced families grasp the female immediately behind their front limbs. This position is known as axillary amplexus and is the one taken up by all the common North American frogs and toads. In a few species there is no amplexus—the male simply sits over the clump of eggs and fertilizes them after they have been laid. As the eggs emerge from the female in clumps or strings of spawn, he releases sperm to fertilize them. The eggs hatch into free-swimming tadpoles that grow legs, lose their tail, and emerge on land as miniature replicas of their parents.

In other parts of the world, however, frogs do not always follow this pattern. Some diverge from it in truly amazing ways. Some species, for instance, use the small pools of water that collect in the center of bromeliads, or air plants, while others breed in tree holes. In both cases these frogs avoid the possibility of fish eating their eggs.

Other species tackle this problem from another angle. They lay their eggs on leaves that overhang ponds. When they are ready to hatch, the tadpoles

⊖ ⊕ *Right:*
A pair of toads in
axillary amplexus.
Below: Axillary
amplexus in
Sphaenorhynchus
lacteus.

wriggle until they slide off the leaf and into the water, where they can continue to develop in the normal way.

Some frogs make even better parents by carrying their eggs around with them. Sometimes it is the male that does the babysitting by wrapping the string of eggs around his hind legs, as in the case of the Midwife Toad, and at other times it is the female, as in the case of the South American marsupial frogs, such as the Riobamba Marsupial Frog (Gastrotheca riobambae). The female has a special pouch on her back into which the male pushes the eggs as he fertilizes them. She then carries the eggs until they have hatched into tadpoles or, in some species, until they have metamorphosed into baby frogs.

Frogs and toads that live in places where there are no suitable pools or streams may skip the swimming tadpole stage. There are many of these, including over 600 Central and South American species of rain or leaf litter frogs (Eleutherodactylus), Gardiner's Frog from the Seychelles, and the New Zealand frogs, such as Hochstetter's Frog (Leiopelma hochstetteri).

All these species find a damp place to lay their eggs, often among moss. The eggs have a thicker than normal outer capsule which also helps prevent them from drying out. The egg inside develops into a tadpole

⊕ *Competition for females means several males may try to mate with one female, forming a "mating ball."*

that feeds on its yolk and develops into a miniature frog before breaking out and becoming independent.

If this seems strange, consider the frogs that carry the developing eggs inside their body. Male Darwin's Frogs *(Rhinoderma darwinii)* from South America pick up their eggs and carry them in their mouth while they develop. The tadpoles live in the male's vocal sac and feed on a "milk" produced from the lining of his mouth, and the male does not spit them out until they are fully formed little frogs. The Gastric-brooding Frogs *(Rheobatrachus silus)* from Australia go one stage farther. They swallow the eggs and hold them in their stomach, where they develop. The eggs are not digested by the parent because it can "switch off" the production of digestive juices. When they are fully formed, the adult regurgitates them. Finally, a small

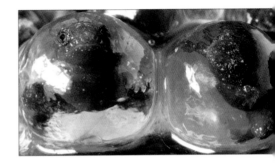

⬆ Eleutherodactylus *rain frogs complete their metamorphosis in the egg.*

➡ *A Strawberry Poison Dart Frog* (Dendrobates pumilio) *carries a tadpole to a bromeliad plant.*

number of frogs fertilize their eggs before they are laid (internal fertilization). Females of these species, one from Puerto Rico and four from West Africa, give birth to live young that have developed inside their oviducts.

Frog and Toad Survival
The 20th century was a bad time for frogs, and things are likely to get worse. Frogs and toads have specific

⬅ *Male Midwife Toads* (Alytes obstetricans) *carry strings of eggs around their hind legs until they hatch.*

requirements. In particular, most species need clean, unpolluted water in which to breed and complete the first stage of their life cycle, and a suitable habitat with plenty of food and cover in which to live after they have metamorphosed. This makes them doubly vulnerable to habitat disturbance. Draining of ponds and ditches, or pollution of the water through the run-off of chemicals from nearby roads and intensive agricultural spraying, have made many former breeding sites unsuitable. Pesticides kill the frogs' food supply.

⊖ *Now extinct, Golden Toads* (Bufo periglenes) *used to be seen in large numbers in Costa Rica.*

Clearance of land for development, agriculture, or logging is destroying many of the adult frogs' habitats. Introduced animals, such as cats and rats, have wiped out some populations, and the Cane Toad has done the same thing in Australia.

At least six or seven species have become extinct in recent years. The real number is probably far higher, however—more like six or seven *dozen*—because there are many areas where frogs and toads are hardly studied. Although some extinctions and drastic reductions in numbers of other species can be put down to human activities, others are more mysterious. When frogs disappear in places as far apart as the United States, the rain forests of Costa Rica, and the mountain ranges of Australia, it seems that the causes are more widespread. Perhaps acid rain is polluting these places, or it may be the harmful effects of ultraviolet radiation on the adults, eggs, or tadpoles caused by the hole in the ozone layer. Diseases, including a fungal infection known as chytrid, iridioviruses, and bacterial infections have also been spreading, perhaps because frogs' resistance to them has been reduced through other effects.

One sad case is that of the Costa Rican Golden Toad *(Bufo periglenes)*, an almost unbelievably colorful species that was only discovered in the 1960s. In 1987 more than 1,000 were seen in one place when they gathered to breed, but three years later only 11 turned up. Since then, none has been seen. In the same country numbers of the Lemur Leaf Frog *(Phyllomedusa lemur)* have been declining dramatically since 1995, and it now appears to be extinct there, although small populations linger on in neighboring countries.

The most worrying thing about these extinctions is that Costa Rica has a greater proportion of protected land than any other country and, superficially at least, its rain forests seem perfectly preserved. The same can be said of the eastern mountain ranges of Australia, where the gastric-brooding frogs and several torrent frogs have almost certainly disappeared in recent years. Scientists are working hard to find out the causes of the declines and try to stop them happening. Even so, it seems likely that many more frogs and toads will become extinct in the next hundred years.

Species' Profiles

⊖ *Wild populations of the beautiful but Critically Endangered Panamanian Golden Toad* (Atelopus zeteki) *are under threat from loss of habitat and fungal infection. Large numbers have also been collected illegally for the pet trade, but the toad is now protected by law in Panama.*

Oriental Fire-bellied Toad

Common names	Oriental Fire-bellied Toad, Oriental Bell Toad
Scientific name	*Bombina orientalis*
Family	Bombinatoridae
Size	1.97 in (50 mm).
Key features	A warty-backed toad with a slightly flattened head and prominent eyes. Back bright green with irregular black spots, some of which are elongated. Underneath it is brilliant carmine red with a varying number of black spots and reticulations. The tips of its toes are also bright red. Males have more heavily built forearms and develop spiny patches on their hands during the breeding season.
Habits	Aquatic, usually resting at the water's surface. Sometimes active on land.
Breeding	Clutches of 50–100 eggs are laid singly and sink to the bottom of shallow pools. Females may breed repeatedly throughout the spring and summer.
Diet	Invertebrates, especially flying insects and aquatic insect larvae.
Habitat	Open shallow ponds, ditches, streams, and flooded fields, including paddy fields.
Distribution	Eastern China; Korea.
Status	Thought to be common.
Similar species	None in the region. The Giant Fire-bellied Toad *(B. maxima)*, also from China, has a gray back and its warts are numerous and larger.

This is an almost unbelievably colorful little toad that is camouflaged when seen from above but displays warning coloration when it feels threatened.

The warts of this species produce a toxin that can cause death or discomfort in larger animals. In humans it can cause sneezing and sore eyes if the toad is handled carelessly. Its first line of defense is camouflage, and it is difficult to see when it is resting on the surface of a weed-covered pond. If it thinks it has been discovered, however, it is quick to arch its back and display the brightly colored underside of its belly, hands, and feet. This is known as the Unken reflex. Other amphibians that have an Unken reflex include the other *Bombina* species and several newts with orange or red undersides.

Fire-bellied toads begin breeding in the spring, as soon as the water has warmed up enough. Males develop rough black patches of skin (nuptial pads) on the insides of their front feet and forearms, and the forearms become thicker. On warm, sunny days they float on the surface of the water and make their repetitive calls throughout the day and into the evening to attract mates.

Spawning begins several hours later. The eggs are laid in ones or twos or in small groups, and they sink to the bottom of the pool or become loosely attached to water plants, dead twigs, and so on. The eggs are small, dark, and have a thin capsule of jelly around them. Hatching takes from three to seven days, depending on the species and on the temperature of the water. The newly hatched tadpoles have external gills at first and cling to the jelly capsule for two or three days before they swim off to look for more food. They work their way over stones, twigs, aquatic plants, and the surface film of the water.

As the tadpole's limbs grow, light cream or yellow patches begin to appear on the soles of its feet. Tadpoles grow to a maximum of 0.8 inches (20 mm) before they begin to absorb their tail, and the newly metamorphosed toadlets are only slightly larger than a bluebottle fly.

They stay near the water, hiding under stones around the edges of the pool. Their diet switches from vegetable material to small aquatic invertebrates, and the pale patches on their undersides gradually turn bright red as substances in their food, especially small crustaceans, produce the necessary pigments.

⊕ *The Oriental Fire-bellied Toad from Southeast Asia.*

Yellow-bellied Toad

Common name	Yellow-bellied Toad
Scientific name	*Bombina variegata*
Family	Bombinatoridae
Size	1.97 in (50 mm).
Key features	A warty-backed toad with a flat body and head and prominent eyes. Its eyes are heart-shaped or triangular. Its back is gray or olive brown, and it has large yellow or orange blotches on its underside. The palms of its hands are also this color.
Habits	Active by day, always in or near water, typically resting with the top of its head and eyes just above the surface.
Breeding	Males call after rain with a soft "poop, poop, poop" sound. Females lay clutches of 120–170 eggs in small clumps, often among submerged grass. Females may breed up to three times throughout the spring and summer.
Diet	Invertebrates, especially flying insects.
Habitat	Shallow ponds, pools, ditches, and flooded fields, and also in water-filled tire tracks and hoof prints.
Distribution	Central and E Europe, from France to S Italy, Greece, and the Carpathians.
Status	Very common in places.
Similar species	The range of the Fire-bellied Toad (*B. bombina*) overlaps in a few places, but this species is darker and has bright reddish orange blotches on its underside.

Yellow-bellied Toads often live in hilly or mountainous regions—at up to 7,000 feet (2,100 m) in the south of their range. They are very sociable, and many toads can often be found together in one small pool or in a series of pools formed from hoof prints or tire tracks. They typically rest with their legs spread out, their bodies floating just below the water, and only the tops of their heads and their eyes above the surface. Any disturbance sends them scurrying to the bottom, where they hide in the mud or among submerged tussocks

of grass or aquatic vegetation—but soon reappear on the surface once the danger has passed. If caught, they raise their arms and legs and arch their back, displaying their brightly colored belly and palms of their hands. This warns predators of the toxic substances produced in glands in their skin. At the same time, a milky-white, pungent-smelling substance may be produced.

There are variations in the amount and shade of yellow on the belly. For example, toads from southern Italy have almost entirely yellow bellies but black throats. In the mountain foothills in the Danube Basin, where this species occurs alongside the Fire-bellied Toad (Bombina bombina), hybrids sometimes occur, with characteristics that are intermediate between the two species.

The Yellow-bellied Toad from southeastern Europe blends perfectly with its surroundings until it reveals its vivid yellow underside.

37

Majorcan Midwife Toad

Common name	Majorcan Midwife Toad
Scientific name	*Alytes muletensis*
Family	Discoglossidae
Size	1.57 in (40 mm).
Key features	A small toad with smooth skin and long slender legs. It is dirty yellow above with many small, roundish, dark blotches or, alternatively, a marbled pattern resulting from many blotches joined together.
Habits	Nocturnal and secretive.
Breeding	Strings of 7–20 eggs are laid, which the male wraps around his back legs, as in other midwife toads. The tadpoles can take up to 3 years to complete their development.
Diet	Invertebrates.
Habitat	Narrow canyons in limestone mountains, with small streams running along the bottom.
Distribution	Majorca in the Balearic Islands.
Status	Rare, and with a limited range.
Similar species	None in the region.

The Majorcan Midwife Toad was first discovered as a fossil in 1977 and was discovered as a living species two years later. It survived in remote limestone mountain valleys by living in places that were inaccessible to its main predator, which appears to be the Viperine Snake *(Natrix maura)*, which was introduced to Majorca in ancient times.

Males carry a string of eggs around their back legs in true midwife-toad fashion but, unlike other species, they rarely carry more than one string. They hide in a damp crevice for two to three weeks before the eggs hatch, and then release them into the small pools that are left by the gradually drying streams in the bottom of the canyons.

The tadpoles apparently "freeze" when Viperine Snakes are nearby, in order to avoid detection. Adults have no toxic secretions, unlike other midwife toads, and consequently do not have the small granular glands on the surface of their skin. The loss of this defensive mechanism is thought to have come about because they live on an island where there are no natural predators.

When it was first discovered, the toad was named *Baleophryne muletensis*, and it is sometimes still listed under this name in older publications.

⊖ *The Majorcan Midwife Toad from Majorca is a relatively new and rare species. It is hoped that its numbers will increase, however, as a result of several captive-breeding programs that have been initiated.*

Midwife Toad

Common names	Midwife Toad, Common Midwife Toad
Scientific name	*Alytes obstetricans*
Family	Discoglossidae
Size	1.5–1.97 in (38–50 mm).
Key features	Body plump and round; limbs short; eyes prominent with vertical pupils. A row of small wartlike glands down each side of its back; a larger gland behind each eye. Warts pinkish or yellow. Body pale gray, brown, or olive with small dark markings.
Habits	Nocturnal, terrestrial. Usually hides under stones, logs, or in crevices by day, or may dig a short burrow with its front limbs.
Breeding	In spring, on land. Male carries the eggs until they hatch.
Diet	Small invertebrates.
Habitat	Varied, including open woods, fields, parks, old quarries, and drystone walls.
Distribution	Europe (N Spain and Portugal, France, Belgium, S Netherlands, parts of Germany and Switzerland; several introduced colonies in England).
Status	Common in suitable habitats; rapidly disappearing in the north of its range, through habitat disturbance and, possibly, climate change.
Similar species	There are three other midwife toads, two of which occur in the Iberian Peninsula: Iberian Midwife Toad *(A. cisternasii)* and Midwife Toad of Hillenius *(A. dickhilleri).* One is confined to Majorca.

The Midwife Toad gets its name from its breeding habits. The males carry one or more strings of eggs wrapped around their hind legs until they are ready to hatch. Males call at night or on rainy or cloudy days, often from a hidden place away from water. Their melodious calls have given them the alternative name of Bell Toad.

Females are attracted to larger males, which they can

identify by their deeper calls. After about half an hour the female lays a string of eggs, which the male winds around his hind legs. After spawning, the male may continue to call on subsequent nights and may eventually end up carrying two to four strings of eggs at the same time. He prevents the eggs from drying out by selecting a moist microenvironment in which to hide, such as a burrow. If the weather becomes dry, he may enter a small pool or puddle to dunk them occasionally.

After three to eight weeks the eggs will have developed to the point of hatching, and the male takes them to water. They continue to develop in the normal way and often overwinter before metamorphosing into toadlets when they are about 1 inch (2.5 cm) long.

A male Midwife Toad, photographed in Spain, carrying a string of eggs wrapped around its hind legs.

Montane Litter Frog

Common name	Montane Litter Frog
Scientific name	*Leptobrachium montanum*
Family	Megophryidae
Size	1.81–2.56 in (46–65 mm).
Key features	This frog has a wide head with bulging eyes, and short limbs. It is brown in color with a darker marking on its back. The eyes have a conspicuous white ring around them.
Habits	Nocturnal and terrestrial.
Breeding	In still pools and backwaters along forest streams.
Diet	Invertebrates such as insects.
Habitat	Montane rain forests above 3,000 ft (900 m).
Distribution	Borneo.
Status	Probably common in suitable habitat, though rarely seen.
Similar species	The other 14 or so species of litter frogs *(Leptobrachium)* are similar in general body shape. Most come from lowland forests.

Like other members of their family, litter frogs have short limbs that are seemingly out of proportion to the rest of their body. In particular, their small hind limbs do not enable them to leap, and they therefore move in short hops. When threatened, these frogs tend to crouch down into the leaf litter.

Litter frogs live among the dead leaves and the other debris that forms the forest floor in rain forests, and they forage at night. They do not congregate to breed, and it is rare to find more than one or two of them on a single night.

Males call with a single squawking note, usually from a position near a stream. The females lay their eggs in quiet pools or backwaters, and the tadpoles hide under rocks at the bottom of the pools. They feed on dead leaves that fall into the water, using their horny beaks to bite off large pieces. As they grow, they develop large dark markings on their bodies, and these markings vary from among the different species. All litter frogs have very large eyes and are totally nocturnal. A few species, including

Leptobrachium hendricksoni and *L. hasselti*, have orange eyes.

Lowland species live in rain forests. Where these have been cleared, the frogs may move into plantations and live among dead leaves and piles of palm fronds.

⬆ *Montane Litter Frogs from Borneo spend their lives among dead leaves and debris on the rain forest floor.*

Asian Horned Toad

Common names	Asian Horned Toad, Large Horned Toad
Scientific name	*Megophrys nasuta*
Family	Megophryidae
Size	2.76–5.51 in (7–14 cm).
Key features	The wide head, pointed extensions over the eyes and snout, and cryptic "dead-leaf" coloration make this toad instantly recognizable. It has huge black eyes and a black mask on either side of its head. Ridges running up the back resemble leaf veins, while irregular deep black patches on its back even imitate holes in the "leaf."
Habits	Nocturnal and terrestrial.
Breeding	In relatively still pools and backwaters along forest streams.
Diet	Large invertebrates and small vertebrates, including smaller frogs.
Habitat	Tropical lowland rain forests.
Distribution	Sumatra, Borneo, and the Malaysian Peninsula.
Status	Common in suitable habitat, though rarely seen.
Similar species	The seven other species of *Megophrys* are smaller and have smaller skin projections over the eyes. The Solomon Islands Leaf Frog *(Ceratobatrachus guentheri)* is similar in shape for the same reason, but its range does not overlap that of *Megophrys*.

The ability of this species to camouflage itself is legendary. When it crouches among the dead leaves that cover the forest floor it almost disappears from sight, and finding one at night is one of the hardest tasks a frog-hunter can undertake. During the day these toads hide under logs and rocks, emerging at night to forage or look for mates.

Their short back legs are unable to propel them forward in a jump, so they crawl slowly and deliberately across the forest floor, making short hops only if they are in a hurry. If they feel threatened, they crouch down with their chin resting on the ground and their limbs tucked under their body. In this position, the cryptic nature of their shape and markings work to full advantage. When looking for food, they raise their head up on their front limbs so that their body is at about 45 degrees to the ground, and their raised "eyebrows" give them a startled expression.

Horned toads have extremely wide gapes— the width of their mouth is equivalent to about two-thirds of their body length— and they will snap up large invertebrates such as adult cockroaches and even snails with relish. They also eat small frogs and other vertebrates, such as young lizards and snakes. When

⊖ Megophrys montana, *another horned frog from Indonesia, is a little smaller than* M. nasuta.

they first spot their prey, they bend their head down slightly as if studying it, then lean forward quickly to seize it in their mouth before swallowing. This species looks most uncomfortable when it swallows, since it uses the undersides of its eyeballs to push prey down its throat; its pointed "eyelids" also dip down.

Apart from being colored and shaped to resemble dead leaves, this toad's back has a bony shield (called an osteoderm) embedded in the skin. (This shield is also present in South American horned toads, *Ceratophrys* species.) In addition, the Asian Horned Toad has two parallel ridges of skin down each side of its back and small bony tubercles that look like the small galls made on leaves by insects.

⊕ *Seen from the side, this Asian Horned Toad in the Danum Valley, Sabah, Borneo, demonstrates its remarkable ability to disguise itself as a dead leaf.*

Common Spadefoot Toad

Common name	Common Spadefoot Toad
Scientific name	*Pelobates fuscus*
Family	Pelobatidae
Size	3 in (76 mm).
Key features	Plump and smooth-skinned; eyes large and prominent with copper-colored irises; pupils vertical. There is a bony lump on top of its head. Back feet fully webbed and have a "spade" (a pale, crescent-shaped, sharp-edged tubercle) on the heel. Body color variable: often dark to light brown, but sometimes gray, reddish, or yellowish with darker markings.
Habits	Burrowing; mostly nocturnal (sometimes diurnal in the breeding season).
Breeding	In spring, usually in response to rain. Amplexus is inguinal.
Diet	Insects and other small invertebrates.
Habitat	Lowlands; on dunes, heaths, pine forests, and fields.
Distribution	Central and E Europe, from France to the Ural Mountains. Also in the Po Valley in northern Italy.
Status	Common.
Similar species	Two other spadefoot toads occur in Europe, but their ranges do not overlap; the Western Spadefoot Toad (*P. cultripes*) occurs in Spain, Portugal, and extreme SW France; the Eastern Spadefoot Toad (*P. syriacus*) lives in Greece, Turkey, and neighboring parts of SE Europe.

Spadefoot toads spend most of their lives below the surface avoiding hot dry weather. They emerge only at night to feed, or during the breeding season, when they can sometimes be seen out during the day.

The bony "spade" on the heel of spadefoot toads helps them burrow rapidly into the ground. They use the spades on each foot alternately so that, as they gradually sink from view, they appear to be marking time, rotating slightly from side to side as they go. Their burrows go straight down, sometimes to 3 feet (1 m), and the toads rest at the bottom where the soil retains some moisture. When they emerge, the toads use the bony plate on top of the head to push their way back up to the surface. In some places they live in the burrows of rodents or under stones.

They often emerge in large numbers during rainstorms to search for food but disappear back underground before dawn. This species favors cultivated fields, although it also lives in less disturbed habitats such as dunes and heaths, where the soil tends to be sandy and easy to burrow in. However, it can also cope with heavier soils such as clay.

In dry places these toads are usually concentrated around bodies of water, but elsewhere they can live half a mile (0.8 km) or more away from

→ *Common Spadefoot Toad, Russia. Its hind legs are modified with "spades" that enable it to burrow rapidly.*

⊖ *This form of the Common Spadefoot Toad, photographed in Hungary, has larger dark blotches.*

permanent water. Although the species occurs in huge numbers in some of the former Soviet countries, populations farther west in Europe and, in particular, the isolated Italian population, subspecies *Pelobates fuscus insubricus*, are less numerous.

Couch's Spadefoot Toad

Common name	Couch's Spadefoot Toad
Scientific name	*Scaphiopus couchi*
Family	Pelobatidae
Size	2.17–3.54 in (55–90 mm). Females are larger than males.
Key features	A plump toad with soft, fairly smooth skin. It has large eyes with yellow irises and vertically elliptical pupils. Its limbs are short and powerful, and the hind ones have hard black ridges on their "heels," which they use to burrow backward into the ground. Yellowish or greenish brown in color; females have brown mottled markings on the back; males are plain colored; in both sexes the underside is white.
Habits	Nocturnal and terrestrial, spending most of its life underground.
Breeding	In temporary pools following rain.
Diet	Invertebrates.
Habitat	Plains, vegetated deserts, and other semiarid places.
Distribution	Southern United States and N Mexico, including Baja California.
Status	Common but rarely seen.
Similar species	There are another four or so spadefoot toads in North America, but Couch's is the only one with yellow coloration.

Because summer storms can be short-lived and localized, and the breeding grounds can therefore change from year to year, the loud choruses of these toads are an important way of bringing breeding animals together. Many parts of the dry American Southwest reverberate with the calls of Couch's Spadefoot Toads following heavy summer rains. Choruses can number several thousand calling males, and the sound they produce can be heard more than 1 mile (1.6 km) away.

The toads, which can be present in high densities, spend most of their lives underground, in cocoons they make from several layers of shed skin. This helps prevent dehydration, and they may spend many months in a form of "suspended animation" during dry weather. As soon as the summer rains fall, however, they quickly dig their way to the surface to take advantage of temporary pools that form in the desert. At these times the ground may be covered with spadefoot toads.

Spadefoot toads are good examples of explosive breeders, species in which all individuals breed within a short space of time. Females of explosive breeders do not "choose" their mates—unlike other species, in which males may be spaced out along a pond or stream edge, for instance. Instead, each male tries to elbow his way to a female and gain one or more matings before the brief breeding season is over; this is known as "scramble competition." In the case of Couch's Spadefoot Toad a breeding season can last just two or three days, with every female toad in a given locality having dug its way to the surface, found a mate, and produced eggs.

Couch's Spadefoot Toad, Arizona. These toads spend most of their life underground in cocoons made from shed skin.

Dwarf Clawed Frog

Common names	Dwarf Clawed Frog, Dwarf Aquatic Frog
Scientific name	*Hymenochirus boettgeri*
Family	Pipidae
Size	1.26–1.38 in (32–35 mm).
Key features	A small chubby frog with a gray body covered in dark pointed warts. The hind limbs are much longer and more powerful than the front limbs, which are not used for swimming. The front and hind feet are fully webbed. The head and body are flattened, and the head is pointed.
Habits	Totally aquatic.
Breeding	Females lay about 100 tiny eggs (the smallest of any frog) that float on the water's surface. Spawning pairs perform a series of somersaults in the water. Females may breed repeatedly throughout the spring and summer.
Diet	Aquatic invertebrates. The small tadpoles are also carnivorous.
Habitat	Pools and shallow backwaters.
Distribution	West Africa, from Nigeria to the Congo Basin.
Status	Probably common, but they live in a little-explored region.
Similar species	There are three other species in the genus—*H. boulengeri*, *H. curtipes*, and *H. feae*—all of which are similar. In particular, *H. curtipes* is virtually indistinguishable from *H. boettgeri* and comes from Gabon.

The natural history of these little toads is poorly known, and much of our knowledge comes from captive animals. They are popular pets, obtainable through aquatic suppliers, although they are not necessarily suitable for housing with tropical fish. They eat only living invertebrates such as *Daphnia* and they are secretive, spending the day beneath dead leaves or other debris on the bottom, or in dense vegetation.

Their breeding habits are very unusual. Males call from beneath the surface and make a long, drawn-out, buzzing sound, like a watch being wound up. Amplexus involves the male grasping the female immediately in front of her hind limbs, and the pair swims about in this position for up to 24 hours. When they are ready to spawn, they swim up to the surface of the water and the female releases a few eggs. The male fertilizes them, and they float. This process is repeated several times until all the eggs have been laid, and they form a raft on the surface.

The eggs hatch after two to three days, and the young tadpoles attach themselves to vegetation for another four or five days, absorbing their yolks. When they are ready to feed, they hunt for minute aquatic invertebrates and they finally metamorphose after one to two months into toadlets measuring about 0.4 inches (10 mm).

⊖ *The Dwarf Clawed Frog from West Africa has the smallest eggs of any amphibian, measuring just 0.003 inches (0.75 mm).*

Dwarf Pipa Toad

Common name	Dwarf Pipa Toad
Scientific name	*Pipa parva*
Family	Pipidae
Size	1.5–2.17 in (38–55 mm).
Key features	Pear-shaped frog with a gray body covered in small pointed warts. The hind limbs are much longer and more powerful than the front limbs. The hind feet are heavily webbed, but the front feet have no webbing. The head is flattened and the eyes are very small.
Habits	Totally aquatic.
Breeding	Males call from under the water and grasp females in front of their hind legs. The eggs are laid during sorties to the surface, and are stuck to the female's back.
Diet	Aquatic invertebrates. The tadpoles are also carnivorous.
Habitat	Shallow, colored waters in ponds, streams, and the edges of lakes.
Distribution	Northern South America (Colombia and Venezuela).
Status	Probably common, but difficult to find.
Similar species	There are six other members of the genus, but *P. parva* is the smallest.

Superficially, this species resembles the African dwarf clawed frogs belonging to the genus *Hymenochirus*, but its relationships and breeding behavior are different. It lives in ponds, backwaters, and lakes in lowland regions of northeast Venezuela and northwest Colombia, in the Lake Maracaibo region, and can occur in high densities at times. Muddy and tannin-stained waters mean that it must hunt by touch and smell rather than by sight.

Despite being aquatic, this species can spread throughout the countryside after heavy rains, invading new ponds. These include artificial ponds created by fish farmers, and there is some evidence that the frogs have an impact on fish production—if not eating the eggs and fish larvae directly, then by competing with the fish for food.

The stomach contents of this and similar species have included insects and insect larvae, as well as the eggs and larvae of other frog species. Some of these are frogs that lay their eggs out of the water, suggesting that the small pipas will leave their ponds to forage around the banks, perhaps during rain.

Breeding is similar to that of the Surinam Toad *(Pipa pipa)*, except that females release their young while they are still tadpoles. The filter-feeding tadpoles take tiny plant and animal material, and metamorphose about two months after falling off their mother's back.

⊕ *A pair of Dwarf Pipa Toads spawning at the bottom of a pond in South America.*

Surinam Toad

Common name	Surinam Toad
Scientific name	*Pipa pipa*
Family	Pipidae
Size	5.12–7.87 in (13–20 cm).
Key features	Body rectangular when seen from above; the head is triangular with tiny eyes. The hind legs are thickly built and end in massive webbed feet, while the front limbs are thinner and end in elongated fingers with no webbing. The back and sides are sprinkled with tubercles and flaps that help disguise the toad's outline. The whole animal is brown or grayish brown in color, with irregular mottled markings, making it look like a dead leaf, a resemblance that is enhanced by its flatness.
Habits	Completely aquatic.
Breeding	The female carries her developing eggs on her back until they hatch into miniature toads.
Diet	Aquatic invertebrates, fish, and tadpoles.
Habitat	Blackwater streams and oxbow lakes, with tea-colored water caused by decayed organic material.
Distribution	Northern South America as far south as Amazonian Ecuador. Also Trinidad, West Indies.
Status	Probably common.
Similar species	Six other species in the genus, but they are mostly smaller.

This is the world's flattest frog. Surinam Toads look as though they have been trodden on or run over by a heavy vehicle. They are not attractive animals.

Strange as the Surinam Toad may look, it is well adapted for life in the murky blackwater streams and swamps where it is found. Its resemblance to a dead leaf makes it almost invisible as it hangs motionless in the water, waiting for prey to swim within range. Its massively webbed hind feet give it maneuverability and acceleration and, despite its clumsy appearance, it is an efficient hunter, catching small fish with ease.

On its forelimbs each finger ends in a small star-shaped organ that is sensitive to touch. The toad uses these organs to trawl through silt and forest detritus on the stream bed. Catching food is just a matter of opening its wide mouth quickly—water flows in, carrying prey with it. If the prey is not completely engulfed at the first attempt, the toad uses its front feet to manipulate it.

Surinam Toads have unusual breeding habits. The male uses its hind feet, with toes spread widely, to position the eggs carefully onto a spongy pad located on the female's back. A full complement may consist of just over 100 eggs in a large female. Once all the eggs have been laid the pair separates, and the female's back begins to swell around the eggs. After 24 hours they are only just visible, each contained in its own cell. The surrounding skin

⊖ *A clutch of eggs can be seen on the back of this female Surinam Toad in South America. The eggs form individual cells in which the tadpoles develop.*

contains many capillaries, and the outer capsule of the eggs fuse to the wall of the chamber, enabling gaseous exchange to take place between the tissue of the female and the embryos. The tadpoles develop in these cells for 77 to 136 days, by which time they are fully metamorphosed miniature versions of the adults.

Just before their "birth" the young toads move about inside their cells, often poking a head or a limb out into the water. Complete emergence can be a struggle, and the female may help by flexing her body. The small toads float to the surface at first but soon learn to swim up and down in the water.

Tropical Clawed Toad

Common name	Tropical Clawed Toad
Scientific name	*Silurana tropicalis*
Family	Pipidae
Size	1.97 in (50 mm).
Key features	The body is pear-shaped, and the hind legs are long and powerful, ending in heavily webbed feet. The front limbs are smaller and the fingers are not webbed. It is brown in color, with conspicuous "stitches" along each side, marking the lateral line organs. Its eyes are small and positioned on the top of its head.
Habits	Totally aquatic but able to make short journeys across land when necessary.
Breeding	The female scatters her eggs over the bottom, loosely attached to stones, twigs, and aquatic vegetation.
Diet	Aquatic invertebrates.
Habitat	Pools in gallery forest.
Distribution	West Africa, from Senegal to the Congo Basin.
Status	Common.
Similar species	Clawed frogs belonging to the genus *Xenopus*, especially the small *X. muelleri*, are similar.

The Tropical Clawed Frog lives and breeds in small ponds in gallery forest, but during the dry season it migrates to nearby riversides and lives under flat stones at the water's edge, or in holes in the bank. If there is no river nearby, it buries itself in the mud and waits for the rains to return. As soon as the rainy season is underway, it migrates into the forests to look for suitable spawning sites; these can include small bodies of water such as buckets.

Spawning, however, takes place mostly in larger bodies of water where there is plenty of floating vegetation. The adults hide under submerged logs during the day and come out at night to feed. They eat anything they can overpower, including small animals that fall onto the surface of the water. They also eat tadpoles, although it is unclear whether they eat those of their own species.

The developing tadpoles form huge shoals, often in sunlit parts of ponds. Tadpoles swim on the spot, lying parallel to each other, with their heads pointing downward and the tips of their tails beating continuously. They apparently take about two months to develop into small toads, and they grow quickly, probably reaching maturity within one year.

⊖ *Tropical Clawed Toad, West Africa, showing its characteristic powerful hind legs and pear-shaped body.*

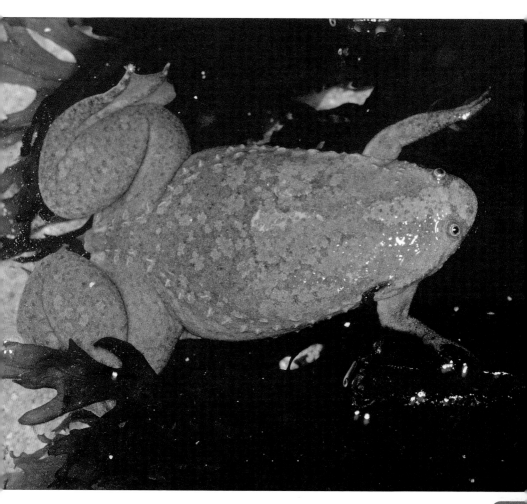

African Clawed Toad

Common names	African Clawed Toad, Common Platanna
Scientific name	*Xenopus laevis*
Family	Pipidae
Size	2.36–5.12 in (60–130 mm).
Key features	Clawed toads have roughly pear-shaped bodies when seen from above but are slightly flattened from top to bottom. They have powerful hind legs and massive webbed hind feet. The three innermost toes end with small black horny claws. Their front legs are smaller and their fingers are not webbed. Their eyes are small and point upward, and have rounded pupils and no eyelids. They are brown or gray in color, and have a limited ability to become lighter or darker according to the conditions.
Habits	Completely aquatic but may move from one pond to another by "swimming" across the ground during heavy rain.
Breeding	Amplexus is inguinal, and the eggs are laid on aquatic vegetation.
Diet	Anything that will fit into its mouth.
Habitat	Any body of water, no matter how large, small, or stagnant.
Distribution	Most of Africa south of the Sahara.
Status	Extremely common.
Similar species	Other species of *Xenopus* are similar, although some have distinctive markings. *Silurana* species are also similar but have a fourth cornified claw.

Although it originates in Africa, the African Clawed Toad has also colonized parts of the United States, Chile, Ascension Island, Wales, and England. It owes its success to several factors. Firstly, it can thrive in a wide range of conditions—it can tolerate brackish water and a temperature range of 36–95°F (2–35°C) or more. Secondly, if the pond in which it is living dries up, the toad may move overland to another one, or it can burrow down into the mud to estivate.

Females can produce up to 2,000 eggs several times each year. The young can reach sexual maturity within a year and can live for 20 years.

With their large webbed back feet, streamlined body shape, and lateral line organ, African Clawed Toads are well adapted to life in the water. They have relatively large lungs, so they can stay underwater for long periods of time.

The diet of African Clawed Toads normally consists of aquatic invertebrates, but they will take fish, other frogs, and tadpoles. They will also eat tadpoles or juveniles of their own species—a food source that can tide them over long periods when other food is in short supply (although they have been known to survive for a year without food). These toads are survivors!

→ *Albino African Clawed Toad, photographed in southern Africa.*

Tailed Frog

Common names	Tailed Frog, Coastal Tailed Frog
Scientific name	*Ascaphus truei*
Family	Ascaphidae
Size	0.98–1.97 in (25–50 mm).
Key features	Males have a short "tail" consisting of an extension of their cloaca, which they use in transferring sperm into the cloaca of the female. In other respects this frog is fairly ordinary-looking, with slightly rough skin and brown, olive, gray, or reddish brown coloration. There is a dark stripe through the eye and some irregular mottling on the body.
Habits	Nocturnal and semiaquatic or terrestrial.
Breeding	Fertilization is internal; the larvae take several years to metamorphose.
Diet	Invertebrates.
Habitat	Cold clear rocky streams flowing through ancient forests.
Distribution	North America (Pacific Northwest from S British Columbia, Canada, to N California), with many separated populations.
Status	Rare and endangered in Canada but without protection in the United States.
Similar species	A second species, the Rocky Mountain Tailed Frog (*A. montanus*), is sometimes recognized, but its differences from *A. truei* are small.

This unique little frog is the most primitive species in the world. Along with the New Zealand Frogs (*Leiopelma* species), adults retain the same tail-wagging muscles that allow tadpoles to swim.

The Tailed Frog reproduces by internal fertilization, accomplished by means of the male's "tail"—a fleshy tubular extension of its cloaca that becomes swollen during amplexus and is inserted into the cloaca of the female in order to transfer sperm.

The tadpoles are highly adapted for life in fast-flowing streams. They have a broad body with a large, round, suckerlike disk on the underside, with which they attach themselves to stones—they stick so tightly to the rocks that they are difficult to remove. Without this disk, they would be in danger of being swept away.

The tadpoles feed on the bacterial and algal slime that develops on rocks and, to a lesser extent, on organic material suspended in the water. They shun the light, hiding away during the day and becoming more active at night. Despite this, in places where they occur in the same streams, larvae of the Pacific Giant Salamander (*Dicamptodon ensatus*) prey heavily on them—Tailed Frog tadpoles may make up 14 percent of the salamander's diet.

The tadpoles grow slowly and take from two to four years to metamorphose. It can be another five or

six years before they are large enough to breed. Adult Tailed Frogs remain in the vicinity of the streams in which they breed, but they sometimes stray as far as 25 yards (23 m) from the water's edge at night to feed. During dry weather, however, they stay close to the side of the stream. They feed on a wide variety of small invertebrates.

The tiny Tailed Frog does not have a true "tail." Males have a tail-like organ that is used for transferring sperm, and all adults have tiny tail-wagging muscles, a reminder of the fact that they evolved from tailed ancestors.

New Zealand Frogs

Common name	New Zealand Frogs
Scientific name	*Leiopelma* species (3 or 4 species)
Family	Leiopelmatidae
Size	1.18–1.89 in (30–48 mm). Archey's Frog (*Leiopelma archeyi*) is the smallest species; Hamilton's Frog (*L. hamiltoni*) is the largest.
Key features	Small frogs found only in New Zealand. Mostly brown, sometimes with a reddish or greenish hue. They have no tympanum (external eardrum) or vocal sac, and their toes are only slightly webbed. Eyes are large and have vertically elliptical pupils.
Habits	Very secretive and rarely seen; they live under rocks and logs and are active only at night.
Breeding	Eggs are laid in damp places and undergo direct development.
Diet	Small invertebrates.
Habitat	Rock piles; leaf litter.
Distribution	New Zealand (two species in the north of North Island; one or two species on islands in the Cook Straits).
Status	One or two species are endangered. The IUCN lists *L. archeyi* as Critically Endangered, *L. hamiltoni* as Endangered, and the other two species as Vulnerable.
Similar species	None, but closely related to the Tailed Frog (*Ascaphus truei*) of North America.

This family consists of three, possibly four, species: Hochstetter's Frog (*Leiopelma hochstetteri*), Archey's Frog (*L. archeyi*), Hamilton's Frog, or Stephen's Island Frog (*L. hamiltoni*), and Maud Island Frog, or Pakeka Frog (*L. pakeka*). The last species is not universally accepted, however.

These tiny frogs are the only ones native to New Zealand, and their existence was overlooked for many years. Their ranges are very small, so new colonies may yet be awaiting discovery.

The first species to be discovered was Hochstetter's Frog, in 1852. However, it was not described to science until several years later. The first colony lived in the Coromandel Mountain Range on New Zealand's North Island, and several additional colonies were found in the same area over the next 10 years or so. Hamilton's Frog was described and named in 1915 after a group was discovered on Stephen's Island in the Cook Straits. Then in 1958 a colony of very similar-looking frogs was found on nearby Maud Island, and named *L. pakeka*. Archey's Frog—the smallest species—was named in 1947 after scientists realized that some of the frogs living alongside Hochstetter's Frogs were different.

Three of the species live away from water— under stones, logs, and leaf litter in places that are mostly damp. (Archey's Frog lives on mountain ridges that catch moisture-laden air as it passes over them, resulting in frequent mists that provide the frogs with the moisture they need.) Hochstetter's Frog sometimes lives near streams under stones and logs. Like Archey's Frog, it occurs occasionally near the entrance of old mine shafts.

⬅ *Hochstetter's Frog* (Leiopelma hochstetteri) *was the first of the New Zealand frogs to be discovered. Further colonies possibly await discovery, but searching for these frogs is difficult, since they are very small and well camouflaged.*

All *Leiopelma* frogs lay eggs that develop directly into young frogs, having gone through the tadpole stage inside the egg capsule. Females lay clusters of two to 11 (but occasionally up to 23) eggs in the spring or summer, under stones or logs. In addition, Hochstetter's Frog may use the old mud burrows of emerging giant dragonflies *(Uropetala cavorei)* in which to lay its eggs.

In Archey's Frog, and possibly in Hochstetter's Frog as well, the male sits on top of the egg mass, guarding it against predators and other sources of danger until the eggs hatch five or six weeks later. When they hatch, the baby frogs measure 0.3 to 0.5 inches (8–12 mm) long and have short tails, which they absorb over the following three to four weeks. The young frogs take three to four years before they reach breeding size.

Parsley Frog

Common name	Parsley Frog
Scientific name	*Pelodytes punctatus*
Family	Pelodytidae
Size	1.97 in (50 mm) maximum.
Key features	A slender frog that has long limbs and toes with little or no webbing to the toes. Its eyes are large and have vertical pupils. It has warts scattered over its back, sometimes arranged in irregular lines, and is pale brown, buff, or gray in color with randomly distributed, bright green or olive spots.
Habits	Nocturnal and terrestrial. A good swimmer and climber.
Breeding	Throughout the spring and summer, in small, often temporary, ponds and ditches.
Diet	Small invertebrates.
Habitat	Open woods, cultivated land, at the base of walls and rock piles, especially in sandy regions.
Distribution	Europe (France, N Spain, and extreme NW Italy).
Status	Has become scarce.
Similar species	The Iberian Parsley Frog (*P. ibericus*) from southern Spain and Portugal is a recently separated species (2000) that is similar but smaller and has a different call; and the Caucasian Parsley Frog (*P. caucasicus*).

The Parsley Frog gets its name from the scattered green markings on the upper part of its body, which make it look as though it has been generously sprinkled with a parsley garnish.

There are three species of parsley frogs altogether and they form a separate family, found only in Europe and the Caucasus Mountains. They are rather mysterious frogs because, although they have a fairly wide range, they are hard to find. *Pelodytes punctatus* seems to have suffered serious declines, especially on the northern fringe of its range—it was formerly found in parts of Belgium and Luxembourg, where it is now almost or completely absent.

Elsewhere it seems to prefer areas with plenty of cover in the form of sparse forests, including pine forests, and among bushes. It spends the day in dense vegetation, under rocks, inside drystone walls and fissures in rock faces, and it also likes to burrow in sandy or limestone-rich soil. In Spain it is sometimes found in gypsum mines. It is a good climber and uses its moist belly to stick temporarily to smooth surfaces. It sometimes rests in bushes and on top of boulders at night.

The Parsley Frog breeds in small bodies of water, and it can tolerate brackish water. During the breeding season the male develops nuptial pads in the form of patches of black tubercles on the chest, arms, and the first two inside fingers. He may also develop short dark spines on his throat and belly to help him grip the female during amplexus.

The female produces a single string of about 40 to 360 eggs, which she twists around the stem of a submerged plant with her hind legs. The eggs hatch after three to 19 days, and metamorphosis takes between three and eight months.

The other two members of the Pelodytidae are the Iberian Parsley Frog *(P. ibericus)* from southern Spain and Portugal and the Caucasian Parsley Frog *(P. caucasicus)* from the Caucasus region. The Iberian species was only separated from *P. punctatus* in 2000, on the basis of a slightly smaller size and differences in the proportions of its limbs and the shape of the

tubercles on its feet. The Caucasian species is similar to the other two but darker. It lives in the forested mountains of the Caucasian isthmus, between the Caspian and Black Seas, in deciduous and mixed forests. Like the other species, it seems to be declining, probably because of habitat change resulting from human development and pollution.

⬇ *The Parsley Frog is agile and graceful, with large eyes. It is mainly nocturnal, but in the breeding season it is active during the day.*

Mexican Burrowing Frog

Common name	Mexican Burrowing Frog
Scientific name	*Rhinophrynus dorsalis*
Family	Rhinophrynidae (of which it is the only member)
Size	2.56–3 in (65–76 mm).
Key features	Unmistakable. Adults are almost as broad as they are long, with a tiny head and blunt, cone-shaped snout. Limbs are short, better suited to burrowing than locomotion. It is dark gray in color with a few scattered white or pinkish white spots around its face and on its flanks, and a conspicuous orange or pink stripe down the center of its back.
Habits	Strictly burrowing, emerging only during heavy rain.
Breeding	In temporary pools and flooded fields after heavy rain.
Diet	Ants, termites, and their larvae.
Habitat	Lowland forests and coastal plains.
Distribution	Central America, barely entering the United States along the Gulf Coast of Texas, extending along the east coast of Mexico into the Yucatán Peninsula, Costa Rica, and just making it to NE Honduras.
Status	Common, though rarely seen.
Similar species	None. Although some of the narrow-mouthed toads, Microhylidae, have the same body shape, they are significantly smaller and lack the brightly colored dorsal stripe.

Immediately after heavy rainstorms, males of this strange species emerge from the ground to call. They are opportunistic breeders, emerging from their underground chambers to mate and lay eggs whenever torrential rain floods the flat countryside where they live.

Their front legs are short and lack webbing, but the hind legs are heavily webbed for swimming and have two elongated tubercles, or "spades," for digging. When they are not calling, their body is flaccid and their skin seems to be several sizes too large for them.

Males have a pair of internal vocal sacs. They inflate themselves like balloons and float on the surface of the flooded land while calling. They make a loud, resonant "whooooooo....." call and form large choruses that can be heard over half a mile away. Females are larger than males. They lay several thousand small eggs following a period of inguinal amplexus. The eggs float to the surface and hatch a few days later.

The tadpoles live in midwater, maintaining a horizontal position by constantly vibrating their tail. They feed by filtering large quantities of water and extracting suspended organic material from it. They tend to live in large shoals of 50 to several hundred individuals, all pointing the same way and moving in synchrony with each other. Although each individual can produce its own current, a large number working together can increase the flow and therefore the amount of food. In experiments, scientists have found that tadpoles kept together in shoals grew more quickly than those raised individually.

They have flattened heads, and eyes positioned on either side of the mouth. The mouth itself is wide, slitlike, and is surrounded by 11 sensitive barbels that presumably help direct the food particles into the mouth. They have no teeth, nor do they have the hard bony beak that most tadpoles use to scrape food from rocks and other hard surfaces. In many respects, the tadpoles of this species are like those of the clawed frogs *(Xenopus)*, and their relatives.

The adult frog has an unusual method of feeding, possibly unique among frogs. The frog's tongue is flat and triangular in shape when contracted, but it can be made stiff and rod-shaped by increasing the hydrostatic pressure in a chamber, or sinus, within it. The tongue can then be protruded through a small groove at the front of the lower jaw. Because it feeds underground, the technique has never been observed, but scientists think that the frog probably pushes its hard calloused snout through the wall of a termite's nest or tunnel and flicks out its tongue to capture the prey inside. Its diet consists mainly of ants, termites, and their larvae.

Mexican Burrowing Frogs are well adapted for their underground lifestyle, with spadelike hind feet and toes and a flattened body. Their tongue is also modified for a specialized diet of ants and termites.

Ghost Frogs

Common name	Ghost Frogs
Scientific name	*Heleophryne* species (5 species)
Family	Heleophrynidae
Size	1.18–2.56 in (30–65 mm). The Natal Ghost Frog *(H. natalensis)* is the largest species.
Key features	They have flattened heads and bodies for squeezing into cracks, and long limbs with adhesive pads on the tips of their toes for climbing wet rocks. The toes of their hind limbs are extensively webbed, and they are good swimmers. Coloration varies among the species; three are tan with darker markings, one is dark brown with yellow markings, and the other is green with reddish brown reticulations.
Habits	Nocturnal; climb among wet boulders.
Breeding	In streams, laying their eggs under rocks and stones.
Diet	Invertebrates.
Habitat	Fast-flowing streams, cascades, and waterfalls in mountainous places.
Distribution	Southern Africa. Each species has a very restricted range—four in the southern Cape region and one in the Natal Drakensberg.
Status	Rare. Hewitt's Ghost Frog *(H. hewitti)* and Table Mountain Ghost Frog *(H. rosei)* are listed by the IUCN as Critically Endangered.
Similar species	None.

Ghost frogs have a very specialized lifestyle and are found in just one type of habitat—waterfalls and fast-flowing streams and torrents—to which they are well adapted.

The whole family occurs in southern Africa, and only in streams that never dry out. Most of these are found on mountain slopes and are fast-flowing and clean. Ghost frogs are active at night, clambering over rocks at the edge of streams and behind waterfalls and torrents in search of food. During the day they may hide under rocks at the water's edge but are more likely to squeeze into the horizontal cracks and crevices between the mossy rocks alongside and behind the waterfalls. One species, the Natal Ghost Frog *(Heleophryne natalensis)*, may live a short

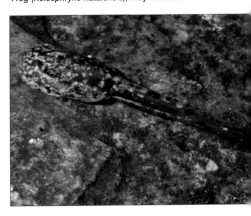

⊕ The tadpoles of ghost frogs are known as "stream-type." They have small tail fins to reduce drag and suckerlike mouths with which to attach themselves to stones.

⊕ Heleophryne rosei *has one of the most restricted ranges of any South African amphibian. Found only on Table Mountain, it lives in streams and damp forested gorges.*

distance away from the streams and has been found hiding in holes made by ground woodpeckers.

The four Cape species breed in the spring, but for the Natal Ghost Frog the season is later, toward the end of summer. Mating in all the species takes place in quiet backwaters and pools, and amplexus is inguinal.

The tadpoles of all the species have streamlined shapes and large suckerlike mouths that help them cling to stones and rocks, thereby avoiding being swept away in the current. Apart from grazing over stones and rocks on the bottom of streams and pools, ghost frog tadpoles can climb vertical surfaces using their mouths and even work their way up waterfalls.

They take at least two years to develop into adult frogs, which means that the streams in which they develop must last throughout the year. If they were to dry up, all the tadpoles would die.

The need for permanent streams makes these frogs vulnerable to environmental changes, especially habitat destruction. Fortunately, all the species gain some protection from living in a type of habitat (mountain fynbos) that is now recognized as being unique and worth saving.

Marsh Striped Frog

Common names	Marsh Striped Frog, Brown Marsh Striped Frog, Brown Frog
Scientific name	*Limnodynastes peronii*
Family	Limnodynastidae
Size	2.56 in (65 mm).
Key features	An agile frog with long hind limbs and a pointed snout. It is brown in color with a light-colored stripe starting at the tip of the snout and running down the center of its back. There are darker stripes on either side of this and a dark mask across its eyes. There is some variation in overall color, with some being nearly uniform dark brown.
Habits	Terrestrial and nocturnal.
Breeding	It forms a floating foam nest in shallow water.
Diet	Invertebrates.
Habitat	Near permanent water, especially swamps and marshes but also streams and ponds. May be found in large numbers in urban situations.
Distribution	Tasmania and the coastal parts of E Australia.
Status	Common.
Similar species	Other marsh frogs tend to be more heavily built. The Salmon-striped Frog (*L. salmini*) is the only species that is likely to be confused with it, and then only with especially pale individuals.

The Australian marsh frogs occupy a similar niche to the European and North American grass frogs (*Rana*). Many of them—but not the Marsh Striped Frog —are burrowing species that have sharp ridges on the bottom of their hind feet.

The Marsh Striped Frog is more generalized in its habits and lives in a wide variety of places, always near water but preferring shallow swamps and marshes. It is also quick to colonize garden ponds and other urban and suburban habitats. It tends to live under vegetation and debris near the water and does not have the heavily webbed feet of a dedicated swimmer.

Like other members of its genus, it lays its eggs in foam masses that float on the surface. Males call from the water with just their heads showing. If there are already rafts of foam floating on the surface, they may call from beneath them. Females use their front feet to whip up the jelly mass into a foam nest, in which they lay up to 1,000 eggs.

⊙ *The Marsh Striped Frog is one of the most common frogs of the eastern coast of Australia.*

Northern Banjo Frog

Common names	Northern Banjo Frog, Scarlet-sided Pobblebonk, Northern Bullfrog
Scientific name	*Limnodynastes terraereginiae*
Family	Limnodynastidae
Size	2.95 in (75 mm).
Key features	This is a heavily built species, with relatively short legs and a rounded body. Each hind foot has a sharp ridge, or "spade," for digging. It is gray above with some small dark speckles. It has darker "mask" markings, and a line of cream or pale orange runs from the upper jaw to the base of each arm. There is a stripe of the same color on each flank. There are also bright red flash markings on the insides of the hind legs and on the thighs.
Habits	Burrowing and nocturnal.
Breeding	It forms a foam nest attached to vegetation in shallow water.
Diet	Invertebrates.
Habitat	Dry forests and open woodlands.
Distribution	Australia (coastal parts of Queensland and NE New South Wales).
Status	Moderately common.
Similar species	Only the Western Banjo Frog *(L.dorsalis)* and the Giant Banjo Frog *(L. interioris)*, but the ranges of the three species do not overlap. Otherwise, the contrasting stripes on its sides help identify this frog.

Also known as the Scarlet-sided Pobblebonk, this frog lives in dry areas near streams and ponds, only emerging onto the surface following rain. Males call from submerged holes in the banks and are well known for their call, which is a single "plonk" repeated every few seconds. To some people it sounds like a badly-tuned banjo string being plucked, hence its common name.

Females lay their eggs on the surface of the water. Flanges of skin around the edges of their inner fingers help them whip up the egg mass into a frothy foam. They lay up to 1,000 eggs each year, and the tadpoles are large and dark brown. They take 70 to 90 days to complete their development and a further two to three years to reach breeding size.

Although figures are not available, there are concerns in some quarters that the populations of this frog may be under pressure from water pollution, clearance of vegetation, and the invasion of foreign plants. Its range overlaps that of the introduced Cane Toad *(Bufo marinus)*, and the tadpoles may suffer from competition with that species.

⊝ *Usually seen on the surface only after rain, Northern Banjo Frogs are found in coastal areas of Queensland and New South Wales, Australia.*

Desert Spadefoot Toad

Common name	Desert Spadefoot Toad, Desert Shovelfoot
Scientific name	*Notaden nichollsi*
Family	Limnodynastidae
Size	2.36 in (60 mm).
Key features	Plump, almost globular in shape, with short limbs and a short head. Gray, brown, or olive above with a few indistinct paler blotches and speckles.
Habits	Burrowing and nocturnal.
Breeding	In temporary bodies of shallow water.
Diet	Invertebrates, especially ants and termites.
Habitat	Deserts.
Distribution	Central Australia.
Status	Not easily found.
Similar species	None in the area, although there are other spadefoot toads, including three other species of *Notaden*, in Australia.

Spadefoot toads (*Notaden* species) are Australian versions of the African rain frogs *(Breviceps)*. They live in the same type of habitat and are similar in appearance and behavior.

These frogs are adapted for burrowing. They have sharp-edged tubercles on the heels of their hind feet. During burrowing, they shuffle their feet alternately, using the "spades" to displace the soil. They are "circular burrowers," turning through 360 degrees as they gradually descend below the surface. They remain underground until it rains heavily, at which point they dig to the surface to breed in temporary shallows.

The eggs, numbering up to 1,000, are laid in a long string and wound around submerged vegetation. They hatch quickly, and the tadpoles grow and develop equally quickly, completing their metamorphosis in 16 days, before all the water has dried up.

Spadefoot toads have an unusual defensive mechanism. If molested, they exude a white milky substance from their skin. It is extremely sticky and is thought to deter biting insects in particular—they become trapped as surely as if they had landed on fly paper.

The Desert Spadefoot Toad inhabits the dry areas of Central Australia.

Moaning Frog

Common name	Moaning Frog
Scientific name	Heleioporus eyrei
Family	Myobatrachidae
Size	2.36 in (60 mm).
Key features	A chubby frog with short limbs, no webbing on the hands, and little or no webbing on the hands and feet. It has prominent raised eyes and vertical pupils. Brown, with indistinct darker and paler markings in the form of marbling or fine speckling.
Habits	Nocturnal and terrestrial. Semiburrowing.
Breeding	In flooded burrows.
Diet	Invertebrates.
Habitat	Sandy and peaty bogs and swamps.
Distribution	Extreme SW of Western Australia.
Status	Probably common.
Similar species	A related species, the Sand Frog (H. psammophilus) from the same region, is practically identical.

The Moaning Frog is typical of species that live semiburrowing lives in wet, sandy soil. It is thickset and has short but powerful limbs. It lives in burrows that it digs itself, and males call from inside their burrows. Females approach the males, and they mate and lay their eggs inside the burrow, suspending them in a frothy mass that the female whips up with her feet. The eggs may hatch but remain in this foam mass until the burrow floods and fills with water after heavy rain, often a considerable time after laying. The rain releases the tadpoles, and they continue to develop in the normal way.

The Sand Frog (Heleioporus psammophilus) is an almost identical frog from the same region. Females of the two species are almost impossible to distinguish, and males can only be identified on the basis of their calls. Whereas the Moaning Frog's call is a drawn-out, high-pitched moan, that of the Sand Frog consists of a pulsating "peeping" sound that is repeated at short intervals.

Species that look identical and can be separated only with difficulty are known as cryptic species. Because a frog's call is an essential part of the mate-selection process, males that produce different calls must belong to different species, even if they look alike.

⊖ *Moaning Frogs from Western Australia get their name from the long, high-pitched call of the males.*

Great Barred Frog

Common names	Great Barred Frog, Great Barred River Frog
Scientific name	*Mixophyes fasciolatus*
Family	Myobatrachidae
Size	3.15 in (80 mm).
Key features	A heavily built frog with long, powerful limbs and strongly webbed feet. It is brown or gray with a dark line passing through its eye. Its legs are marked with darker bars.
Habits	Terrestrial and mainly nocturnal.
Breeding	In a large clump on land at the edge of water.
Diet	Invertebrates and small vertebrates.
Habitat	Found in rain forests.
Distribution	Australia (coastal mountain ranges of Queensland and New South Wales).
Status	Common.
Similar species	There are several other *Mixophyes* species that look similar and whose ranges overlap that of *M. fasciolatus*. The markings on the back, spots on its side, and dark brown iris may help distinguish this one.

These large frogs are generalists, living in wet forest habitats and preying on almost anything they can catch and swallow. They often hide in leaf litter near permanent fast-flowing streams.

Males call (a deep, harsh "wark" sound) in spring and summer from the banks of streams. Mating takes place at the water's edge; once the eggs are fertilized, the female pushes them up onto the bank. The eggs are sticky, and fix easily to leaves, rocks, and grasses.

After hatching, the tadpoles drop into the water or get washed in when it rains. They are large and dark golden brown to gray brown in color, with a streamlined shape. In flowing water they attach themselves to rocks and other surfaces by the mouth.

Females are believed to reproduce for the first time after two to three years and produce between 200 and 1,000 eggs per year.

The species seems to tolerate disturbance and changes in habitat, as long as some forest remains. It may breed in farm dams and water holes. Overall, numbers may have increased slightly in recent years.

⊙ *A Great Barred Frog at night in a Queensland rain forest.*

Turtle Frog

Common name	Turtle Frog
Scientific name	*Myobatrachus gouldii*
Family	Myobatrachidae
Size	2.36 in (60 mm).
Key features	A blob-shaped frog with stumpy limbs and a tiny head. Gray or brown in color with few, if any, markings. Its name comes from its appearance, which is like a turtle that has lost its shell.
Habits	Lives underground in burrows. Unlike most frogs, this species burrows head-first.
Breeding	Underground. The young develop directly without a free-living tadpole stage.
Diet	Termites.
Habitat	Beneath logs in sandy areas.
Distribution	Extreme SW of Western Australia.
Status	Difficult to estimate, since they are secretive and do not congregate to breed.
Similar species	Unmistakable.

The Turtle Frog is a very strange frog that lives under the surface in the open areas of Western Australia, among sparse trees or scrub, on sandhills or where the soil is sandy. It appears to feed exclusively on termites, and its preferred habitat is always associated with termite nests. It burrows down into the soil using its short but powerful front legs, or rests beneath logs and rocks that are partially embedded in the soil. Its snout is calcified and is used as a ram for pushing through the soil.

These frogs appear on the surface only in spring and summer after rainstorms, when they breed. Males call from the surface or from a partially buried position. Amplexus does not take place on the surface, so presumably the pair burrows into the soil to mate underground.

The eggs are very large and are laid in clusters of about 40, in a chamber 3 to 4 feet (1–1.2 m) beneath the surface. The young frogs develop directly inside the egg capsule without going through a free-living tadpole stage.

The Turtle Frog bears some similarities in behavior and body shape to the African rain frogs of the genus *Breviceps* and the pig-snouted frogs (*Hemisus* species).

⊖ *The Turtle Frog from Western Australia can often be found in the nests of termites, which are the only items in its diet.*

Corroboree Toadlet

Common name	Corroboree Toadlet
Scientific name	*Pseudophryne corroboree*
Family	Myobatrachidae
Size	1.18–1.57 in (30–40 mm)
Key features	Stout with short limbs, a slightly warty skin, and small parotid glands. It has bold black and yellow spots and stripes over its body and limbs and is instantly recognizable.
Habits	Active during the day as well as at night. Mostly terrestrial, but may burrow.
Breeding	Eggs laid in damp sphagnum moss.
Diet	Small insects, including ants and termites.
Habitat	In wet or flooded grasslands and marshes and in sphagnum bogs, at high altitudes (above the tree line).
Distribution	Australian Alps around Mount Kosciusko, New South Wales.
Status	Thought to be one of Australia's most endangered frogs. The IUCN lists it as Critically Endangered.
Similar species	*Pseudophryne pengilleyi*, described in 1985, is very similar and is listed by the IUCN as Endangered.

The Australian toadlets include a number of brightly colored frogs, all of which are thought to be poisonous to predators. The Corroboree Toadlet is the brightest of all. Startlingly marked in yellow and black, it gets its name from the corroborees, traditional Aboriginal gatherings in which the participants paint their skin with stripes of yellow ocher.

The Corroboree Toadlet and its closest relative, the Northern Corroboree Toadlet *(Pseudophryne pengilleyi)*, live in upland sphagnum bogs. Males occupy tunnels in the moss, arriving several weeks before breeding starts in fall and calling from tunnels in the moss. The females lay between six and 40 large eggs, and the males usually stay with the eggs for up to four weeks. The eggs do not develop immediately, but wait

until rain inundates the burrow, so the total time to hatching is four to six months. The tadpoles take another six to eight months to reach metamorphosis.

Most frogs and toads have some degree of protection against predators through poisons they secrete from glands in their skin. They accumulate these toxins through eating mildly poisonous insects (which, in turn, obtain them from poisonous or distasteful plants). The poisons involved belong to the alkaloid group of compounds and are called pumiliotoxins. If these species are deprived of their normal diet,

they gradually lose their toxicity. At least some of the Australian toadlets are different, though: recent research has shown that they manufacture their own poisons. This is highly unusual, possibly unique, among frogs.

Scientists found that wild frogs contained mostly pumiliotoxins but also traces of different substances, which they called pseudophrynamines. When held in captivity and therefore denied access to toxic insects, the pumiliotoxins disappeared from the frogs' systems as expected, but the amounts of pseudophrynamines increased.

The rare Corroboree Toadlet is found only in a very small area of New South Wales, Australia.

Chacoan Horned Frog

Common names	Chacoan Horned Frog, Cranwell's Horned Frog
Scientific name	*Ceratophrys cranwelli*
Family	Leptodactylidae
Size	4.92 in (12.5 cm).
Key features	Large, round-bodied toad with a huge mouth and short "horns" above the eyes. Its limbs are short and it can move only clumsily by short hops. Coloration usually a shade of brown or tan with symmetrical darker markings on its back. Widely bred in captivity, but many of the examples sold are hybrids between this species and Bell's Horned Toad *(C. ornata).*
Habits	Terrestrial. It lies in wait for its prey, relying on its camouflage, and is not normally very active.
Breeding	Females lay 1,000–2,000 eggs in shallow water. The tadpoles are carnivorous and grow quickly, leaving the water after 1–2 months as miniature versions of the adults and with similarly hearty appetites.
Diet	Invertebrates and small vertebrates.
Habitat	Seasonally dry flat plains, known as *chaco.*
Distribution	Lowland regions of Argentina, Bolivia, Brazil, and Paraguay.
Status	Widespread and abundant.
Similar species	Other species of *Ceratophrys,* although there are differences in coloration and the size of the "horns."

Many of the areas where Chacoan Horned Frogs live have a prolonged dry season. If their ponds dry up, they dig themselves into the mud and form a cocoon with several layers of shed skin. They remain in this state for several months until summer storms or floods occur, when they make their way back to the surface.

Breeding takes place after rains and is opportunistic. Males make a loud metallic call, and the female scatters between 1,000 and 2,000 eggs over the bottom of the pond. The tadpoles grow very large—up to 2.8 inches (7 cm), despite having a short tail. In contrast to most other species they are carnivorous, eating small aquatic invertebrates, the tadpoles of other frogs, and each other. They grow rapidly and metamorphose after about a month. Rapid growth and development may be necessary to avoid being stranded in shrinking pools.

Chacoan Horned Frogs have become popular pets. They are attractive, and as new color forms become available through selective breeding and hybridization, it could almost be considered a domestic animal. It has plenty of character, and its "attitude" appeals to certain people (although captives are nearly always placid). Large specimens are very impressive. It is relatively tough and easily cared for with the minimum of outlay and attention, although being a tropical species it requires some supplementary heating.

⊖ ⬆ Above: The Chacoan Horned Frog from South America.
Left: This Horned Frog, or Escuerzo, is a hybrid between the
Chacoan Horned Frog and Bell's Horned Frog (C. ornata).

Amazonian Horned Frog

Common name	Amazonian Horned Frog
Scientific name	*Ceratophrys cornuta*
Family	Leptodactylidae
Size	Males to 2.83 in (72 mm); females to 4.72 in (120 mm).
Key features	A rounded frog with short limbs. The hind limbs in particular look incapable of supporting the frog's weight. The horns over this species' eyes are long and very characteristic. It is variable in color and may be shades of green, tan, brown, or beige, with darker and paler stripes and blotches.
Habits	A sit-and-wait predator that relies on camouflage to escape detection.
Breeding	In pools and flooded areas after heavy rain. The tadpoles are large and carnivorous.
Diet	Invertebrates and small vertebrates, such as other frogs and rodents.
Habitat	Rain forests.
Distribution	Amazon Basin.
Status	Widespread but rarely seen.
Similar species	Other horned frogs. This species has very long horns.

This frog's mouth is more than one and a half times as wide as its body is long. The Amazonian Horned Frog is an eating machine and will attack and overpower other animals almost as large as itself. It can also give a painful bite to humans. Its skull is bony, with many of the smaller bones fused together.

The Amazonian Horned Frog lives in all the countries within the Amazon Basin, giving it the widest range of any of the South American horned frogs, but its camouflage is so effective that it is rarely seen. It lives in forests, including those that are inundated with floodwater during the rainy season, and its strategy is to wait, half-buried among leaves, until a likely victim passes by. It takes its prey with a sudden lunge and grasps it in its mouth.

It feeds on anything small enough to fit into its large mouth, including ants and beetles as well as smaller frogs, lizards, snakes, and small mammals. Analyzing the stomach contents of some of these frogs, scientists found that large prey can account for more than half of their diet.

Adults are active mostly at night, but juveniles may be active in the day as well. Breeding takes place at the start of the rainy season, and males have loud calls. The tadpoles are armed with a bony beak and feed mainly on other tadpoles. They metamorphose when they reach about 1 inch (25 mm). Assuming they can find enough food (which sometimes includes other metamorphosing frogs of their own species), they grow quickly.

⊖ *The Amazonian Horned Frog is cryptically marked and usually lurks among leaves to ambush its prey.*

Bell's Horned Frog

Common names	Bell's Horned Frog, Argentine Horned Frog, Ornate Horned Frog, Pacman Frog, Escuerzo
Scientific name	*Ceratophrys ornata*
Family	Leptodactylidae
Size	4.92 in (12.5 cm).
Key features	Almost as wide as it is long, Bell's Horned Frog is one of the most distinctive frogs. Its plump body is almost spherical and its legs are short. Its mouth is huge, stretching the full width of its body. Its eyes are situated toward the top of its head and have small fleshy projections, or horns, over them. It is brown in color, with darker brown, green, and red markings consisting of blotches and streaks, sometimes with pale borders.
Habits	Terrestrial. It is never very active but is more likely to be seen on the move at night.
Breeding	Seasonal, laying eggs in ponds and flooded areas in the wet season.
Diet	Any living thing that fits into its mouth.
Habitat	Open forests and semidesert flatlands.
Distribution	Argentina, Paraguay, Uruguay, and S Brazil.
Status	In decline; Near Threatened (IUCN).
Similar species	There are seven other species in the genus, all of similar build, but the coloration and distribution of Bell's Horned Frog set it apart from the others.

Owing to its shape and its voracious appetite, Bell's Horned Frog is often known as the "pacman" frog in the pet trade. It has also been described as a stomach on legs.

Its massive bony head and huge gape are suited for a single purpose: capturing and swallowing prey. Few frogs have evolved toward such a dedicated "eat everything" philosophy.

It is a classic sit-and-wait predator, ambushing prey from a hidden location, usually partly buried in soil or leaf litter with just its eyes exposed. This frog rarely strays far from a favored hunting site and will take on almost any prey that happens to pass, lunging forward suddenly and using its mouth as a trap.

It has formidable fanglike teeth that point slightly backward, making escape difficult for its victims, and any small animal unfortunate enough to be captured is unlikely to survive. In the wild its prey is largely unknown, although other frogs form a large proportion

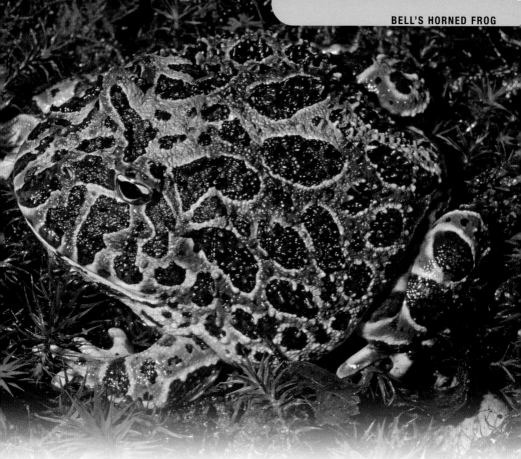

of their diet. They are also cannibalistic, eating smaller members and tadpoles of their own species. Captives will eat large insects such as adult locusts and small vertebrates such as mice.

In their natural range local people think Bell's Horned Frogs are venomous. This belief has arisen because of the frogs' aggressive temperament. If they

⊕ *The distinctive huge mouth of Bell's Horned Frog from South America stretches the full width of its body and is designed to swallow any living thing that comes within reach.*

are threatened, they open their mouth wide and may jump at their enemy. Getting bitten by a horned frog is no laughing matter.

Perez's Eyelash Frog

Common name	Perez's Eyelash Frog
Scientific name	*Edalorhina perezi*
Family	Leptodactylidae
Size	1.18 in (30 mm).
Key features	A small frog with a blunt snout. It has a number of conical tubercles on each eyelid, forming a fringe or frill, hence its common name. Its body is flattened and has a prominent ridge along each flank. It is marked in shades of brown, with dark and light blotches and spots, which provide effective camouflage against the forest floor.
Habits	Terrestrial and diurnal.
Breeding	In temporary pools.
Diet	Invertebrates.
Habitat	Lowland tropical forests.
Distribution	Amazon Basin, from Colombia to Bolivia.
Status	Common.
Similar species	None known. The only other species in the genus, *E. nasuta*, is known only from a few specimens in central Peru.

This unusual frog is poorly known. Its "eyelashes" are very distinctive but their purpose is unclear—they may simply help break up the frog's outline when it is resting among leaf litter and general debris on the forest floor. A few species of snakes and lizards have similar ornamentation that is also thought to be connected with disguise.

The breeding habits of Perez's Eyelash Frog are fairly typical of leptodactylids. Males call from among leaves on the forest floor. When a male has attracted a female, the pair goes into amplexus and moves into a small temporary pool. They lay up to 100 eggs in a foam nest, which they create by kicking their back legs as the eggs are laid. The nest is rounded and floats on the surface of the water. The tadpoles wriggle free of their foam "meringue" shortly after they hatch and continue their development in the water.

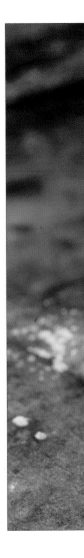

⊖ *The cryptic coloring of Perez's Eyelash Frog, seen here in Ecuador, enables it to blend well with leaf litter on the forest floor. © Arthur Georges.*

Coqui Frog

Common names	Coqui Frog, Common Coqui
Scientific name	*Eleutherodactylus coqui*
Family	Leptodactylidae
Size	2.05 in (52 mm).
Key features	Small frog with disks on the ends of its fingers and toes for climbing. Usually brown in color and with a darker line running through each eye and a faint pattern of darker speckles on its back.
Habits	Nocturnal and mostly terrestrial, although it will climb into low shrubs and bushes, and even into tall trees.
Breeding	On land, with direct development.
Diet	Small invertebrates.
Habitat	Forests and disturbed habitats.
Distribution	Puerto Rico. Also introduced into several West Indian Islands, Hawaii, and the American mainland.
Status	Common.
Similar species	Other *Eleutherodactylus* species. Identification is best made on distribution.

The Coqui Frog has become a pest species in places where it has been introduced, especially in Hawaii. In its native Puerto Rico it occurs alongside about 20 other species of *Eleutherodactylus* frogs, and a biological balance between populations is maintained. On Hawaii, however, where it was first heard in the mid- to late 1990s, it has no competitors and has spread unchecked.

It occurs on "Big Island," Maui, and Oahu, in gardens, parks, plant nurseries, and forest edges. It seems to prefer disturbed habitats, and populations often increase after hurricanes have brought down tall vegetation. The main problem associated with it is the incessant calls of high densities of males. Their two-part calls—"cock-eee"—give the species its

common name. It belongs to a genus of frogs *(Eleutherodactylus)* known collectively as robber frogs.

The species owes its success to its high breeding potential. Females lay up to six clutches of 25 to 30 eggs each year. Fertilization is internal, and males guard the eggs. The young hatch as fully formed froglets after 17 to 26 days. The time between generations is about eight months. Numbers can build up quickly, and estimates of 20,000 frogs per hectare have been made.

Accidental introductions of the frog into other parts of the region are made when potted

plants harboring eggs are transported from one place to another. Several other robber frogs have been spread in this way, including the Greenhouse Frog *(E. planirostris)* and the Martinique Robber Frog *(E. martinicensis)*, but because their calls are quieter, they often go unnoticed.

⊕ *Populations of Coqui Frogs have grown rapidly in Hawaii, where the species was first introduced in the 1990s.*

Martinique Robber Frog

Common names	Martinique Robber Frog, Lesser Antilles Robber Frog
Scientific name	*Eleutherodactylus martinicensis*
Family	Leptodactylidae
Size	To 1.85 in (47 mm).
Key features	Small frog with obvious disks on the ends of its fingers and toes. Brown in color, with a dark "mask" across each eye. It has a speckled dark brown marking on its back.
Habits	Nocturnal and mostly terrestrial, but occasionally climbs into low bushes.
Breeding	Out of water, with direct development.
Diet	Small invertebrates.
Habitat	Forests and forest edges.
Distribution	The Lesser Antilles, West Indies, and introduced to Maui, Hawaii.
Status	Widespread and common.
Similar species	The commonest species of robber frog in the region.

This is a very adaptable species of robber frog. Its natural habitat is rain forest. It also lives in dry forests, although in smaller numbers. It seems to be most common, however, in disturbed habitats, including gardens, sugarcane fields, banana plantations, and inside houses. It forages mostly on the ground but calls from low bushes and bromeliad plants (air plants) during the night. It lays its eggs on the ground, among moss and leaf litter. As in all species of robber frogs, the eggs hatch directly into small adult frogs.

The Martinique Robber Frog's main claim to fame is its ability to crop up far away from its natural home, having stowed away in produce, especially bananas. By this method it occurs with great regularity in all the countries that import bananas from the smaller West Indian islands.

In temperate countries its life span is obviously limited, but in some places it thrives to the point of being considered a nuisance. In Hawaii, for example, it has become widely established. As with the Coqui Frog *(Eleutherodactylus coqui)*, there are concerns that it will compete with small birds on the island for food and will contribute toward the decline of native forest birds. In addition, its deafening choruses are beginning to disturb the sleep of Hawaiian residents.

→ *A male Martinique Robber Frog inflates his vocal sac, calling to establish a territory and attract a mate.*

Noble's Robber Frog

Common names	Noble's Robber Frog, Noble's Leaf Litter Frog
Scientific name	*Eleutherodactylus noblei* (*Craugastor noblei*)
Family	Leptodactylidae
Size	1.69–2.6 in (43–66 mm).
Key features	Larger than many robber frogs but still quite small, with obvious disks on the ends of its fingers and smaller ones on its toes. Brown in color, with a dark "mask" across each eye. It has a dark brown marking on its back, often in the shape of an hourglass.
Habits	Nocturnal and mostly terrestrial, but occasionally climbs into low bushes.
Breeding	Out of water, with direct development.
Diet	Small invertebrates.
Habitat	Forests and forest edges.
Distribution	Central America, from Honduras to Panama.
Status	Widespread but not common.
Similar species	There are several similar species in the region and identification can be difficult.

Noble's Robber Frog is found throughout the forested parts of Central America. It occurs from sea level up to montane foothills but is absent from grasslands and swamps. Unusually, males of this species do not call (in many robber frogs males are very vocal and highly territorial, and will fight if another calling male encroaches on their territory). Eggs are laid on the ground or among moss-covered tree trunks, where they develop directly into tiny froglets the size of bluebottle flies.

Robber frogs form the largest genus of frogs in the world, with more than 600 species occurring from Mexico to Brazil and including most West Indian islands. They have also been introduced into other tropical areas.

Populations of robber frogs in many parts of Central and South America appear to be declining, even in habitats that are largely undisturbed (but Noble's Robber Frog is too poorly studied to know if it is affected). The reasons are not clear, but infection with chytridiomycosis fungus, the suspected cause of declining amphibian populations elsewhere in the world, is a possibility. Populations on Trinidad have not been studied.

There are recent proposals to reclassify the robber frogs and some of their close relatives, moving them from the Leptodactylidae into the Brachycephalidae, a family that at present holds just three species. It may take a little while before this is generally accepted by herpetologists.

⊖ *In a Costa Rican rain forest a Noble's Robber Frog makes a good job of mimicking a dead leaf.*

Greenhouse Frog

Common names	Greenhouse Frog, Cuban Litter Frog
Scientific name	*Eleutherodactylus planirostris*
Family	Leptodactylidae
Size	0.39–4.13 in (10–105 mm).
Key features	A small frog that may have a pair of stripes down either side of its back or may be mottled in different shades of brown, cream, and tan. Overall, it often has a reddish or pinkish tint.
Habits	Mostly nocturnal and terrestrial, although it will climb into low vegetation.
Breeding	Terrestrial breeders, with direct development.
Diet	Small invertebrates.
Habitat	Deciduous forests, rain forests, plantations, gardens, and parks.
Distribution	From extreme S Texas and Arizona through Central America and the West Indies to Argentina and Brazil. Introduced to Florida and Louisiana.
Status	Very abundant.
Similar species	Distinguishing between different species of *Eleutherodactylus* can be very difficult.

The Greenhouse Frog is a West Indian species from Cuba and several small islands and island groups. It was introduced to Florida in 1875 and has spread throughout most of the state, including the Keys, where it is the commonest frog in many places. It also turned up in Louisiana in 1975, exactly 100 years after the Florida introduction, and may have arrived among soil or plants that were moved from Florida to a large nursery near New Orleans.

Wherever it goes, the greenhouse frog is a success. It lives among leaves, boards, and other debris, often in greenhouses, gardens, and parks. At night or during rainstorms males make a short chirping noise, like a quiet cricket, and are easily overlooked. They breed throughout the warmer months, usually May to September in Florida.

The female lays between three and 26 eggs in a small cluster on damp soil and stays nearby for 13 days, after which time they hatch. The newly hatched froglets are 0.16 to 0.24 inches (4–6 mm) in length and they feed on tiny invertebrates.

Adults of the species eat ants, beetles, spiders, and other arthropods. They have long slender toes with no webbing but with squared-off, expanded tips. This is a dimorphic species, with two patterns—mottled and striped—of which the former is more common in most populations.

⊖ *The Greenhouse Frog is a dainty, agile species with long limbs and toes. This frog was photographed at Pinar del Rio, Cuba.*

Other *Eleutherodactylus* Species

⊖ *Right:* Eleutherodactylus conspicillatus, *Ecuador.*
A conspicuous forest inhabitant, this frog is found in
Brazil, Colombia, Ecuador, and Peru.

⊖ ⊖ *Opposite page:* Eleutherodactylus croceoinguinis *(seen*
here in Río Palenque, Ecuador) is a nocturnal species found on
low vegetation in dense forests in Colombia, Ecuador, and Peru.

⊕ Eleutherodactylus malkini, *Ecuador. This species is known*
from lowland forest in western Brazil, southeastern Colombia,
eastern Ecuador, and eastern Peru.

Budgett's Frog

Common name	Budgett's Frog
Scientific name	*Lepidobatrachus laevis*
Family	Leptodactylidae
Size	Females to 3.94 in (100 mm); males about half this size.
Key features	A wide, flattened frog with very wide mouth, rounded body, small eyes on the top of the head, and short limbs. The back is smooth and gray or greenish in color, with darker blotches that have orange outlines. Male has a dark throat.
Habits	Nocturnal and semiaquatic, but burrowing in the dry season.
Breeding	In shallow temporary pools. The tadpoles develop quickly to emerge before the water dries up.
Diet	Other frogs, small reptiles and mammals, and invertebrates.
Habitat	*Chaco* (arid plains with seasonal rain).
Distribution	Argentina, Bolivia, Paraguay.
Status	Common but rarely seen.
Similar species	Two other species in the genus (*L.asper* and *L. llanensis)* are similar but lack the orange markings.

Even in a family of strange-looking frogs, Budgett's Frogs stand out as the most bizarre of all. The Budgett's Frog (named for its discoverer) is highly adapted for life in the extreme conditions of South American *chaco* habitats. During the dry winter months these frogs remain underground in a cocoon that is made up of several layers of shed skins, which helps protects them from desiccation.

Heavy rains at the beginning of spring create many temporary pools, and the frogs emerge from their underground retreats and begin to feed and breed. They are sit-and-wait predators, submerging themselves in the water or mud with only their eyes above the surface. Possible prey include other frogs, large invertebrates, and snails.

Females lay up to 1,400 eggs that hatch quickly into carnivorous tadpoles with formidable jaws. They feed on each other or on other tadpole species, swallowing them whole in the same way as the adults feed. Development is a race against time, and many batches of tadpoles dry up before they have a chance to metamorphose.

Budgett's Frogs are very aggressive. If disturbed, they inflate their body and raise themselves up on their legs. If all else fails, they open their mouth, emit a loud shriek like a cat in pain, and launch themselves at their tormentor, using two large tusks in the lower jaw to bite. They can draw blood and may be difficult to dislodge.

⊕ *The eyes and nostrils of Budgett's Frog point upward, and the snout slopes sharply down. With its enormously wide mouth, it is a bizarre-looking frog.*

Llanos Frog

Common names	Llanos Frog, Dwarf Budgett's Frog
Scientific name	*Lepidobatrachus llanensis*
Family	Leptodactylidae
Size	2.56–3.94 in (65–100 mm).
Key features	Unmistakable. A rounded, bloated frog with small limbs, a wide gape, and small bulbous eyes on the top of its head. Gray or grayish brown in color with no markings, although it has a few small irregular warts on its back.
Habits	Aquatic.
Breeding	In shallow pools.
Diet	Large invertebrates and small vertebrates, including smaller frogs.
Habitat	Temporary shallow pools in seasonally wet floodplains, known as the *chaco*.
Distribution	Argentina and northern Paraguay.
Status	Common at times but vulnerable to habitat changes.
Similar species	Two other species in the genus, *L. laevis* and *L. asper*, are similar in general appearance but differ in their proportions and the shape of their pupils; *L. laevis* is also significantly larger.

Llanos Frogs live an unusual lifestyle in shallow pools which form during the seasonal heavy rains that occur in the Argentine *chaco* region from October to February. The pools form on clay soil, and the water becomes turbid, suiting sit-and-wait predators such as Llanos Frogs. They sink into the soft mud with just their bulbous eyes showing, waiting for other frogs, large insects, and snails to come within range. They are aggressive feeders, lunging forward suddenly to grasp their prey in a huge mouth that is armed with large fanglike teeth.

Like Budgett's Frogs (*Lepidobatrachus laevis*), they inflate their body and straighten their legs to keep themselves clear of the ground if disturbed, and will lunge at their predator with an open mouth. The local name for the frog translates as the "toad that shrieks."

Breeding takes place as soon as the rains fill the shallow pans in which the frogs live. Females can lay more than 1,000 eggs, which develop rapidly. They hatch into voracious, predatory tadpoles that begin feeding immediately. Their jaws have adaptations that allow them to spread sideways, producing a huge gape with which they engulf prey nearly as large as themselves. They prey on other tadpoles, including those of the same species. They grow and develop quickly so that they can leave the pools before they dry up.

Llanos Frog, Argentina. The rounded body of these strange-looking frogs is gray, broken up only by the small prominent eyes on top of the head.

Basin White-lipped Frog

Common names	Basin White-lipped Frog, Mustached Frog
Scientific name	*Leptodactylus mystaceus*
Family	Leptodactylidae
Size	1.85–2.05 in (47–52 mm).
Key features	A powerful frog with long, muscular back legs. It has large eyes positioned on top of its head and horizontally elliptical pupils. Its eardrum is about the same size as its eyes and very prominent. Color varies, but it is usually gray with a darker "mask" across its eyes. It may have a lighter stripe down the center of its back.
Habits	Rarely found far from water. Nocturnal.
Breeding	During the rainy season, in underground chambers near ponds and lakes.
Diet	Invertebrates and small vertebrates.
Habitat	Large and small ponds, swamps and neighboring forests, plantations and clearings in lowland forests.
Distribution	South America, in the Amazon Basin.
Status	Common.
Similar species	Several other *Leptodactylus* species are similar in appearance.

This is a common frog found throughout much of the Amazon Basin, where it lives in burrows or beneath logs or stones, emerging at night to hunt. Large numbers can often be found in puddles, including those on roadways, during heavy rain.

During rainy weather the males call from underground chambers, which they dig themselves. The chambers are positioned at the edge of a pond or a flooded area. Each chamber is slightly larger than the frog, and several may be connected to form an extensive gallery reaching up to 3 feet (1 m) across. This probably allows the frogs to escape if predators enter or dig up their burrows.

Females visit the males and lay their eggs in the chambers, whipping up a mass of foam around them. When the young hatch, they feed on the foam at first but soon make their way to the pond and become free-living. Tadpoles of other species of *Leptodactylus* (and possibly this one) form dense shoals and move around in the water like a ball, with one of the parents, usually the female, in

attendance. This is a form of parental care and is thought to prevent predators from attacking the tadpoles.

⊙ *Basin White-lipped Frog, Pastaza, Ecuador. This small but powerful frog is a nighttime hunter.*

Smoky Jungle Frog

Common names	Smoky Jungle Frog, South American Bullfrog
Scientific name	*Leptodactylus pentadactylus*
Family	Leptodactylidae
Size	To 3.94 in (100 mm).
Key features	A large, heavily built frog with prominent ridges of skin along either side of its back. Grayish brown in color with darker blotches on its face and dark bars on the thighs. It has a pair of raised glands in the lumbar region, and there is often a reddish or orange blotch on each of its flanks.
Habits	Nocturnal and terrestrial.
Breeding	In foam nests floating on water or on flooded land.
Diet	Invertebrates and small vertebrates.
Habitat	Lowland forests.
Distribution	Central and South America, from Honduras to Ecuador and Brazil.
Status	Common and widespread.
Similar species	Several other *Leptodactylus* species occur in the region, but this is the bulkiest.

Smoky Jungle Frogs live in tropical regions along the edges of primary and secondary forests. They hide in burrows, under logs, or between the roots of large forest trees during the day and emerge at night to feed. They are large, aggressive frogs that eat other frogs, small reptiles, nestling birds, and bats.

If they feel threatened, they release large amounts of mucus from glands in their skin. Apart from making them difficult to hold, this may also induce sneezing and swelling of the eyes in a potential predator. Touching the mucus leads to more serious symptoms, so any predator intending to swallow the frog would think again. The frogs also make a loud shriek if grasped.

This adaptable species breeds in small ponds, trickles of water, flooded roads, forests, and swamps. Males have spines on their thumbs and chest to help them keep a grip on females during amplexus. They form a large, floating foam mass during egg-laying, and this contains about 1,000 eggs.

Rain washes the tadpoles free of the foam and into ponds or streams, although some may stay in flooded burrows or holes and complete their development there. The tadpoles are carnivorous and cannibalistic, although they will also eat plant material if necessary. They metamorphose in about 28 days.

⊕ *The large, aggressive Smoky Jungle Frog, seen here in Amazonian Ecuador, defends itself from would-be predators by secreting toxic substances from glands on its flanks.* © Arthur Georges.

Other *Leptodactylus* Species

⊖ Leptodactylus stenodema *occurs in tropical forests of the Amazon Basin in Brazil, in Colombia, south to Peru, and east to the Guianas.* © Arthur Georges.

⊖ Leptodactylus rhodomystax *is found in tropical forests in the Guianas, Brazil, Peru, Bolivia, and Ecuador.* © Arthur Georges.

⊕ Leptodactylus troglodytes *is limited to northeastern Brazil, where it inhabits dry and moist savanna, agricultural land, and dune systems.*

Painted Ant Nest Frog

Common names	Painted Ant Nest Frog, Gold-striped Frog
Scientific name	*Lithodytes lineatus*
Family	Leptodactylidae
Size	2.2 in (56 mm).
Key features	Slender, with a long pointed head and moderately long limbs. It is dark brown to black with a pair of yellow stripes starting at the snout, passing over the top of each eye and ending in the groin.
Habits	Terrestrial and nocturnal.
Breeding	In underground water bodies.
Diet	Invertebrates.
Habitat	Lowland tropical forests.
Distribution	Northern Amazon Basin, from Brazil and Bolivia to Colombia, Venezuela, and the Guianas.
Status	Uncommon.
Similar species	Similar to some poison dart frogs (Dendrobatidae).

Some experts suspect that the bright colors of this frog are intended to mimic several poisonous dart frogs (*Phyllobates* species) that have similar colors and markings. Another species in the Leptodactylidae, *Eleutherodactylus gaigei*, is thought to have a similar strategy. Mimicry of this sort is common among snakes but rare in frogs.

The Painted Ant Nest Frog has an interesting life history, although it has not yet been fully studied. It lives in the nests of leaf-cutter ants (*Atta* species), and it seems that the frog gives off chemicals that prevent the ants from attacking it. The frog benefits by living in a controlled environment and being largely immune to attack from predators, which the ants drive away. The ants benefit from the frog's diet, which includes parasitic insects that would otherwise lay their eggs in the nest. The frogs apparently resist the temptation to eat the ants as museum specimens never have ants in their stomach.

Males call from inside the nests, which can measure several yards in diameter. Within the nest there are tunnels leading to underground water sources. Scientists suspect that the frogs lay their eggs in the water and that the tadpoles feed on fungal spores that fall into it. So far, this is the only known example of a symbiotic relationship between a frog and an insect.

⊌ The Painted Ant Nest Frog, seen here in Amazonian Ecuador, lives in the nests of leaf-cutter ants, to mutual benefit.
© Arthur Georges.

Chilean Four-eyed Frog

Common name	Chilean Four-eyed Frog
Scientific name	*Pleurodema thaul*
Family	Leptodactylidae
Size	1.97 in (50 mm).
Key features	Short and stocky with a buff, gray, or greenish body marked with darker irregular blotches. On the lumbar region, near the position of the knees when the frog is at rest, is a pair of rounded glands, each with a black center.
Habits	Nocturnal.
Breeding	In shallow ponds and flooded areas, where gelatinous egg masses are laid among aquatic plants.
Diet	Invertebrates.
Habitat	Generalists, living in a wide range of natural and disturbed habitats.
Distribution	Central Chile.
Status	Common.
Similar species	There are 12 species of four-eyed frogs, of which *Pleurodema bufonina* is similar but has larger lumbar glands and lives in the Patagonian lowlands.

The conspicuous lumbar glands of this species discharge toxic substances if the frog is alarmed. Before doing so, it turns its back on a predator and straightens its hind limbs, raising its backside to display the brightly colored glands. These glands look like large eyes, hence the frog's common name. Other animals that have similar so-called startle behavior include several species of caterpillars and moths. In the case of the frog, however, the threat is real, since predators eating it will be affected by the toxins.

This is a very versatile species, found from the dry regions of the Atacama Desert to the beech forests in southern Chile, close to the Antarctic circle, and from sea level to nearly 7,000 feet (2,100 m). It adapts to the varied conditions by altering its breeding season to the most favorable months of the year, depending on temperature and rainfall. Other four-eyed frogs produce foam nests that float on the surface of the water.

⊙ *The highly adaptable Chilean Four-eyed Frog makes its home in forests, deserts, grassland, and even urban habitats, and can reproduce in all types of water bodies.*

Other *Pleurodema* Species

⬆ *Peter's Four-eyed Frog*
(P. diplolistris) *is widely distributed in the savannas of northeastern Brazil. It spends much of its time underground, emerging to breed in temporary water.*

⬅ *The cryptic Andean Stone Frog*
(P. marmorata), *photographed on a stony slope at 12,500 feet (3,800 m) in the Andes, Bolivia.*

➡ *In the Andes a Foam Nest Frog*
(P. cinerea) *whips up a frothy mass in which to lay its eggs.*

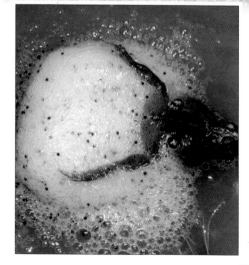

117

Tungara Frog

Common names	Tungara Frog, Canal Frog, "Poon-la-la"
Scientific name	*Physalaemus pustulosus*
Family	Leptodactylidae
Size	1.18 in (30 mm).
Key features	A chubby frog with a very warty skin. The fingers and toes are not webbed, but the toes have a fringe along the edge. It is gray or brownish gray in color, with darker markings on the back, often coinciding with rows of warts.
Habits	Secretive and nocturnal, but heard frequently during and after rain.
Breeding	In puddles, flooded fields, ditches, and drains. It produces a small foam nest that floats on the surface.
Diet	Small invertebrates.
Habitat	Savannas and other open places, including airfields, agricultural fields, roadsides, clearings in jungles, etc. Often found near human habitations.
Distribution	Central and South America, from S Mexico to the Amazon Basin.
Status	Very common.
Similar species	There are many other small grayish frogs in the region, including several other *Physalaemus* species, but few are as common as this one.

On warm still nights the call of this species typifies those parts of Central and South America where it lives. Many males may gather together over a large open area, and their chorus can be heard for up to a mile. One of its many local common names, the "poon-la-la," is derived from its call.

These charming frogs are found wherever humans have disturbed the natural habitat, even in muddy pools around building sites and kitchen and laundry drains. They breed in shallow puddles that collect during rainstorms, and their characteristic foam nests, about the size of a large walnut, can be found in wheel ruts and animal hoof prints, as well as in gutters and drainage channels in towns.

Each nest contains about 300 small eggs. They hatch after about 72 hours, although the tadpoles may stay in the foam for up to seven days unless rain washes them out. The foam is thought to help prevent them from drying out and may also give the tadpoles some protection against predators.

Breeding in temporary pools also avoids the possibility of predation by fish. Tadpoles are eaten by tadpoles of other species, freshwater crabs, and dragonfly larvae, however. The adults are heavily preyed on by the frog-eating bat *Trachops cirrhosus*, which occurs in the same region and which apparently locates calling males by sound.

⊖ *Right: A male Tungara Frog* (Physalaemus pustulosus) *calling in Arima, Trinidad. Inset: The related* P. petersi *is much less common and is restricted to the western Amazon Basin. It is nocturnal and its diet consists exclusively of termites.* © Arthur Georges.

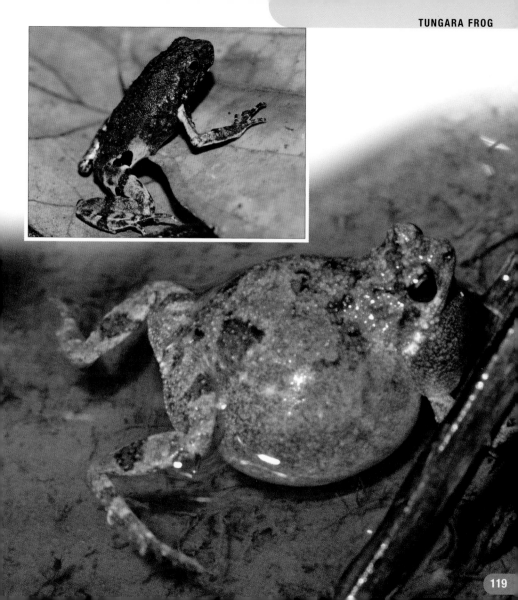

⬅ Proceratophrys cristiceps *is common in northeastern Brazil, where it is found among dry savanna and in secondary forests.*

⬅ *Far left:* Adenomera martinezi *from Brazil. It occurs above 1,970 ft (600 m) in the states of Pará, Mato Grosso, Tocantins, and Goiás.*

⬇ *Another common Brazilian species,* Barycholos ternetzi, *lives in the leaf litter of gallery forests and open areas in the* cerrado.

Other Leptodactylids

⬅ *Another foam-nesting leptodactylid,* Adenomera andreae, *from the Amazon Basin, seen here in Ecuador. © Arthur Georges.*

➡ Vanzolinius discodactylus *is found throughout much of Amazonian Peru and, as here, Ecuador. © Arthur Georges.*

⬇ Odontophrynus salvatori *is known only from three areas of Brazil but is presumed to occur more widely.*

Malaysian Slender Toad

Common name	Malaysian Slender Toad
Scientific name	*Ansonia malayana*
Family	Bufonidae
Size	0.79–1.06 in (20–27 mm).
Key features	A small skulking toad with a slender body and limbs and a bony back covered in warts. Dark brown with some indistinct lighter markings.
Habits	Nocturnal and secretive, hiding among leaf litter and under logs, etc., during the day.
Breeding	In rocky streams.
Diet	Small invertebrates.
Habitat	Montane forests.
Distribution	Hills of the Malaysian Peninsula and S Thailand.
Status	Probably common in suitable habitat.
Similar species	Other species of *Ansonia*, which are very difficult to differentiate without locality data.

All slender toads are restricted to primary rain forest or old secondary forests, in mountainous or hilly country in Southeast Asia. The Malaysian Slender Toad occurs up to about 4,000 feet (1,220 m) but is also found at lower altitudes. These frogs live on the forest floor, where their somber coloration makes them very hard to see. Occasionally, they climb up to the lower leaves of small shrubs and bushes.

When they are ready to breed, males call from rocks or other vantage points next to fast-flowing clear mountain streams. Their call is a high-pitched metallic trill or chirp. Little is

known about the spawning process, but the tadpoles are elongated and streamlined so they can cling to rocks and live in torrents and small cascades without being washed away.

Only one species, the Brown Slender Toad *(Ansonia leptopus)* from Borneo, is found in lowland forests. Its tadpoles differ from those of the rest of the genus, being less streamlined and living among dead leaves on the bottoms of slow-moving streams and backwaters.

⤵ *Malaysian Slender Toad, Bukit Larut, West Malaysia.*

Peruvian Stubfoot Toad

Common names	Peruvian Stubfoot Toad, Peruvian Harlequin Toad
Scientific name	*Atelopus peruensis*
Family	Bufonidae
Size	1.18 in (30 mm).
Key features	A small toad with smooth skin on its back, a stocky body, and pointed head. Its color is mainly green on top, yellowish below with white-spotted black flanks.
Habits	Unknown, but probably terrestrial and predominantly diurnal like other *Atelopus* species.
Breeding	Presumed to breed in streams, where they lay their eggs in short strings attached to the bottom.
Diet	Small invertebrates.
Habitat	Lightly wooded valleys and gullies on mountain slopes.
Distribution	Peru, South America.
Status	Listed by the IUCN as Critically Endangered.
Similar species	*Atelopus* is a large genus with more than 70 species, but the Peruvian Stubfoot Toad is the only one with predominantly green coloration.

Stubfoot, or Harlequin, Toads are among the most endangered in the world. All montane species, which account for half the genus and include *Atelopus peruensis*, are declining rapidly.

Although the causes are not completely known, a fungus known as the chytrid fungus appears to be implicated. It has become a serious pest in frog species throughout the world, especially in populations from mountains. Other threats, such as habitat destruction for logging, oil exploration, and agriculture, are also present but are less important at the present time than the fungus. Some species, such as the Ecuadorian Black

⬆ *Inset: The Ecuadorian Black Stubfoot Toad, or Jambato Toad* (Atelopus ignescens), *has been listed as Extinct by the IUCN since 2001.*

Stubfoot Toad *(A. ignescens),* have not been seen since 1988, and others that were common are now rare.

From the little we know of the Peruvian Stubfoot Toad, it lives among mosses and in leaf litter alongside streams running down gullies in Andean forests and *paramos* (high, treeless plateaus). Each major valley is separated from the next by a mountain spur that acts as a barrier, thereby isolating each population. The males of

↑ *The increasingly rare Peruvian Stubfoot Toad from Peru is the only member of the genus that is predominantly green.*

some stubfoot toads attach themselves to females several days or even weeks before egg-laying takes place, in order to ensure a successful mating. The pair eventually visits a shallow mountain stream, where their eggs are attached to stones on the bottom.

Harlequin Toad

Common names	Harlequin Toad, Harlequin Frog
Scientific name	*Atelopus varius*
Family	Bufonidae
Size	1.06–1.89 in (27–48 mm).
Key features	A slender toad with very long spindly arms and legs. Its skin is smooth and free of the glandular warts found on most bufonid toads. Its color and pattern are highly variable, but it is mostly black with a combination of yellow, lime green, orange, or red blotches or stripes.
Habits	Diurnal and terrestrial.
Breeding	In water, with eggs attached to stones on the bottom.
Diet	Small invertebrates.
Habitat	Lower montane forests.
Distribution	Central America (Costa Rica and Panama).
Status	Formerly common but now extinct in many localities and listed by the IUCN as Critically Endangered.
Similar species	Other *Atelopus* toads from the region have glandular skin. Otherwise, there is nothing similar.

The small Harlequin Toads live alongside fast-flowing streams, but they rarely enter the water. They are active by day and sit on the banks or on rocks in the stream. They congregate around the streams in the dry season but disperse into the surrounding forests in the wet season, when males become especially territorial, calling repeatedly to warn off intruders. If this fails to work, they chase and wrestle with each other until one gives way. Females are also territorial, especially in the dry season, and chase away other females as well as males. They feed on small invertebrates, including spiders, small flies, and caterpillars.

Like most *Atelopus* species, they go into amplexus long before the eggs are laid, with the female carrying the male for up to a month before entering the water and attaching short strings of eggs to rocks and stones on the bottom. The tadpoles probably attach themselves to rocks by means of suckers on their underside.

The population of the Harlequin Toad is declining dramatically and has disappeared completely from several localities where it was formerly common. Various color forms are sometimes considered to be separate species, but most authorities

⊖ *This bright little Harlequin Toad was photographed in cloud forest in Costa Rica.*

consider them to be merely different races of the same, highly variable, species.

⊙ *Also Critically Endangered, the Yellow Harlequin Toad* (A. oxyrhynchus), *seen here in a Venezuelan rain forest, is a warningly colored diurnal species.*

Panamanian Golden Toad

Common names	Panamanian Golden Toad, Panamanian Golden Frog, Golden Frog
Scientific name	*Atelopus zeteki*
Family	Bufonidae
Size	1.06–1.97 in (27–50 mm).
Key features	Slender, with very long spindly arms and legs. Its skin is smooth and free of the glandular warts found on most bufonid toads. It is golden orange in color, with dark blotches on its back and limbs. These blotches often take the form of ovals or chevrons with rounded edges.
Habits	Diurnal and terrestrial.
Breeding	In water, with eggs attached to stones on the bottom.
Diet	Small invertebrates.
Habitat	Montane forests.
Distribution	Central America (Panama).
Status	Formerly common but now extinct in many localities and listed by the IUCN as Critically Endangered.
Similar species	Some forms of *Atelopus varius* are similar, but *A. zeteki* is more heavily marked.

The ecology of this toad is similar to that of the Harlequin Toad *(Atelopus varius)*. It lives alongside fast-flowing streams that run through forests on mountain slopes, and its tadpoles are flattened and streamlined to avoid being washed away when feeding on the alga-covered stones on the stream beds. Also like the Harlequin Toads, numbers of the

Panamanian Golden Toad have declined dramatically in the recent past. In fact, it may become extinct in the next few years. This is a famous species, once common on the montane rain forests in the west of the country. Now it is in real trouble, facing the multiple threats of infection by chytridiomycosis fungus, pollution, and especially deforestation for agricultural development. The latter has resulted in the silting up of the rivers in which the tadpoles live.

The Golden Toad is not only a charismatic amphibian but also a cultural symbol, revered by indigenous people of the region who made talismans (known as *huacos*) of these toads in precious metals. Legend has it that the frogs transform into golden effigies of themselves when they die, and the places where they lived became places of pilgrimage. Anyone seeing a live Golden Toad was considered to be lucky—the same can be said today, but for different reasons.

⊕ *Environmental and human threats have brought the Panamanian Golden Toad close to extinction.*

River Toad

Common names	River Toad, Spiny Toad, Rough Toad, Asian Giant Toad
Scientific name	*Bufo asper*
Family	Bufonidae
Size	2.76–5.51 in (70–140 mm). Females larger than males.
Key features	A large toad with very many, slightly spiny, warts over its body. The parotid gland behind the eye is small and rounded. Overall brown or reddish brown in color.
Habits	Mainly terrestrial but may also climb.
Breeding	In rivers and streams.
Diet	Small and large invertebrates.
Habitat	Primary rain forest and well-grown secondary forest.
Distribution	Southeast Asia.
Status	Common.
Similar species	The only other large species in the region is the Giant Toad *(B. juxtasper)*, which has much larger, elongated parotid glands.

The River Toad is strongly associated with rivers that run through forests, although occasionally it occurs in disturbed places and may be found in caves, gardens, plantations, and at the side of paths and roads through suitable habitat. Young toads occasionally climb up tree trunks and can be found several feet off the ground. Adults do not move about much, and the same individual can often be found in exactly the same place night after night.

They are sit-and-wait predators, preferring to ambush their prey rather than go hunting for it. Because of their large size, they are able to tackle a wide variety of invertebrates such as cockroaches, beetles, and caterpillars, and probably take smaller frogs and lizards as well.

The main threat to the species comes from deforestation and the subsequent silting up of the rivers in which they breed. Larvae are specialized and are unable to feed on riverbeds in which the spaces between pebbles become clogged with silt.

Breeding takes place in backwaters of rivers and streams. Nothing is known about the eggs, but they are probably stuck to stones or pebbles on the bottom. Tadpoles grow to a large size and attach themselves to stones by means of a large suckerlike mouth. They metamorphose when they reach about 0.6 inches (15 mm).

⊕ *The River Toad, photographed here in Gombak Forest, West Malaysia, is one of the largest toads in the region.*

European Common Toad

Common name	European Common Toad
Scientific name	*Bufo bufo*
Family	Bufonidae
Size	3.15–7.87 in (8–20 cm). Females larger than males (which have thicker forearms).
Key features	A typical toad with warty skin and short back legs. Parotid glands are large, elongated, slightly crescent-shaped. Males have thick forearms but no vocal sac. Drab brown, gray, or reddish with no markings; eyes copper colored.
Habits	Terrestrial; mainly nocturnal, but sometimes active on damp overcast days or when moving to breeding sites.
Breeding	An explosive breeder in spring.
Diet	Invertebrates, including insects and slugs.
Habitat	Very adaptable. Common in gardens and other disturbed habitats but also in sparse woodland, meadows, and heaths.
Distribution	Throughout most of Europe (except extreme N Scandinavia, Ireland, and some Mediterranean islands). Also in NW Africa and throughout Central Asia to Japan.
Status	Common.
Similar species	Natterjack Toad (*B. calamita*) is smaller, has a yellow stripe down its back and pinkish warts on its flanks. Green Toad (*B. viridis*) has green or olive blotches on a putty-colored background. The Japanese form is sometimes regarded as a separate species, *B. japonicus*.

The European Common Toad holds the record for being the highest and the lowest amphibian: it has been found at over 26,000 feet (8,000 m) in the Himalayas and at 1,115 feet (340 m) below ground level, in a coal mine.

It is familiar to gardeners and naturalists across Europe and central Asia in a variety of habitats, often in fairly dry places, including woods, heaths, gardens, and agricultural areas. Because toads eat pest species, enlightened gardeners often encourage them to live in their gardens, greenhouses, or allotments, although the use of chemicals in such situations has reduced the urban population in many places.

In general, toads can tolerate drier conditions than frogs, thanks to their relatively thick skin, and they may burrow down into the soil during excessively dry weather. Although they need a body of water in which to breed, they disperse widely at other times and make annual breeding migrations. These can take place over several successive nights, during which they can cover a total distance of many miles. In winter they hibernate in burrows or sometimes in mud at the bottom of ponds.

Because they are secretive and largely nocturnal, European Common Toads are seldom seen (even in places where they are common) except at breeding time, when large numbers congregate. Usually they hide away in crevices, rodent burrows, or under logs. Individuals often favor a particular hiding place, returning to it after each night's foraging and even going back to it after a prolonged period of absence during breeding time.

Their enemies include dogs, cats, hedgehogs, birds of prey, and grass snakes. Powerful skin toxins are their most important means of defense, and many predators learn to avoid them, or quickly drop them as soon as they taste the toxin. Grass snakes seem immune to this deterrent, so the toad adopts a different strategy by inflating its

body and raising itself off the ground on stiff legs. This is intended to fool the snake into thinking that the toad is too large to swallow, and it often works.

↓ *The adaptable European Common Toad is common in gardens and other disturbed habitats.*

Natterjack Toad

Common name	Natterjack Toad
Scientific name	Bufo calamita
Family	Bufonidae
Size	2.76–3.54 in (70–90 mm).
Key features	A stocky toad with short limbs and a distinctive yellow stripe down the center of its back. Brown or olive in color, often with some pinkish warts on its flanks.
Habits	Terrestrial and nocturnal.
Breeding	Over an extended period in spring or summer, in warm shallow water; sometimes in temporary pools and occasionally brackish water.
Diet	Invertebrates, including insects.
Habitat	Lowland areas, including heaths and sand dunes, often near the sea. In southern Europe it sometimes lives a long way from the coast and may occur in hilly country.
Distribution	Northern and western Europe as far east as the Baltic region.
Status	Common overall but very localized in Britain.
Similar species	The Green Toad (B. viridis) is its closest relative but has large blotches over its body.

The Natterjack Toad is among the few species that can tolerate brackish water. It often breeds in the shallow pools that collect between sand dunes, known as dune slacks, where there is little or no vegetation and where the water warms up quickly. It breeds later in the year than the European Common Toad (Bufo bufo), and lays up to 7,500 eggs in a single string of spawn that can measure up to 6 feet (2 m) long.

The males' calls are very loud and last for several seconds. Large choruses of males produce a volume of sound that carries for long distances across open countryside, audible up to a mile or more away. On occasion, the breeding pools dry up before the tadpoles metamorphose and they are all lost. At other times they emerge from the water in large numbers, and hundreds of them swarm around the edges of pools and the surrounding vegetation. They reach maturity in two to three years.

As adults they may live in burrows in sand or sandy soil, which they dig using their front legs. Sometimes they use mouse burrows or hide under stones and logs. Natterjacks move by running in short bursts rather than hopping, and are rather mouselike in their movements, especially in half-light when they first become active. Many coastal sites are threatened by development for the tourist industry.

⊕ *The Natterjack Toad gets its common name from the loud rasping call made by males during the breeding season.*

American Green Toad

Common names	American Green Toad, Green Toad, Eastern Green Toad, Western Green Toad
Scientific name	*Bufo debilis*
Family	Bufonidae
Size	1.18–1.97 in (30–50 mm).
Key features	A small flat-bodied toad with a bright green or yellowish green back, scattered with black spots, bars, or reticulations.
Habits	Burrowing, secretive, and nocturnal.
Breeding	In temporary pools and streams following rains.
Diet	Invertebrates, including insects.
Habitat	Arid lowland areas, usually with sandy soil, with mesquite bushes, grasses, or without vegetation.
Distribution	South-central United States and adjacent parts of N Mexico.
Status	Probably common but only apparent after heavy rains.
Similar species	The Sonoran Green Toad (*B. retiformis*), is similar but slightly bigger, has more black markings, and occurs in a small area to the west.

This desert toad spends most of its life deep underground in burrows, cracks in the ground, or beneath rocks and logs, where the soil holds some moisture. It breeds only after heavy rains, when the land floods and small temporary streams flow again. It may travel long distances to suitable breeding sites, which vary from year to year according to rainfall.

Males call from the base of a grassy tussock or other vegetation and can be difficult to find, even though their loud buzzing call lasts several seconds and is repeated frequently. Calling takes place whenever rain falls, usually just a few nights each season. Clutch size is small, averaging about 25 eggs. They hatch quickly in the warm water, and

⊕ *The Great Plains Toad* (Bufo cognatus) *from south-central United States. When stressed, the toad makes a wide gape.*

the larvae develop in a few weeks, although some undoubtedly perish when their pools dry up.

During localized rainstorms this species is often found alongside other desert toads such as spadefoot toads *(Scaphiopus* species), Red-spotted Toads *(Bufo punctatus)*, and Colorado River Toads *(B. alvarius)*. At these times driving can be difficult, since toads spill over from the desert onto roads. Breeding pools also attract

⬆ *The nocturnal American Green Toad, photographed here in Arizona, is most likely to be seen after periods of heavy rainfall.*

the attention of predators. Checkered Garter Snakes, for example, may eat several toads in one night. Young snakes may also benefit from the abundance of small toads later in the year, when they are leaving the water.

Karoo Toad

Common name	Karoo Toad
Scientific name	*Bufo gariepensis*
Family	Bufonidae
Size	To 3.74 in (95 mm); males are smaller.
Key features	A thick-set toad with a deep body. It is covered in prominent warts; those behind the eyes—the parotid glands—are very large. Light or dark brown in color, sometimes with darker blotches.
Habits	Terrestrial and nocturnal.
Breeding	In permanent or temporary pools following rains.
Diet	Invertebrates.
Habitat	Deserts, semideserts, and dry grasslands.
Distribution	Arid parts of SW South Africa.
Status	Common.
Similar species	Several other toads live in the area, but the Karoo Toad is distinct in having few or no markings on its back.

This toad lives in dry rocky and thorny places. It derives its scientific name from the Gariep River (more commonly known as the Orange River), where it was first described. It is a large species that adapts well to arid habitats, including sand flats with little vegetation and rocky areas in the Karoo region, where the main plants are succulents and drought-tolerant shrubs. It has a walking or running gait, although it can hop for short distances when necessary.

Its breeding season is dependent on rain. In parts of its range this falls during the summer, but its range also includes a small area that has winter rainfall, and here the toad shifts its breeding season accordingly. It breeds in any body of water it can find, either permanent or temporary, including streams, bogs, water holes, and ponds created for cattle. Males call during the early part of the night or, in overcast weather, during the day, spacing themselves out along the water's edge.

The eggs are laid in strings of about 100, and the tadpoles live in small shoals on the bottom and metamorphose quickly—usually in about 20 days—into small toadlets. Rapid metamorphosis helps them evacuate their ponds before they dry up.

⊙ *The large parotid glands on the neck behind the eyes can be seen clearly in this Karoo Toad from Kamieskroon, Namaqualand, South Africa.*

Cane Toad

Common names	Cane Toad, Marine Toad, Giant Toad
Scientific names	*Bufo marinus*
Family	Bufonidae
Size	3.9–9.4 in (10–24 cm). The largest specimen weighed 3 lb (1.36 kg).
Key features	A huge toad, possibly the world's largest, with a big head and elongated parotid glands on its neck. There are also large poison glands on its thighs, and the whole of its back is liberally sprinkled with warts. It is brown in color, often plain but sometimes with a pattern of slightly darker blotches.
Habits	Nocturnal and terrestrial.
Breeding	In water, with females laying up to 35,000 eggs in a long string.
Diet	Most things edible, which includes insects, small vertebrates, and even static items such as dog food.
Habitat	Absent from very few habitats within its range, including villages and towns.
Distribution	Its natural distribution is in Central and South America, just reaching the United States in extreme S Texas, but it has been deliberately introduced to numerous other countries, most notably Australia.
Status	Common, to plague proportions in places.
Similar species	Several other large brown toads, including the Rococo Toad *(B. paracnemis)*, live in the same region.

The Cane Toad was introduced to Australia in 1935 to control a pest species, the Cane Beetle. The results were disastrous. From an initial group of 101 toads they spread rapidly in the absence of any predators and ate all before them, including beneficial insects as well as the pest species. By 1974 they occupied about one-third of the state of Queensland and continue to spread today.

What makes the Cane Toad such a good colonizer? In a word, adaptability. Cane toads are like rats: they are able to modify their lifestyle, diet, and breeding habits according to whatever is available. Although they originate in tropical rain forests, they are equally at home in fields, plantations, parks, golf courses, and gardens. They even occur in the heart of cities, hiding under buildings by day and emerging at night to sit around the bases of street lamps and snap up insects that have been attracted to them.

Their feeding habits are legendary. They will eat anything they can fit in their mouth. This includes not only all the usual insects and other invertebrates but also smaller frogs and toads, lizards, small snakes, mammals, and birds. The most significant factor in their feeding habits, though, is their ability to recognize food that is not moving. They recognize the smell of dog food, for instance, and will even learn when it is due to be placed out in a bowl. They congregate in numbers, along with the dog, waiting for the bowl to arrive, just as they wait at the entrances of bee hives, ready to pick

off returning bees. They also visit refuse tips and eat vegetable scraps such as corn on the cob, broccoli, and rice.

They are not greatly troubled by predators themselves because of very powerful toxins they produce in the large glands on their neck and legs.

⊘ *The Rococo Toad* (Bufo paracnemis), *also from South America.*

⊙ *Cane Toad, Simla, Trinidad. These toads were introduced to the West Indies in the 19th century.*

Black-spined Toad

Common names	Black-spined Toad, Asian Common Toad, Black-spectacled Toad, Southeast Asian Toad
Scientific name	*Bufo melanostictus*
Family	Bufonidae
Size	2.36–3.35 in (60–85 mm).
Key features	A stocky toad with a small head and short hind limbs. It has bony crests over its eyes and on its snout and these are edged in black. It is gray, dirty yellow, or reddish brown in color.
Habits	Terrestrial and nocturnal.
Breeding	In permanent or temporary pools following rains.
Diet	Invertebrates.
Habitat	Forests and open places, but most often in disturbed habitats such as plantations and gardens.
Distribution	South and Southeast Asia, from China and Pakistan through Indo-China to Malaysia, Borneo, and Indonesia.
Status	Very common.
Similar species	The black ridges on its head separate this toad from others in the region.

This toad has adapted with great success to human disturbance. It is rarely found in forests or natural areas now but is common around villages, gardens, plantations, and even in the center of large cities. Black-spined Toads have learned to sit under street lamps and the lights of outdoor restaurants, feasting on the flying insects that are attracted to the lights before dropping to the ground. Because they often occur in high densities, their impact on insects and other pests of cultivated crops must be considerable. However, chemical control of pests, as well as other destructive agricultural practices, may affect the toads' survival, which is a possible cause for concern.

Breeding takes place at the onset of monsoon rains where they occur; elsewhere, the toads breed throughout the year after rain. A variety of water bodies are used including, in towns and villages, drains and puddles in the road.

Males are much smaller than females and greatly outnumber them. Large aggregations of calling males often result in scrambles and tussles as each tries to gain access to a receptive female. The tadpoles are black and feed in shoals, often around the edges of pools where algae accumulate.

Black-spined Toad, Hunas Falls, Sri Lanka. Black-spined Toads are associated with humans and are often regarded by gardeners as beneficial, since they eat insect and mollusk pests.

Gulf Coast Toad

Common name	Gulf Coast Toad
Scientific name	*Bufo nebulifer* (formerly known as *B. valliceps*, a name that is now reserved for a closely related species occurring farther south, in Mexico).
Family	Bufonidae
Size	1.97–3.94 in (50–100 mm).
Key features	Less warty than most other toads in the region and with a distinctive broad dark stripe down each flank, bordered above by a thin light-colored stripe. The back is gray with another thin light stripe down the center of its back. These light stripes may be cream, yellowish, or reddish in color.
Habits	Terrestrial and nocturnal.
Breeding	In water, in a variety of situations.
Diet	Invertebrates.
Habitat	Prairies, beaches, and even the outskirts of towns in storm drains.
Distribution	Southeastern United States.
Status	Common in suitable habitat.
Similar species	There are several other toads that occur in the region, but the dark stripe down the flanks easily identifies this one.

This toad is among the most adaptable in North America and can be found breeding in a wide variety of drainage channels and irrigation ditches as well as natural pools and marshes. It tolerates brackish water and is quick to move into artificial pools and cattle tanks, often within one year of their being constructed. It often occurs around towns and may hunt for flying insects by stationing itself near street lights. It sometimes climbs into low bushes and may hide in tree holes and is frequently found under pieces of rubbish such as boards, discarded carpets and sacking, or in rodent burrows. Unlike most amphibians, it does not seem to react adversely to habitat disturbances such as felling of trees or clearing or development, provided there is somewhere for it to breed.

Breeding takes place in spring or summer, in response to rain. Males make a trilling or rattling call, lasting two to six seconds, repeated over and over. Numerous males may call from the same pond, resulting in a loud chorus that carries for many hundreds of yards. The eggs are laid in still, shallow water, and each female can lay up to 2,000 eggs, divided among a number of short double strands that float near the surface.

⊖ *The light stripe running down the center of the back and the two dorsal stripes are distinctive features of the Gulf Coast Toad, seen here in Texas.*

Golden Toad

Common names	Golden Toad, Monte Verde Toad, Orange Toad, Sapo Dorado
Scientific name	*Bufo periglenes*
Family	Bufonidae
Size	1.57–2.2 in (40–56 mm).
Key features	A spectacular toad. Males are uniform orange or reddish and females are black or dark green with large red spots. This species also has large parotid glands and bony crests on the head.
Habits	Terrestrial and nocturnal.
Breeding	In small shallow pools.
Diet	Invertebrates.
Habitat	Lower montane rain forest (cloud forest).
Distribution	Costa Rica.
Status	Listed by the IUCN as Extinct.
Similar species	None.

The Golden Toad of Costa Rica was probably the first species to alert the scientific community to the fact that frogs and toads were in serious trouble. Discovered in 1966, this spectacular species could be found in large numbers at its breeding pools up until 1987. In 1988, however, only eight males and two females were seen; and in 1989 only one male was found. Since then no Golden Toads have been found, despite thorough searches of the area they lived in. The hope is that colonies of the toads have lingered on in remote places and await discovery but, in view of their distinctive coloration, this seems increasingly unlikely.

Assuming there are any left, males emerge from their hiding places toward the end of the dry season and migrate to suitable pools. Females join them following thunderstorms, and a breeding frenzy takes place: males frantically try to find unattached females or attempt to dislodge males that have already been successful. Males outnumber females by about 10:1, and large breeding "balls" result, with a single female at the center.

Once the female has laid her eggs she leaves the pool, but males may hang around for several nights in the hope of further matings. The eggs are laid in long strings and hatch after several days. The tadpoles feed on algae and other plant material if it is present, but in the absence of suitable food they will continue to grow and develop, nourished only by their yolk. The juveniles begin to attain the bright coloration of adults shortly after metamorphosis.

↓ *The Golden Toad exhibits an extreme form of sexual dimorphism: the males are a striking orange or reddish color, while the females are black overall with yellow-edged scarlet blotches.*

Red-spotted Toad

Common name	Red-spotted Toad
Scientific name	*Bufo punctatus*
Family	Bufonidae
Size	1.5–3 in (38–76 mm).
Key features	A small, relatively slender toad with a flattened head and a rounded parotid gland behind each eye. It is gray or brown in color, but its most distinctive feature is the large number of reddish or orange warts covering its back. Toads living on pale substrate, such as limestone, tend to be lighter in color than those living on a dark substrate.
Habits	Terrestrial and nocturnal, but sometimes active in the day during the breeding season.
Breeding	In permanent or temporary pools following rains.
Diet	Invertebrates.
Habitat	Desert, dry grasslands, and open woodland.
Distribution	Arid parts of SW and S North America (United States and Mexico).
Status	Common.
Similar species	Several other small toads live in the area, but the red warts make this species unmistakable.

Red-spotted Toads are the most widespread of the American desert species and live from below sea level in Death Valley up to 6,500 feet (2,000 m) in the mountains of Colorado. They are frequent around oases and in rocky places where springs and seepages occur throughout the year. They may also live near cattle tanks. By day and throughout the coldest and driest parts of the year they hide in rodent burrows or beneath rocks. Their flattened body allows them to retreat into deep crevices.

They will breed throughout the summer, depending on rainfall, moving to permanent pools in rocky places or temporary pools with muddy bottoms. A typical clutch contains about 1,500 eggs, laid singly or in small clusters. They hatch in three days. The tadpoles grow slowly compared with other desert species, often taking up to 60 days to complete their development. During this time they are prone to predation from carnivorous tadpoles with which they share their ponds, such as those of spadefoot toads (family Pelobatidae).

⊖ *A Red-spotted Toad in Arizona. These small rock-climbing toads have slightly flattened bodies that help them retreat into deep crevices.*

Oak Toad

Common name	Oak Toad
Scientific name	*Bufo quercicus*
Family	Bufonidae
Size	0.75–1.3 in (19–33 mm).
Key features	A tiny toad with a brown back and a white, yellow, or orange stripe down the center of its back. Dark markings either side of this stripe may be edged in white. They show a tendency to change color according to temperature (going lighter when warm) and substrate.
Habits	Terrestrial and largely diurnal.
Breeding	In permanent or temporary pools, usually during or after rains.
Diet	Invertebrates.
Habitat	Sandy pine scrublands and dry pine or oak hammocks.
Distribution	Coastal plain of SE United States.
Status	Common in suitable habitat.
Similar species	None: the small size and pale mid-dorsal line are unmistakable.

W here the habitat is suitable, such as raised areas of open pine and oak woods with dry sandy soil, this toad can occur in large numbers. It does not adapt well to urban development, however, and usually disappears within a few years of such habitat change. Rapid expansion of houses and roads into its habitat will reduce the areas over which it can make a living and ultimately deplete the number of toads.

They breed in temporary pools, flooded fields, and roadside ditches. Males call on humid summer evenings, with a loud, high-pitched peeping sound, made

repeatedly. They have large sausage-shaped vocal sacs, and when a large number of males are calling together the sound can be almost painful to the ears. Females lay about 300 to 500 eggs in a number of short strands that may float or stick to vegetation such as submerged grass blades. The tadpoles are grazers and eat algae and decaying animal material. They take about four or five weeks to develop, and metamorphose at a small size—less than 0.4 inches (10 mm).

A calling male Oak Toad in Sarasota, Florida.

Raucous Toad

Common names	Raucous Toad, Ranger's Toad
Scientific name	*Bufo rangeri*
Family	Bufonidae
Size	To 4.53 in (11.5 cm).
Key features	A large toad with long legs and prominent parotid glands. It is variable in color and can be quite bright. The background color is brown or cream and there are a number of well-defined large dark blotches on the back. Warts along the back and flanks may be tinged with pink.
Habits	Terrestrial and nocturnal.
Breeding	In deep permanent pools or rivers, in the summer.
Diet	Invertebrates.
Habitat	Very adaptable, being found in dry and well-watered habitats.
Distribution	South Africa.
Status	Common.
Similar species	Several other toads occur in the region, and this species may be confused with some of them.

The Raucous Toad is a familiar sight in gardens, agricultural areas, foothills, and the outskirts of towns and villages. Its coloration and markings vary from place to place, with the most brightly colored examples coming from the west of the range. In places it may take up residence in termite mounds.

It lives away from water for most of the year but migrates to rivers, ponds, and dams in the spring and summer. Males have loud calls, hence their name, and may call singly or in large choruses during the night or daytime.

Eggs are laid in double rows in long strings, which may be wrapped around vegetation

or simply allowed to drift downstream. The tadpoles take five weeks or more to metamorphose. A related species, the Guttural Toad *(Bufo gutteralis)*, is gradually extending its range and replacing the Raucous Toad in parts of northeastern South Africa. Recent research using DNA analyses has shown that the two species may hybridize where their ranges meet.

A similar, but more brightly colored, species was described as recently as 1996 from the arid Richtersveld region of South Africa. This species, the Paradise Toad *(B. robinsoni)*, lives near springs in rocky outcrops.

Raucous Toad, Clanwilliam, South Africa. This toad breeds in rivers and ponds but spends most of its time away from water.

Southern Toad

Common name	Southern Toad
Scientific name	*Bufo terrestris*
Family	Bufonidae
Size	1.5–3 in (38–76 mm).
Key features	This toad has bony knobs over each eye and bony crests running forward from the knobs toward its snout, where they converge but do not touch. It varies in color and may be brown, reddish, or olive, sometimes with a light mid-dorsal stripe and sometimes with darker blotches on its back.
Habits	Terrestrial and mainly nocturnal, but sometimes active in the day.
Breeding	In shallow water, in the summer.
Diet	Invertebrates.
Habitat	Found in most places, but especially common in dry sandy areas with open cover, such as pine woods.
Distribution	Coastal plain of the SE United States.
Status	Common.
Similar species	There are several other toads in the region, but the bony head of the Southern Toad is usually distinctive.

This is the most common toad over large parts of the American Southeast. It lives in a variety of habitats, including the outskirts of towns, where it adapts to garden living and may visit street lights in the evening to take advantage of the insect life that is attracted to them. Its diet includes a huge range of invertebrates, such as earwigs, ants, and beetles, and it will also eat honeybees even after being stung.

On the other hand, Southern Toads are prey to a wide range of animals. Hog-nosed snakes (*Heterodon*), which are specialized toad-eaters, prey heavily on them, and water snakes and indigo snakes also include them in their diet. While they are tadpoles they are eaten by aquatic amphibians and dragonfly larvae.

The adults have a number of ways of dealing with potential predators. In particular, they will lower their head and raise the back of their body to display their parotid glands to any aggressor. This also makes them look bigger than they really are. If they are grasped, they discharge a sticky white substance from their skin glands. This substance contains bufotoxin, which proves unpalatable to many predators, including dogs and cats.

⊖ *The Southern Toad spends most of the daylight hours hiding in its burrow, emerging around dusk to feed on insects. This individual was seen at Corkscrew Swamp, Florida.*

Dead Leaf Toad

Common name	Dead Leaf Toad
Scientific names	Bufo typhonius (B. margaritifer, B. alatus)
Family	Bufonidae
Size	1.5–3 in (38–76 mm).
Key features	Small toads with extensions to their snouts. There are probably three or more species going under this name and they vary somewhat in shape and coloration. Some forms have sharp bony ridges running along either side of the nape of the neck, extending onto their pointed snout. Others have a pointed snout but lack the bony ridges. Some forms have a light stripe down the center of the back, and others have markings that resemble dead leaves, including small white-edged, black spots that mimic holes made by caterpillars.
Habits	Terrestrial and mainly nocturnal, but sometimes active in the day.
Breeding	Not known.
Diet	Invertebrates.
Habitat	In tropical forests.
Distribution	South America, in the Amazon Basin.
Status	Common in suitable areas.
Similar species	The pointed snout makes this "species" unique, but differences between populations are harder to establish, and three or four species may be involved.

In certain forms of Dead Leaf Toad the resemblance to a dead leaf is uncanny, rivaling that of the Asian Horned Toad (Megophrys nasuta) and the Solomon Islands Leaf Frog (Ceratobatrachus guentheri).

In some Dead Leaf Toads there may be a diagonal row of tubercles running diagonally from behind the head to the groin, separating the flanks from the back. The back itself may be a different color, giving the appearance of a light brown leaf casting a darker shadow. Some individuals have a light stripe down their back, which serves to break up their outline further, but this may be lacking and the back may be marked with irregular dark blotches.

↑ *The Pinocchio Toad, a form of Dead Leaf Toad from Peru, showing a distinct row of tubercles.*

These markings sometimes resemble the damage caused to leaves by insects.

Little is known of the daily lives of these toads. They are thought to feed mainly on small insects, especially ants, and to climb into the branches of low shrubs to rest. At least one form breeds in slow-moving streams, but the tadpoles are not known.

⊕ *A form of Dead Leaf Toad from Ecuador, showing large bony ridges.*

European Green Toad

Common name	European Green Toad
Scientific name	*Bufo viridis*
Family	Bufonidae
Size	To 3.94 in (100 mm).
Key features	A chunky toad with large parotid glands and a pattern of large green, brownish green, or olive markings on a buff or cream background. The markings may be in the form of separate blotches or they may be grouped into several interconnected blotches. Females, which are larger than males, often have brighter and better-defined markings.
Habits	Terrestrial and mainly nocturnal, but sometimes active in the day.
Breeding	In spring, in a variety of bodies of water.
Diet	Invertebrates.
Habitat	Lowlands, in dry, sandy places, including coastal dunes, fields, and disturbed land.
Distribution	Eastern Europe, N Africa, and SW Asia.
Status	Common.
Similar species	The Natterjack Toad (*B. calamita*) is the closest relative, but it invariably has a yellow line down the center of its back.

This toad is frequently seen around human habitations—on farms, in villages, and even in large towns, where it sometimes waits at the base of street lights in the hope of catching insects that are attracted there. It burrows well and does so to avoid dry conditions. It also lives under rocks or logs, or in rodent burrows. It uses similar places to hibernate for up to six months in the winter.

↱ In parts of North Africa the European Green Toad lives side by side with the similar Moroccan Toad (Bufo mauritanicus), *pictured here.*

It emerges to breed in the spring, the males calling in large choruses from the edges of pools and ditches, even some that are polluted. Their call is a pleasant trill that lasts about 10 seconds. Females visit the pools to lay their eggs and then depart, while the males may spend several weeks at breeding sites, hoping to attract more females as they arrive over successive nights.

As the breeding pair moves over the bottom of the pond, they lay eggs in double strings up to 6 feet (2 m) long. They are wrapped around aquatic vegetation and hatch three to six days later. The tadpoles metamorphose in the summer, but the exact time depends on temperature and availability of food. They probably mature at about three years old.

↰ *European Green Toads are nocturnal and are often found near human habitation.*

Other *Bufo* Species

⤷ As its name suggests, the American Toad, or Eastern American Toad (B. americanus), is found across large parts of North America, with the general exception of the southern states.

⤶ Garman's Toad (B. garmani pseudogarmani), *photographed by night in South African savanna.*

⤋ The Colorado River Toad (B. alvarius) *lives in desert habitats in Arizona, California, and New Mexico.*

Other *Bufo* Species

⊖ *Fowler's Toads (B. fowleri) are common through the United States from the Atlantic coast to the Coastal Plain and the Gulf of Mexico. This toad was photographed in woodland in South Carolina.*

⊖ *A Funereal Toad (B. funereus) demonstrating its effective cryptic coloring on the floor of the Kakamega Forest, Kenya.*

⊕ *The nocturnal Western Giant Toad (B. fustiger / Peltophryne fustiger) is endemic to western Cuba, where it is found along the banks of streams, in fields, forests, and sometimes around houses in rural areas.*

165

Bumblebee Toad

Common names	Bumblebee Toad, Clown Toad
Scientific name	*Melanophryniscus stelzneri*
Family	Bufonidae
Size	0.98–1.18 in (25–30 mm).
Key features	Stout-bodied, with a blunt snout and a flattened head. Its limbs are short. The hands have no webbing, and the feet have webbing only at the base of the toes. Its skin is rough but there are no large glands. Black in color, with many rounded yellow spots on the back, head, and limbs. The underside is black with bright red spots, and the soles of the hands and feet are solid red.
Habits	Terrestrial and diurnal.
Breeding	In streams.
Diet	Small invertebrates such as ants and aphids.
Habitat	Mountain grasslands, alongside streams from 2,950–6,600 ft (900–2,000 m).
Distribution	Argentina. Closely related species live in Brazil, Paraguay, and Uruguay.
Status	Locally common.
Similar species	Several other *Melanophryniscus* species are fundamentally similar in color and markings. Some are considered to be subspecies of *M. stelzneri*, but others are species in their own right.

Bumblebee Toads are brightly colored to warn predators that their skin contains toxins. If they are molested, they will arch their back and display the soles of their hands and feet to show off the brightly colored blotches there. This is known as an Unken reflex and is paralleled by the fire-bellied toads (*Bombina* species) of Europe and Asia.

Bumblebee Toads appear in numbers after the summer rains and hunt for small insects among grass. They do not jump or swim, but scramble about using their short limbs. At breeding time the males call from tufts of grass at the edges of rocky streams, often early in the morning.

Mated pairs go into the water (although they are poor swimmers) and lay their eggs in a jelly mass attached to stems of water plants. The tadpoles grow to about 0.39 inches (10 mm) before completing their development and leaving the water.

→ *The black skin of the Bumblebee Toad allows it to absorb heat, and the bright spots on its body warn its enemies that it is toxic.*

Common Tree Toad

Common names	Common Tree Toad, Malaysian Tree Toad
Scientific name	*Pedostibes hosii*
Family	Bufonidae
Size	2.09–4.13 in (53–105 mm).
Key features	A long-legged toad with a bony ridge behind each eye, connected to a small parotid gland. Its toes are long and slightly expanded at the tips for climbing, and its hind feet are webbed. Males are plain brown in color, but females may be either plain brown, or about half of them may be black or olive green with bright orange spots on the body and limbs.
Habits	Arboreal and nocturnal.
Breeding	On the ground in forest streams.
Diet	Invertebrates.
Habitat	Primary rain forests.
Distribution	Borneo, Sumatra, Thailand, and the Malaysian Peninsula.
Status	Not often seen.
Similar species	The Marbled Tree Toad (*P. rugosus*) is the only close relative in the region. It is more warty than the Common Tree Toad, and both sexes are green with brown markings.

The only genus of arboreal toads in the Bufonidae (a family that otherwise contains heavily built toads that are far more at home on or under the ground) is *Pedostibes*. Modifications on these toads include long limbs and long fingers and toes that end in slightly widened tips for gripping. Yet they do not fit the usual pattern for tree-climbing species and can be found on the ground as well as in trees up to 20 feet (6 m) off the ground. They come down to the forest floor to breed, migrating to clear streams in the forest.

These toads do not form large aggregations to call, but may be stationed at regular intervals along the stream bank for one or two nights before returning to the trees. It is difficult to say what

galvanizes them into activity, since they are not seasonal. The eggs are not known, but the tadpoles live among dead leaves that accumulate in backwaters and other quiet sections of the streams. Adults feed on insects, including the plentiful ants that live in the forests.

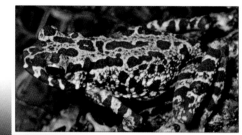

↑ *A juvenile Marbled Tree Toad (Pedostibes rugosus) from the Danum Valley, Sabah, Borneo.*

← *Not all Common Tree Toads are brightly colored. Males and some females are light- to mid-brown in color. This female was photographed in West Malaysia.*

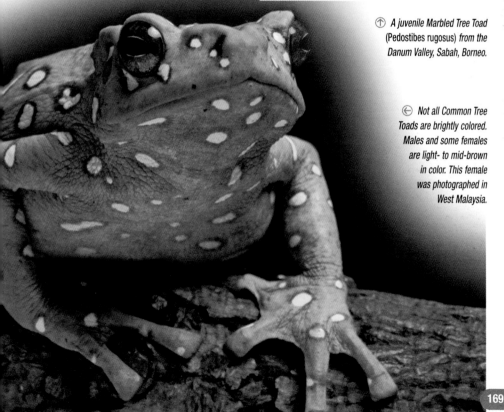

Kinabalu Dwarf Toad

Common name	Kinabalu Dwarf Toad
Scientific name	*Pelophryne misera*
Family	Bufonidae
Size	0.63–0.9 in (16–23 mm).
Key features	A tiny toad that can look like the juvenile of a larger species. However, its hands and feet are fully webbed, which is unusual among bufonid toads. It is dark brown or black in color with small, round, scattered warts.
Habits	Terrestrial and nocturnal.
Breeding	On the ground, in small pools of water.
Diet	Small invertebrates.
Habitat	Montane rain forests.
Distribution	Borneo, in the vicinity of Mount Kinabalu, Sabah, and Mount Marud, Sarawak.
Status	The IUCN lists the Kinabalu Dwarf Toad as Vulnerable.
Similar species	Three other *Pelophryne* species exist in Borneo, and others occur in neighboring countries. They can be difficult to distinguish from one another without locality information.

Dwarf toads, sometimes known as flat-head toads, are small, secretive species about which little is known. The Kinabalu Dwarf Toad has been found inside the vessel of a large pitcher plant (*Nepenthes* species) on Mount Kinabalu. This may have been coincidental, or the toads may use the water in these pitchers for breeding.

They lay small clutches of eggs—six to 16 have been recorded—in shallow pools. The eggs have no pigment, and the tadpoles do not feed, so they draw on the egg yolk during their development.

These small toads are easily overlooked. Their distribution, with several specimens from Mount Kinabalu and one from Mount Marud, Sarawak, probably indicates that they also occur in some of the intervening montane forest. Logging for timber and clearance of large tracts of forest to make way for oil-palm plantations is a serious problem in Borneo, and small amphibians are vulnerable to extinction. The region around Mount Kinabalu, however, is a national park, so this particular species may be safe for the time being.

⊖ *A tiny Kinabalu Dwarf Toad inside pitcher plants. Among the distinguishing features of this toad are the fully webbed hands and feet. In addition, the tips of its fingers are narrow.*

Cuban Toad

Common name	Cuban Toad
Scientific names	*Peltophryne peltocephala*
Family	Bufonidae
Size	5.12–6.42 in (130–163 mm).
Key features	A large toad covered in many warts. The parotid glands are equally large. Adults are reddish brown with cream or yellow reticulations, but the juveniles are very different, being either bright green or reddish brown with three large conspicuous blotches.
Habits	Terrestrial and nocturnal.
Breeding	In slow-moving streams and flooded areas.
Diet	Invertebrates.
Habitat	Forests, fields, and disturbed areas.
Distribution	Central and E Cuba.
Status	Common.
Similar species	There are two other species of *Peltophryne* in Cuba, but neither is as common as *P. peltocephalus*.

This very large toad can be mistaken for the Cane Toad *(Bufo marinus)* at first glance. Its toxic secretions are equally potent, and most local people are reluctant to handle it; others, however, think it is a cure for bacterial skin diseases and rub the toad on the infected parts.

Toads that feel threatened can inflate themselves to a huge size, with the intention of intimidating predators. They also straighten their limbs so that they are standing high off the ground and tilt their bodies in the direction of the attack.

Cuban Toads live under rocks and logs, in cracks in soil, in holes in the ground that they dig themselves, and in holes that other animals have dug, including those of the Burrowing Owl *(Athene cunicularia)*. They will also set up home in drainpipes and culverts taking storm water under roads, and are well adapted to life in an urban environment. Several individuals often live together in a single underground chamber. They are hard to find in dry weather, but after rains they emerge onto fields and roads to feed and breed.

Males call from the edges of slow-running streams, flooded ditches, and irrigation channels around the edges of sugar-cane plantations. Their call—a melodious "Pa, pa, pa, pa"—sounds like a kettle drum, a characteristic that has given them the local name of *timbrero*, which means drummer.

The eggs are laid in long double strings. The newly transformed young are more brightly colored than the adults and may occur in huge numbers.

⊝ *The large Cuban Toad can be seen in fields and roads after heavy rain, when it emerges to breed and feed.*

Rocket Frogs

Common name	Rocket Frogs
Scientific name	*Colostethus* species and other genera
Family	Dendrobatidae
Size	0.98–1.97 in (25–50 mm).
Key features	Small frogs with thin limbs and long thin digits. Similar in body shape to the brightly colored members of the family but dull (usually some shade of brown) with stripes down their flanks and sometimes more brightly colored undersides.
Habits	Terrestrial and diurnal.
Breeding	The eggs are laid on the ground and are guarded by the male, female, or both. The tadpoles climb onto the parents' back when they hatch.
Diet	Small invertebrates, especially ants.
Habitat	Lowland and montane forests, usually close to streams or rivers.
Distribution	Central and South America.
Status	Some species are common, while others are known from just a handful of specimens. One species is thought to be extinct, and several are listed by the IUCN as Critically Endangered.
Similar species	There are about 143 species of *Colostethus*, 12 of *Mannophryne*, and 8 of *Nephelobates*.

The *Colostethus* species, collectively known as rocket frogs, are the poor relations within the Dendrobatidae. Whereas the better-known species are brightly colored to warn predators of the toxins in their skins, the rocket frogs are relatively dull in color. They are day-active, however, and may contain toxins even though they do not advertise the fact.

They also follow the same life cycle as the others, with females laying their eggs on the ground, usually on a large leaf, where they remain until they hatch. The tadpoles climb onto the back of the male or female (depending on species) and are carried to a small body of water,

often in the vase of a bromeliad plant. In the case of the Brazilian species, *C. stephensi,* however, the tadpoles lack feeding mouthparts and apparently remain in the place where the eggs were laid, surviving on their yolk. They can live out of water because the humidity is high– usually 95 to 100 percent in the places they live.

In yet another species, *C. degranvillei* from Surinam, the male appears to carry the tadpoles on his back until they metamorphose, rather than depositing them in water.

Left: This Colostethus *frog from western Ecuador lives along wide shallow rivers and in forests behind the rivers. Inset:* Colostethus marchesianus *is native to Brazil, Colombia, Peru, and Venezuela, and occurs in the central, eastern, and upper Amazon Basin. © Arthur Georges.*

Green and Black Poison Dart Frog

Common names	Green and Black Poison Dart Frog, Green Poison Dart Frog
Scientific name	Dendrobates auratus
Family	Dendrobatidae
Size	0.98–1.65 in (25–42 mm).
Key features	A small frog with thin limbs and expanded tips to the digits. It has smooth skin and a slightly hunched back. Usually black with bronzy green markings in the form of large interconnected blotches. Another form has similar markings but in blue. The blue form appears to be restricted to Panama, and there is also a brown and white form, in which most of the body is brown and the lighter markings are restricted to small spots and bars.
Habits	Terrestrial and diurnal.
Breeding	The eggs are laid on the ground and are guarded by the male. The tadpoles climb onto his back when they hatch.
Diet	Small invertebrates, especially ants.
Habitat	Lowland rain forest.
Distribution	Central America, from Nicaragua to NW Colombia.
Status	Common and easy to observe.
Similar species	None with this distinctive pattern.

This beautiful little frog lives in colonies of day-active, lively individuals. They hop around constantly on the forest floor, occasionally climbing up tree trunks and into the canopy, looking for food. Females as well as males are territorial and they interact with each other all the time. Males call from hidden places, usually in the early afternoon, and two males that call too close to each other will wrestle to establish territory. Females also wrestle and fight over males, chasing competing females away to prevent a rival from mating with "their" male.

Courtship lasts several hours, with the pair hopping around each other and touching frequently. Eventually, the female lays between five and 13 eggs in the leaf litter and leaves the male to guard them and keep them moist. When the eggs hatch, the male encourages the tadpoles to wriggle up onto his back so that he can transport them to a small body of water, such as a hole in a fallen log or a puddle that has collected in a bromeliad plant, a leaf axil, or even on a curled-up dead leaf.

The tadpoles eat plant material such as algae as well as small aquatic invertebrates and other tadpoles. They will even eat members of their own species, especially if they are overcrowded. The young metamorphose in about eight weeks and grow quickly, becoming mature in about 15 months.

⊖ *The lively little Green and Black Poison Dart Frog is rarely still and is often on the lookout for food. It has excellent eyesight and captures its prey with its sticky, retractible tongue.*

Blue Poison Dart Frog

Common name	Blue Poison Dart Frog
Scientific name	*Dendrobates azureus*
Family	Dendrobatidae
Size	1.18–1.77 in (30–45 mm).
Key features	Unmistakable; a bright blue frog with slender limbs, an upright posture, and a hunched back. The shade of blue varies from the frog's back, which is bright light blue, to its underside, which is dark blue. It has several large rounded spots of dark blue or black on its back and fine dark speckles over most of its body and head. Its digits are expanded at the tips for climbing.
Habits	Terrestrial and diurnal.
Breeding	It lays its eggs on the ground, where they are guarded by the male and sometimes by the female.
Diet	Small invertebrates, especially ants, termites, and small flies.
Habitat	Small isolated patches of forests bordering streams.
Distribution	Surinam (South America).
Status	Common in a few very localized areas, but listed as Vulnerable by the IUCN.
Similar species	The closest relative is the Dyeing Poison Dart Frog (*Dendrobates tinctorius*), but that species invariably has large patches of white or yellow somewhere on its body.

A stunningly beautiful frog, the Blue Poison Dart Frog is perhaps the most colorful in the world, and its bright blue pattern is unique. It lives alongside streams that run through relatively small patches of forest surrounded by dry savanna. Within these forest patches the conditions are warm and humid, and the frogs rarely stray more than a few feet from the edges of the stream.

Blue Poison Dart Frogs are solitary except during the breeding season, which lasts about two months in the wild. At this time, males call to attract females, which may fight each other for the right to mate with a male. The five to 10 eggs are laid within the male's territory, and he guards them until they hatch; occasionally the female will also remain in attendance. Hatching takes place about two weeks after laying, and the tadpoles,

which are elongated, climb up onto the male's back so that he can move them to a small pool of water, usually in the central "urn" of a bromeliad plant. The female may also assist in moving the tadpoles. Because they have cannibalistic tendencies, the tadpoles are often placed singly in their small pools. They metamorphose in about three months and become sexually mature in two years.

⬇ *With its vivid blue coloration* Dendrobates azureus *is possibly the most spectacular of all frogs.*

Harlequin Poison Dart Frog

Common name	Harlequin Poison Dart Frog
Scientific name	*Dendrobates histrionicus*
Family	Dendrobatidae
Size	0.98–1.5 in (25–38 mm).
Key features	A highly variable species. It is most commonly black with red or orange spots but it may also have yellow, white, or even blue markings in the form of spots, reticulations, or bands. Other individuals have such extensive light markings that they are better described as yellow with black reticulations.
Habits	Terrestrial, although it will climb into low vegetation; diurnal.
Breeding	Small clutches of eggs are laid on the ground.
Diet	Small invertebrates such as ants and termites.
Habitat	Rain forest.
Distribution	Northern Ecuador and Colombia.
Status	Common in suitable habitat.
Similar species	There is some confusion over related species that have similar coloration, but the Harlequin Poison Dart Frog is usually the only one with regularly spaced, rounded spots on a darker background.

The Harlequin Poison Dart Frog is one of the species that gives the name poison dart frog to the whole of the genus. In Colombia, the Choco Indians smear the skin secretion of this and one or two other species onto the tips of their blowgun darts. They cut grooves into the tips to improve the amount of toxin that they can hold, and the dart remains potent for up to a year. The toxin is powerful enough to kill small mammals such as monkeys and can harm humans if it gets into the bloodstream.

Parental care in this species goes a stage further than in most other poison dart frogs. Courtship follows the usual pattern, whereby females are attracted to calling males and lay their eggs on a previously cleaned surface. The female guards the eggs, sometimes with help from the male, until they hatch 10 to 14 days later.

Once they are free from the egg membrane, the tadpoles swim up onto the female's back. She takes them to individual pools of water in the center of bromeliad plants, sometimes several feet off the ground. The care does not stop here, however. Tadpoles of this species eat only eggs, so the female must visit each of her offspring every other day and lay an unfertilized egg, sometimes known as a "food egg," into its pool. The tadpoles take up to three months to complete their development.

⊖ *Harlequin Poison Dart Frog, Ecuador. These tiny frogs are able to forage during the day safe from predators thanks to the potent skin toxins that are present over the entire surface of their body.*

Red-banded Poison Dart Frog

Common names	Red-banded Poison Dart Frog, Lehmann's Poison Frog
Scientific name	*Dendrobates lehmanni*
Family	Dendrobatidae
Size	1.38 in (35 mm).
Key features	In its typical form this is a distinctive species, with a black background on which there is a bright red band around the hips and another just behind the head. The limbs are also banded in red, and the fingers have white tips, slightly expanded. In some individuals the background is brown or even orange instead of black.
Habits	Mainly terrestrial but a good climber. Diurnal.
Breeding	Eggs are laid on the ground and guarded by the female.
Diet	Small invertebrates.
Habitat	Dense rain forest at moderate elevations.
Distribution	Western Colombia.
Status	Listed by the IUCN as Critically Endangered because of its small, fragmented distribution.
Similar species	Previously regarded as a form of the Harlequin Poison Dart Frog *(D. histrionicus)* but separated on account of its different color pattern and the chemistry of its skin toxins.

The Red-banded Poison Dart Frog, also known as Lehmann's Poison Dart Frog, is sometimes regarded as a form of the Harlequin Poison Dart Frog *(Dendrobates histrionicus)*, and the two species will interbreed in captivity. However, its coloration of broad red, orange, or yellow bands is distinctive and it lacks histrionicotoxin, one of the components of the skin toxin found in the latter species. Even so, the

secretions of the Red-banded Poison Dart Frog are potent and apparently used by Choco Indians for tipping their blowgun darts.

Its habits are similar to those of the Harlequin Poison Dart Frog, but the Red-banded species is thought to lay its eggs on clean surfaces 3 or 4 feet (1–1.2 m) above the ground. Some reports state that males guard the eggs, but this is unlikely because the tadpoles of this species require unfertilized eggs on which to feed. Obviously, these can be supplied only by the female. It is logical to suppose therefore that it is the female that carries them to the pools of water in which they develop.

This species was formerly imported into North America for the pet trade, but difficulties in keeping it healthy and, in particular, with breeding resulted in it becoming a protected species.

⟵ *A Red-banded Poison Dart Frog in rain forest in Ecuador.*

Black and Yellow Poison Dart Frog

Common names	Black and Yellow Poison Dart Frog, Yellow-headed Poison Frog, Bumblebee Poison Dart Frog
Scientific name	*Dendrobates leucomelas*
Family	Dendrobatidae
Size	1.38–1.97 in (35–50 mm).
Key features	Stocky in build with a unique color pattern. This species is black with wide yellow bands around its body and a large yellow patch on the top of its head. Within the yellow bands are black spots that increase in size and number as the frog grows.
Habits	Mainly terrestrial but will climb into low bushes and onto tree trunks. Diurnal.
Breeding	Eggs are laid on the ground and guarded by the male until they hatch.
Diet	Small invertebrates.
Habitat	Warm lowland rain forests.
Distribution	Northern South America (N Brazil, Colombia, Guyana, and Venezuela).
Status	Common.
Similar species	None. This is one of the less variable poison dart frogs.

This is one of the more robust species of poison dart frogs and, as a result, is popular among amateur frog keepers. It breeds readily in captivity as long as its few, simple requirements are provided for, and there should be no reason to collect these frogs from wild populations. One of the characteristics of captive-raised poison dart frogs is their tendency to stop producing the skin toxins that give them their name. In the wild, they gather these substances from their prey, especially ants, and accumulate them in their skin glands. In captivity, however, if their food does not contain the relevant chemicals their toxicity gradually declines, and individuals hatched and raised entirely in captivity are not at all toxic.

The bright colors of poison dart frogs are a signal to potential predators that they are poisonous. This is known as aposematic coloration and is common throughout the animal kingdom. Wasps and bees are probably the most familiar animals exhibiting this type of coloring; and *Dendrobates leucomelas* is sometimes called the Bumblebee Poison Dart Frog.

The life cycle of this species is similar to that of other *Dendrobates*. The male guards the eggs after they have been laid, and he moves them to a small body of water once the tadpoles hatch out. They feed on algae and a variety of small aquatic invertebrates, including other tadpoles. They take 70 to 90 days to complete their development.

→ *The coloring of Black and Yellow Poison Dart Frogs varies by individual. Each frog has a unique pattern of bands; the number and size of spots inside the bands is also unique.*

Strawberry Poison Dart Frog

Common names	Strawberry Poison Dart Frog, Flaming Poison Frog, Red and Blue Poison Frog
Scientific name	*Dendrobates pumilio*
Family	Dendrobatidae
Size	0.67–0.94 in (17–24 mm).
Key features	A small, bright red frog, with slightly granular skin on its back. Some have black speckling on their backs, but most are plain. The front legs are also largely red but the back legs are black with small blue speckles, or plain blue. Frogs from some areas are completely different: they may be all-red or all-blue; they can even be plain greenish yellow or yellow with black spots.
Habits	Terrestrial and diurnal.
Breeding	Eggs are laid on the ground and guarded by the female.
Diet	Small invertebrates, especially ants.
Habitat	Lowland rain forest.
Distribution	Central America, on the eastern sides of Nicaragua, Costa Rica, and Panama.
Status	Very common in suitable places.
Similar species	*D. granuliferus* is similar in coloration but has a more granular back.

Despite its small size, this is a charismatic little frog that has come to epitomize the Central American "jungle." It is lively and brightly colored, and males constantly stop what they are doing to make their pleasant buzzing call. Their image can be found on postage stamps, T-shirts, and souvenirs, especially in Costa Rica, where it can occur in very high densities—in excess of 800 per 2.5 acres (per 1 hectare).

This species breeds at any time of the year. Males call constantly, often from an exposed position, and will fight off other males that approach. Females that are ready to lay eggs are attracted to calling males and approach them. The male leads the female to a site that he has prepared, usually a large leaf that he has cleaned of debris. There is no amplexus—the two adults sit facing in opposite directions with their cloacae touching.

The female lays up to five eggs (more in captivity) and may lay a clutch every week. After egg-laying and fertilization, the male and female return to the clutch every day. The male moistens the eggs by sitting over them and emptying his bladder. When the eggs hatch, after about seven days, the mother returns. The tadpoles climb on her back, sometimes singly and sometimes several at a time, and she carries them up into bromeliad plants—usually a few feet from the ground on tree branches and fallen trunks. She places a single tadpole in each bromeliad "vase," but only if it is empty to start with.

Following this, the female returns to each bromeliad every day or so, usually in the morning, and lays one to five infertile eggs on *(continued over)*

Two male Strawberry Poison Dart Frogs are locked in combat as they wrestle for dominance over a territory.

Strawberry Poison Dart Frog

which the tadpole feeds. She backs down into the water in the base of the plant until her vent is submerged. The tadpole approaches, stiffens its body, and vibrates. This "begging behavior" is only successful with the tadpole's mother; females refuse to feed tadpoles that are not theirs.

Young tadpoles bite a hole in the jelly and suck out the eggs, but larger tadpoles eat the jelly as well. The tadpoles take 43 to 52 days to develop, during which time they eat as many as 40 infertile eggs. They measure 0.4 inches (10 mm) at metamorphosis and are a uniform, dark blood-red color.

⊖ *Not all Strawberry Poison Dart Frogs live up to their colorful name. Many variations exist, in particular on the small islands off the coast of Panama, as the collection pictured here from Panama exemplifies. Sometimes color variants are mistakenly described as different species.*

Dyeing Poison Dart Frog

Common name	Dyeing Poison Dart Frog
Scientific name	*Dendrobates tinctorius*
Family	Dendrobatidae
Size	1.57–1.97 in (40–50 mm).
Key features	One of the larger poison dart frogs, with long slender limbs and upright posture. Its back is usually dark blue or black with a pair of yellow stripes (sometimes connected with cross bands) down each side. Its limbs and underside are lighter blue and covered with black speckles. Other pattern forms occur (but rarely), including one in which the back is cream or white and one in which the limbs, flanks, and broad dorsal stripes are yellow.
Habits	Mainly terrestrial, but can be found up to 6 ft (1.8 m) from the ground. Diurnal.
Breeding	Eggs are laid on the ground and guarded by the male.
Diet	Small invertebrates, but it can take larger prey than some members of the genus.
Habitat	In humid lowland forests, often isolated within large areas of unsuitable grassland.
Distribution	Northern South America (the Guianas and NE Brazil).
Status	Common in suitable habitat, but this is gradually shrinking.
Similar species	Its closest relative, the Blue Poison Dart Frog (*D. azureus*), is similar in size and shape, but the coloration of the two species sets them apart.

A large, bold species, the Dyeing Poison Dart Frog is capable of tackling somewhat larger prey than many of the smaller poison dart frogs. Even so, ants account for more than half of its diet, and this is where the toxins stored in the frog's skin glands come from. Additional food items found in wild individuals include a wide variety

of small leaf-litter insects, indicating that this species is not a specialist but simply hops around on the forest floor, snapping up anything it can handle. Because most of its food is small, each frog needs to feed more or less continuously, especially when young.

This species' common and scientific names originate from accounts that local Indians used the skin secretions of these frogs to alter the coloration of birds' feathers. Apparently, they would pluck the feathers from young parrots before rubbing the frog against the resulting bare patch of skin. When new feathers grew, they were red or yellow instead of green. The highly prized feathers were used in headdresses.

← *These Dyeing Poison Dart Frogs were seen on a tree trunk in a Guianan forest.*

Yellow-striped Poison Dart Frog

Common names	Yellow-striped Poison Dart Frog, Río Magdalena Poison Dart Frog
Scientific name	*Dendrobates truncatus*
Family	Dendrobatidae
Size	0.98–1.77 in (25–45 mm).
Key features	Black or dark brown with a pair of bright yellow stripes that start at the tip of the snout and run down either side to the rump. There are also yellow stripes on its flanks and limbs.
Habits	Diurnal and terrestrial.
Breeding	On land.
Diet	Small invertebrates.
Habitat	Wet and dry forests, and some disturbed habitats.
Distribution	Colombia, from the Caribbean coast south into the Central Valley.
Status	Common.
Similar species	There are several striped *Phyllobates* species, but none in the same area.

The Yellow-striped Poison Dart Frog, sometimes called the Río Magdalena Poison Dart Frog, is one of the few species that appears to cope with disturbed habitat. Whereas most species live only in primary or well-grown secondary rain forest, this species can also be found in banana plantations and other cleared areas as long as there is some forest cover remaining. It is more terrestrial than some species and is nearly always found on the ground, foraging for small insects such as ants, aphids, and other leaf-litter dwellers.

Breeding begins at the onset of the rainy season, often accompanied by a drop in temperature. The males, which are distinguishable by having slightly larger toe pads than the females, attract mates with a low buzzing call that is barely audible to the human ear. After a prolonged courtship, which includes circling each other with short hops, the female lays between four and 20 eggs on a previously cleaned leaf. Males, females, or both parents often stay with the eggs until they hatch, before carrying them on their backs to a suitable body of water. Metamorphosis takes about four months, and the young are relatively large.

The Río Magdalena suffered a serious pollution incident several years ago, and the area is also being cleared for cultivation on a rapid scale. The frog's ability to adapt may prove to be its lifeline.

⊖ *The Yellow-striped Poison Dart Frog is common in Colombia. The secret of its success may lie in its adaptability to changing environmental conditions.*

Three-striped Poison Dart Frog

Common names	Three-striped Poison Dart Frog, Phantasmal, Poison Dart Frog
Scientific name	*Epipedobates tricolor*
Family	Dendrobatidae
Size	0.75–0.98 in (19–25 mm).
Key features	Small frog with a striped body. Most specimens are basically reddish brown with three stripes of white, cream, or pale green running down the body. The central stripe starts at the snout and ends at the rump, while the side stripes also start at the snout and end in the groin on each side. The limbs are banded and spotted.
Habits	Terrestrial and diurnal.
Breeding	Eggs laid on land and guarded by the male.
Diet	Small invertebrates such as aphids.
Habitat	Andean slopes with dry forests and grasslands. The frogs live alongside small streams.
Distribution	Ecuador, on the Pacific slopes of the Andes; may extend north into SW Peru.
Status	Listed by the IUCN as Endangered from central Ecuador population.
Similar species	None, although the species is sometimes split into other similar species that are probably local races, one example being *E. anthonyi*.

The Three-striped Poison Dart Frog was placed originally in the genus *Phyllobates* before being moved to a new genus, *Epipedobates*, on the grounds that it has different skin toxins from the other groups. It has also been known by several other names, including *Prostherapsis tricolor* and *Colostethus paradoxus*, and is sometimes found under these names in older publications. The frog has an alternative common name, Phantasmal, which means dreamlike or hallucinatory—how this relates to this particular species is not known.

The species has proven useful to science. In 1993 scientists isolated epibatidine, a toxin found only in this and closely related species. It is a minor toxin, but a potent painkiller—200 times

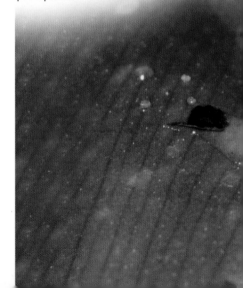

stronger than morphine, and nonaddictive. It has been synthesized, and the U.S. Food and Drugs Administration has approved testing of the substance.

Breeding in this species follows the usual pattern in poison dart frogs. The male's call is a pleasant warbling or whistling sound, sometimes likened to that of a canary. Males guard the 20 to 25 eggs and take them to water when they hatch. The male may carry a whole brood on his back in a single journey, and the tadpoles are deposited in one place since they are not as inclined toward cannibalism as some other members of the family. They metamorphose at a small size after about 60 days and reach sexual maturity in eight months. This is one of the more prolific species in the family, and colonies grow quickly if conditions are suitable.

The Three-striped Poison Dart Frog is less elaborately patterned than many species, but it can occur in other color forms.

Two-toned Poison Dart Frog

Common names	Two-toned Poison Dart Frog, Black-legged Poison Frog
Scientific name	*Phyllobates bicolor*
Family	Dendrobatidae
Size	1.5–1.65 in (38–42 mm).
Key features	This species is large for a poison dart frog and has a bright yellow head and body. Its hind limbs may also be yellow, but more often they are heavily suffused with black speckles. Juveniles are striped at first, and the yellow areas gradually expand as they grow.
Habits	Mainly terrestrial and diurnal.
Breeding	Eggs laid on land.
Diet	Small invertebrates, especially ants.
Habitat	Rain forests, usually near wide streams where the humidity is high.
Distribution	Western Colombia.
Status	Locally common, but listed by the IUCN as Near Threatened as a result of declining habitat.
Similar species	The Golden Poison Dart Frog (*P. terribilis*) is similar but never has black hind legs.

The Choco region of Colombia, where these frogs live, is one of the wettest places on Earth. During the rainy season up to 33 feet (10 m) of rain can fall, turning the wide shallow streams into raging torrents. Since the tadpoles of these frogs also live in the same streams, heavy rains disperse them downstream. Two-toned Poison Dart Frogs are more arboreal than most members of the family and will move up into low bushes and onto the trunks of fallen forest trees. They are very bold.

Although all members of the family are popularly known as poison dart frogs, only three or four species are used for this purpose. The Choco Indians of western Colombia use blowgun darts tipped with the skin secretions of this and two other species, including *Phyllobates terribilis*. The method of obtaining the toxins from the Two-toned Poison Dart Frog is to skewer the animal with a stick, which makes it secrete large quantities of the poisonous substance from its skin. The toxin is then applied to blowgun darts, which can be stored for up to a year.

Like other poison dart frogs, when deprived of its normal diet of ants, termites, and other leaf-litter invertebrates, this species gradually loses its toxicity. However, it does not disappear altogether, possibly because these frogs eat their own shed skins, thereby recycling the toxins. Frogs bred in captivity, however, have little or no toxin in their skin.

⊖ *A pair of male Two-toned Poison Dart Frogs fighting.*

Golden Poison Dart Frog

Common name	Golden Poison Dart Frog
Scientific name	*Phyllobates terribilis*
Family	Dendrobatidae
Size	1.97 in (50 mm).
Key features	A heavily built species with uniform coloration. Most are plain yellow or yellowish orange in color, but some are green.
Habits	Terrestrial and diurnal.
Breeding	Eggs are laid on the ground.
Diet	Small invertebrates, notably ants.
Habitat	Humid rain forest.
Distribution	Colombia.
Status	Locally common, but listed by the IUCN as Endangered because it is found in only five locations or fewer, and its habitat is in decline.
Similar species	The Two-toned Poison Dart Frog (*P. bicolor*) nearly always has black hind limbs and is smaller. Otherwise there are no similar species.

This stunningly beautiful frog is the most toxic animal in the world. It is 20 times more toxic than any of the other poison dart frogs. A single frog can yield up to 1,900 micrograms of poison, and a mere 200 micrograms is thought to be lethal to humans. Just touching a Golden Poison Dart Frog can cause a serious, possibly life-threatening reaction.

This species' toxins are used to tip the darts of blowguns; such small quantities of the poison are needed that the Indians keep the frogs alive in small woven baskets, or tubes of bamboo or sugarcane, and use each one several times. When they need to tip their darts, they pin a frog to the ground with a stick (to avoid the irritation caused by handling it) and simply wipe or roll the dart over its back. The poison is so potent that, when shot, monkeys feel its effects almost instantly and fall from the trees in seconds.

Batrachotoxins are the most potent of all naturally occurring poisons and occur only in the *Phyllobates* species, most notably in *P. terribilis*. They affect the nervous system and the heart, causing arrhythmia and ultimately heart failure. Symptoms in laboratory animals include muscle contractions, convulsions, salivation, and death—even at very low doses. One microgram of batrachotoxin will kill a

mouse in less than a minute and much smaller doses—
as low as 0.05 micrograms—are still fatal. An average
yield from one frog is about 1,100 micrograms, enough
to kill 20,000 mice. Although it is difficult to relate this to
the potential effect on a human, these poisons would
certainly pose a serious threat to life. There is no

⬆ *The harmless-looking Golden Poison Dart Frog from
Colombia is, in fact, the most toxic animal in the world.*

antidote. Almost unbelievably, a frog-eating snake,
Leimadophis epinephelus, may be immune to its toxin
and is probably the frog's only natural enemy.

Golfodulcean Poison Dart Frog

Common names	Golfodulcean Poison Dart Frog, Striped Poison Dart Frog
Scientific name	*Phyllobates vittatus*
Family	Dendrobatidae
Size	0.87–1.22 in (22–31 mm).
Key features	A small frog with a narrow head and bluntly rounded snout. It is mainly black, with a pair of orange stripes running down either side of its back. There are bluish stripes on its lower jaw, and its flanks and limbs are covered with bluish speckles.
Habits	Terrestrial and diurnal.
Breeding	Lays its eggs on leaves above the ground.
Diet	Small insects, including ants.
Habitat	Lowland rain forests, especially near streams.
Distribution	Southwestern Costa Rica. Possibly also in neighboring parts of Panama.
Status	Thought to be relatively common, but listed by IUCN as Endangered because of relatively small, fragmented, and declining habitat.
Similar species	*Phyllobates lugubris* from the same region is similar but smaller.

These small frogs appear to live a wandering life on the forest floor, walking and hopping among the leaf litter in search of food. Unlike many members of the family, they are not territorial. Males make a soft trilling call to attract a female, and during courtship this changes to a series of chirps repeated every few seconds. Courtship lasts several days, during which time the two frogs constantly circle and hop around one another. When the eggs are eventually laid, usually on a living leaf a few inches or more above the ground, the male and female sit facing away from each other with their vents touching. The female lays seven to 21 eggs and, in captivity at least, females lay clutches every week or two. The breeding season lasts for about three months, so they are relatively prolific.

Although in this species the male does not constantly guard the eggs, he visits them several times each day to moisten them with water from his bladder. When they hatch, after 13 to 17 days, he nudges them until some of the tadpoles wriggle up onto his back. He can transport up to about 12 at a time, and returns to the brood until he has moved them all to water. The tadpoles metamorphose after about 45 days.

The common name of Golfodulcean originates from the Golfo Dulce, the large bay in southwestern Costa Rica around which the frogs are found.

This Golfodulcean Poison Dart Frog was photographed in a Costa Rican rain forest.

Other Poison Dart Frogs

⬆ Epipedobates braccatus *originates from Brazil, where it lives and breeds among leaf litter in the savanna habitat known as the* cerrado.

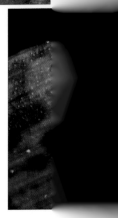

➡ *Color variant of the Three-striped Poison Dart Frog* (Epipedobates tricolor) *in which the central pale stripe is distinctly green and broken up (see also page 194).*

Other Poison Dart Frogs

→ Epipedobates bilinguis *from Colombia and Ecuador lives among leaf litter close to streams in primary and secondary forest.* © Arthur Georges.

← Epipedobates hahneli *is distributed widely in Colombia, Ecuador, Peru, Brazil, the Guianas, and northwestern Bolivia.* © Arthur Georges.

↓ *The Rough-skinned Poison Dart Frog (Dendrobates granuliferus) occurs in a habitat of less than 8,000 square miles (20,000 sq. km) in Costa Rica, and the species is under threat because of forest destruction.*

Darwin's Frog

Common names	Darwin's Frog, Darwin's Toad
Scientific name	*Rhinoderma darwinii*
Family	Rhinodermatidae
Size	0.98–1.18 in (25–30 mm).
Key features	Small and chubby with a pointed snout ending in a short appendage. Its pupils are horizontal. Its hind feet are slightly webbed and have small flaps of skin on the ankles. The frog may be bright green, brown, or reddish brown, with faint spotting of darker hues. Underneath it is black with bright white spots. Its throat is gray.
Habits	Terrestrial and active by day.
Breeding	It has a unique breeding strategy in which males pick up the eggs and hold the developing tadpoles in their vocal sac.
Diet	Small invertebrates.
Habitat	Shallow cold streams running through southern beech *(Nothofagus)* forests.
Distribution	Extreme S Chile and adjacent parts of S Argentina.
Status	Formerly common but becoming scarcer because of habitat reduction. Listed by the IUCN as Vulnerable because of population decline.
Similar species	*Rhinoderma rufum*, from the same region, is similar and is listed by the IUCN as Critically Endangered.

Darwin's Frog has a unique breeding system in which a male guards the eggs and cares for the tadpoles by carrying them in its mouth.

These frogs live along small shallow trickles of water that drain the temperate beech forests of the southernmost tip of South America. Breeding takes place throughout the year but is most frequent between December and March, mid-summer in the Southern Hemisphere. Males call with a high-pitched note similar to birdsong, and amplexus is short and very weak. The female lays a clutch of about 30 to 40 eggs on damp ground and then has nothing more to do with them. The male, however, remains with the clutch after fertilizing them, until they hatch about 20 days later. As soon as the embryos begin to move about, he picks them up in his mouth and moves them to his vocal

sac. Occasionally more than one male may attend a single clutch of eggs and they then share the tadpoles between them. The males carry the eggs for about 50 days while they are developing into froglets. When they are ready to be released, they make their way from the vocal sac into the male's mouth, which he opens so that they can escape. The tadpoles are thought to absorb a nutritious fluid (sometimes called "male's milk") that is produced in the male's vocal sac.

In the only other member of the family, *Rhinoderma rufum*, the male picks up the hatching eggs in the same way as in Darwin's Frogs but merely takes them to water and deposits them, after which they develop in the normal way.

⊖ *An adult male Darwin's Frog stays close to a group of newly emerged froglets.*

Orange-eyed Leaf Frog

Common names	Orange-eyed Leaf Frog, Blue-sided Leaf Frog
Scientific name	*Agalychnis annae*
Family	Hylidae
Size	2.24–3.31 in (57–84 mm).
Key features	A slender frog with heavily webbed hands and feet and large adhesive pads on all its digits. Its eyes have a yellow iris. Mostly uniform bright green in color, with blue flanks and blue or lavender areas on the limbs, hands, and feet.
Habits	Arboreal and nocturnal.
Breeding	Lays its eggs on leaves overhanging ponds.
Diet	Invertebrates.
Habitat	Lower montane rain forests, including nearby disturbed areas.
Distribution	Central Costa Rica.
Status	Formerly common, but its numbers are decreasing. Listed by the IUCN as Endangered.
Similar species	Other *Agalychnis* species are similar in size and shape but differ in coloration of their bodies or eyes. Related *Phyllomedusa* species have less webbing on their hands and feet.

Sometimes called the Blue-sided Leaf Frog, this species lives in one of the more heavily populated areas of Costa Rica, the Central Valley. Despite this, it was relatively common until recently, living in small remnants of rain forest surrounded by development and even surviving in gardens and overgrown plantations. Lately, however, like many frog species from this part of the world, its numbers have fallen dramatically, and it is difficult to find.

Like most other *Agalychnis* species, the Orange-eyed Leaf Frog lays its eggs on the upper surfaces of large leaves overhanging forest ponds. In built-up areas it may make use of ornamental pools in parks and gardens or even swimming pools. The males call throughout the year, except during dry weather, from bushes and trees up to 30 feet (9 m) above the ground. When a female arrives, they go into amplexus and move down to the water, where the female fills her bladder. Then they climb back into the vegetation and look for a suitable large leaf that is 4 to 10 feet (1.2–3 m) above the surface.

The female lays her eggs on top of the leaf or, occasionally, attaches them to a branch or vine. The eggs are pale green and 45 to 126 in number. They hatch in five to seven days, and the tadpoles' movements cause them to slide down the leaf into the water below. The tadpoles take up to nine months to develop fully and are just under 1 inch (20–23 mm) long when they first emerge from the water.

⊕ *Its heavily webbed limbs and sticky toe pads enable the Orange-eyed Leaf Frog to climb over trees and wet surfaces.*

Splendid Leaf Frog

Common names	Splendid Leaf Frog, Flap-heeled Leaf Frog
Scientific name	*Agalychnis calcarifer (Crucihyla calcarifer)*
Family	Hylidae
Size	1.97–3.43 in (50–87 mm). Males are significantly smaller than females.
Key features	A very distinctive leaf frog, this species has a dark green back and bright yellow or orange flanks. Several black or dark purple bars cut across the flanks. The inside surfaces of the legs are similarly orange with darker crossbars. The hands and feet are large, heavily webbed, and the toes end in large adhesive pads. The pupils are vertical.
Habits	Arboreal and nocturnal.
Breeding	Lays its eggs on leaves overhanging water-filled holes in tree trunks.
Diet	Invertebrates.
Habitat	Primary lowland rain forests. This species does not tolerate disturbed habitat.
Distribution	Central America, from E Honduras through Costa Rica, Panama, and into Colombia. and N Ecuador.
Status	Rarely seen.
Similar species	Other *Agalychnis* species are similar in size, but the bold crossbars on this species' flanks are distinctive. Related *Phyllomedusa* species have less webbing on their hands and feet. Other tree frogs have horizontal pupils.

This spectacular frog lives in the tallest trees of the rain forest and is seen only when breeding. Males move down from the canopy to call from trees up to 25 feet (7.6 m) tall, but they move down to lower bushes before mating. Unlike most other leaf frogs, they do not lay their eggs on leaves overhanging ponds but on surfaces such as tree trunks and vegetation

above water-filled cavities. Unless the cavities become clogged with fallen leaves or other debris, the frogs may return to the same site for several years.

The female first goes down to the water to fill her bladder before climbing back up to the egg-laying site. Unusually, she tends to lay her eggs in the morning, in daylight. Clutches contain 10 to 54 bluish green eggs that hatch after five to 10 days, but sometimes take up to a month. The eggs do not all hatch at the same time. When they do finally hatch, the tadpoles fall into the water or are washed there by heavy rain. Only about half the clutches hatch successfully, and most of the offspring perish before they metamorphose. Tadpoles are preyed upon by insect larvae and water boatmen as well as older tadpoles. They take eight months or more to complete their development.

⤓ *The Splendid Leaf Frog, seen here in Costa Rica. Leaf frogs are unusual among tree frogs in having vertical pupils.*

Red-eyed Leaf Frog

Common name	Red-eyed Leaf Frog
Scientific name	*Agalychnis callidryas*
Family	Hylidae
Size	2.8 in (71 mm).
Key features	Red eyes! This species has a slender body, narrow waist, long spindly legs, and heavily webbed feet with large adhesive pads on all the toes. Its eyes are very large and have brilliant red irises with vertical pupils. The flanks have blue and cream markings, although their shape and extent vary from one locality to another.
Habits	Highly arboreal and mostly nocturnal.
Breeding	Eggs are laid on leaves overhanging small pools.
Diet	Invertebrates.
Habitat	Lowland rain forests.
Distribution	Central America from southern Veracruz and the Yucatán Peninsula, Mexico, to the Canal Zone, Panama, mostly on the Atlantic slopes but also in the Pacific lowlands of Costa Rica.
Status	Common in suitable habitat, but declining.
Similar species	Several other *Agalychnis* species occur in the region but only the Small Red-eyed Leaf Frog (*A. saltator*) also has red eyes. The latter is smaller, however, and lacks the brightly colored flanks of this species.

No other frogs characterize the exotic fauna of the rain forests or "jungles" of South America to the same extent as the Red-eyed Leaf Frog. It is instantly recognizable and appears on posters, postage stamps, and in numerous books and magazines throughout the world. It is restricted to primary rain forests, where it lives in the canopies of tall forest trees such as palms or in bromeliads and other epiphytic plants. It rests by day and becomes active at dusk, often descending to lower levels, especially in the breeding season.

The Red-eyed Leaf Frog breeds during the rainy season. Males often call as soon as the sun sets, from high up in the branches where they have spent the day. These preliminary calls are sometimes known as rain calls. As they descend, they stop calling until they take up their positions near the breeding sites. Their calls here are different from the rain calls and consist of single or double note "chock" or "chock-chock." Calling males usually sit at right angles across the stems of shrubs. Sites are typically 3 to 9 feet (0.9–2.7 m) above small pools and, unless the population is very dense, are usually well spaced out.

The male's calls attract females in breeding condition. When a female gets to within a few inches of a male, he stops calling, moves toward her, and climbs on her back. If the female approaches from behind, where the male cannot see her, she places a forelimb on his back. Once they are in amplexus the female first descends to the water to fill her bladder (she uses the water to produce the jelly surrounding her eggs). Then she climbs back into the bush or tree and walks around until she finds a suitable egg-laying

⊕ *The Red-eyed Leaf Frog is recognized worldwide as a symbol of the rain forest.*

site. While this is going on the male, who is substantially smaller than the female, simply hangs on and may close his eyes. Eventually the female walks along a stem until she arrives at a leaf that is hanging over the water. She crawls to the tip of the leaf and turns so that she is facing upward. As she lays her eggs, she moves slowly up the leaf so that the egg mass is elongated. The male fertilizes the eggs while this is happening.

The eggs take about five days to hatch. At the time of hatching the jelly mass begins to liquefy so the tadpoles can move around in their nest. Hatching is usually triggered by rain, and the tadpoles wriggle until they slide down the leaf and drip off the end into the pond below. After hitting the water, they swim to the bottom and remain there for a minute or two before reappearing at the surface. Sometimes things go wrong and the tadpoles miss the water. If the distance is only an inch or two they can usually flip themselves into it. If they hatch during dry weather, they stay in the nest to avoid the possibility of dripping onto mud or into a shrinking pool.

Small Red-eyed Leaf Frog

Common names	Small Red-eyed Leaf Frog, Parachuting Red-eyed Leaf Frog
Scientific name	*Agalychnis saltator*
Family	Hylidae
Size	2.4 in (61 mm).
Key features	Similar to the Red-eyed Leaf Frog (*A. callidryas*) but smaller and lacking the banded markings on its flanks; instead they are uniform dark blue or purple. The eyes of this species appear darker red. The hands and feet are heavily webbed.
Habits	Highly arboreal and nocturnal.
Breeding	Eggs laid on leaves hanging over small pools.
Diet	Invertebrates.
Habitat	Lowland rain forests.
Distribution	Central America, from NE Nicaragua to NE Costa Rica.
Status	Common in suitable habitat, but declining. Listed by the IUCN as Near Threatened.
Similar species	Red-eyed Leaf Frog (*A. callidryas*) (see above).

The Small Red-eyed Leaf Frog is restricted to primary rain forests. Like some other members of the genus, it is a gliding species and uses its webbed feet to parachute down from tall trees. This technique is paralleled by gliding frogs from South East Asia that look similar but are not closely related. The webbed feet of these frogs are not associated with swimming. In fact, leaf frogs are poor swimmers and may even drown if they become stranded in deep water.

The Small Red-eyed Leaf Frog is an explosive breeder. On suitable nights, usually immediately after torrential rain, several hundreds may congregate on vines overhanging suitable ponds. The females plaster their egg masses to clumps of moss surrounding epiphytic plants, or to their roots. Although each clump is separate at the time of laying, the activities of the frogs, both single males and breeding pairs, tend to mix the clutches together into a single mass. The eggs are laid in the early morning, and some pairs are still present at the laying sites at noon the following day. Each female lays 21 to 72 eggs, which hatch after about six days. The eggs may be eaten by snakes, ants, warblers, and capuchin monkeys.

Red eyes are associated with nocturnal species. As well as the species described here, several tree frogs, *Hyla* species, have red eyes. There is also a large Australian red-eyed frog, *Litoria chloris*. On the island of Madagascar a number of frogs belonging to the genus *Boophis* also have red or pink eyes.

⊖ *A Small Red-eyed Leaf Frog photographed in Costa Rica. Like many red-eyed animals, it is a night hunter.*

Spurrell's Leaf Frog

Common names	Spurrell's Leaf Frog, Gliding Tree Frog
Scientific name	*Agalychnis spurrelli*
Family	Hylidae
Size	1.77–2.68 in (45–68 mm). Males are smaller than females.
Key features	The eyes in this species are very dark red or reddish brown. Its hands and feet are large, heavily webbed, and the toes end in large adhesive pads. Its back is bright green and usually has a few random white dots scattered about. Its underside, the inside of its limbs, and its hands and feet, are yellow or orange.
Habits	Arboreal and nocturnal.
Breeding	Lays its eggs on leaves overhanging water-filled holes in tree trunks.
Diet	Invertebrates.
Habitat	Primary lowland rain forests.
Distribution	Central and South America, from S Costa Rica to NW Ecuador.
Status	Rarely seen.
Similar species	The combination of webbed feet, vertical pupils, and green and orange coloration makes this species easy to identify.

This gliding frog has especially large hands and feet, making it well equipped to parachute down from high branches. During a leap it can move horizontally at an angle of about 45 degrees, landing some distance from the base of the tree from which it launched itself. At other times it walks along branches and vines using a deliberate, hand-over-hand method of locomotion, and may pause mid-stride.

This species is an explosive breeder. During or after heavy rain hundreds or even thousands of frogs descend from the canopy to congregate on small trees and shrubs around temporary ponds. They are mostly males because females visit only for a short time—having laid their eggs, they return to the canopy. The males, on the other hand, stay around in the hope of attracting more mates.

Egg-laying continues into the following morning and may not finish until well after dawn. The jelly-covered egg masses are laid up to 25 feet (7.6 m) above the water, but most are lower. Each female lays between 14 and 67 eggs but the total number after a breeding session runs into many thousands. A large number are dislodged by the males, however, and fall into the water prematurely. Otherwise, they begin to hatch after about one week and continue to drip into the water for several days. The tadpoles are large and they hang in the water with their heads pointed up, filtering out microscopic food particles. They may also feed from the surface film.

⊖ *Spurrell's Flying Frog in Costa Rica. Although it can glide, it usually does so only in response to danger.*

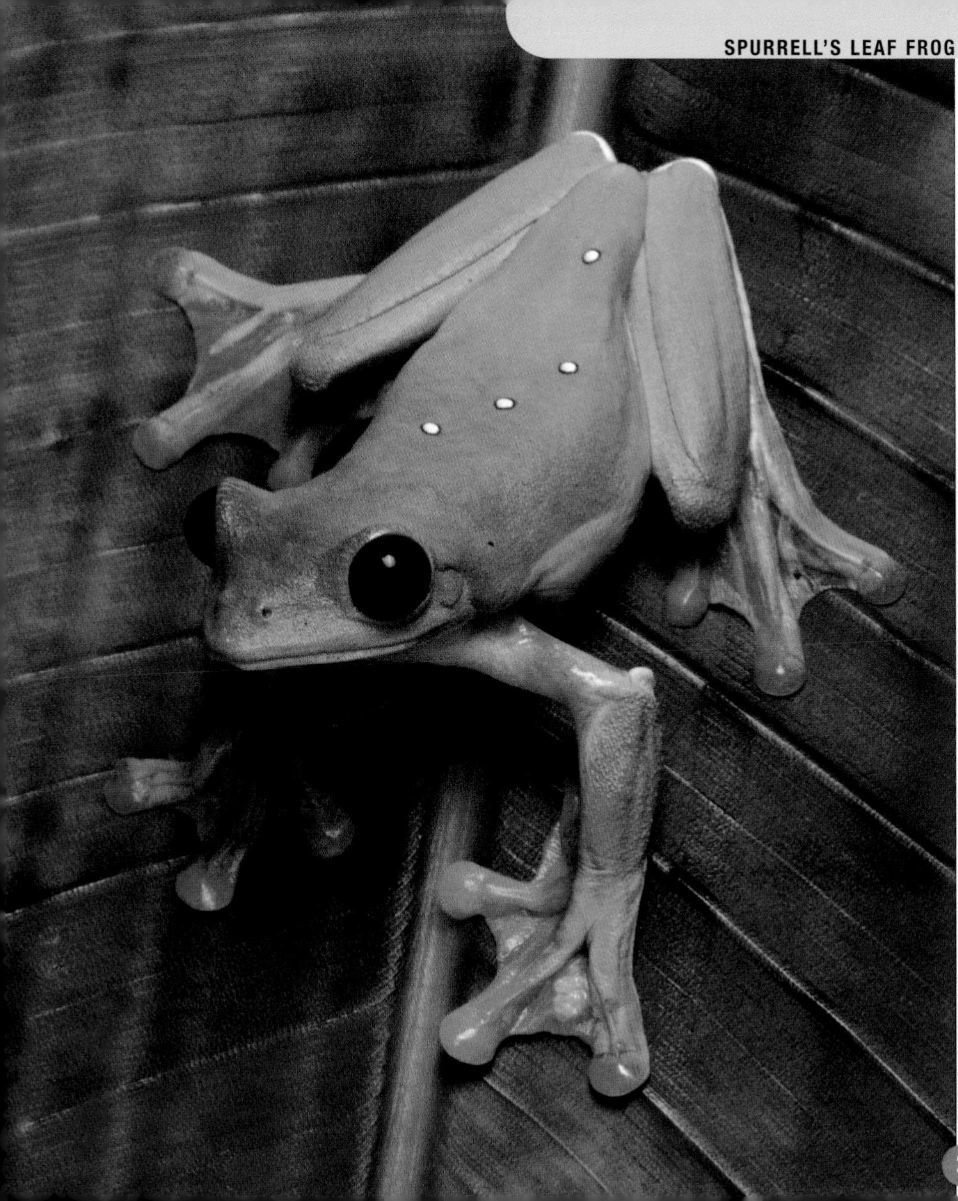

Crowned Tree Frog

Common name	Crowned Tree Frog
Scientific name	*Anotheca spinosa*
Family	Hylidae
Size	2.36–3.15 in (60–80 mm). Males are smaller than females.
Key features	This species is unmistakable. Its large head is bony, with a rim of spiky projections. It is gray or light brown on the back with dark gray or purple flanks. Where the two colors meet, there is a thin white line. The dark coloration extends to the underside, onto the face and limbs, in the form of spots or bars.
Habits	Arboreal and nocturnal.
Breeding	Lays its eggs in water-filled cavities.
Diet	Invertebrates.
Habitat	Primary lowland or lower montane rain forests.
Distribution	Central America, from SE Mexico to Panama.
Status	Very secretive and rarely seen. Listed by the IUCN as Near Threatened because of population and habitat decline.
Similar species	The spiny head ornamentation make this species unique.

One of the more strange-looking frogs, the Crowned Tree Frog has a lifestyle to match its appearance. Males find a water-filled tree hole, bromeliad vase, or other small water body above the ground, and call there every night. During the day they leave and hide elsewhere. When a female arrives at the "pool," the two frogs go into amplexus and dive to the bottom, their heads down and their backsides just above the surface. The eggs are laid in this position and attached to the sides of the pool, just above the surface. On average, the females lay about 150 eggs each. Upon hatching, the tadpoles slide or wriggle down into the pool, but it seems that most of the eggs perish—sometimes fewer than a dozen tadpoles make it to the next stage.

Now things take an interesting turn. After the tadpoles have hatched, the female returns to the pool and floats on the water with her cloaca submerged. She lays large clutches of unfertilized eggs for the tadpoles to eat. When they are young, the tadpoles suck out the contents of each egg, leaving the membrane, but as they grow, they eat the entire egg. It seems that the female will only lay her eggs when she is stimulated by the tadpoles. If subsequent fertile eggs are laid by the same or another female while older tadpoles are still in the water, they are eaten as soon as they hatch. The young grow slowly, taking from two to four months to develop fully. When they first metamorphose, they have a similar coloration to the adults but lack the spiky heads.

Tadpoles that eat infertile eggs provided by their mother also occur among the Dendrobatidae, in species such as the Strawberry Poison Dart Frog *(Dendrobates pumilio)*, and the Rhacophoridae. There are also a couple of other hylid tree frogs that have similar diets.

🔽 *The Crowned Tree Frog, seen here in Turrialba, Costa Rica, lives high in the forest canopy and breeds in small tree holes.*

New Holland Water-holding Frog

Common names	New Holland Water-holding Frog, New Holland Frog, Snapping Frog
Scientific name	Cyclorana novaehollandiae
Family	Hylidae
Size	2.76–3.94 in (70–100 mm).
Key features	A large, stocky, muscular frog with long hind limbs. There is a pair of glandular ridges running down either side of its back and another pair on its flanks. A wide dark "mask" crosses the eye and reaches the angle of the jaw. The body color is buff or pale brown, often marked with green.
Habits	Nocturnal and terrestrial.
Breeding	In shallow temporary ponds.
Diet	Other frogs and large invertebrates, such as beetles and grasshoppers.
Habitat	Open areas, often near water but also in dry places.
Distribution	Most of Queensland and N New South Wales, Australia.
Status	Rarely seen except during or immediately after rain.
Similar species	There are several similar Cyclorana species, including another water-holding frog (C. platycephala) and the Long-footed Frog (C. longipes).

This is one of several related frogs that survive dry conditions by burrowing down into the soil and forming cocoons around themselves. Many of the *Cyclorana* species come from dry semidesert regions. They are unlike other tree frogs in that they are terrestrial, and they do not have the typical tree frog characteristics such as expanded toe disks. They are also heavy bodied and muscular.

During dry weather they burrow down into the soil using bony spades on their hind feet. Their burrows can be up to 3 feet (1 m) long. When cocooned, the metabolic rate of these frogs slows right down, so they can live off their food reserves for months if necessary. This process is known as estivation.

Estivating frogs dig back up to the surface when heavy rains begin. Light rain, which can fall occasionally even in the dry season, does not penetrate the hardened soil in which the frogs are buried, so they do not emerge at the wrong time. Only torrential and prolonged rain soaks down to the frog's layer—it also softens the clay so that the frog can force its way out.

Water-holding frogs are among the first species to breed at the start of the rainy season. They lay large, irregularly shaped clumps of spawn containing up to 7,000 eggs in shallow water covering flooded ground. The water heats up quickly, and the tadpoles can tolerate temperatures of up to 109°F (43°C).

The New Holland Water-holding Frog from Australia is a large burrowing frog.

They develop rapidly so that they can escape from the water before it has a chance to dry up.

Australian aboriginals use the buried frogs as a source of water, unearthing them and squeezing gently. Finding them when they are buried is quite an art, and two methods have been reported. In one, the aboriginals stamp on the ground, and the frogs give themselves away by croaking—presumably because they think the rain has started. In the other method, hunters examine the ground for minute marks left by the frog when it sank below the surface.

221

Riobamba Marsupial Frog

Common name	Riobamba Marsupial Frog
Scientific name	*Gastrotheca riobambae*
Family	Hylidae (now often listed under Leptodactylidae)
Size	1.57–2.36 in (40–60 mm).
Key features	Plump (for a tree frog), with a wide head and blunt snout. The skin on its back is warty, and a raised ridge runs down either side of its back. Its toes are long and have adhesive pads, but they are fairly small. Color can be uniform green or green with brown or bronze patches. The insides of the thighs are often blue.
Habits	Terrestrial and active in the evening.
Breeding	Females carry their eggs in a pouch on their back.
Diet	Invertebrates.
Habitat	A montane species, living in a wide range of habitats, including fields.
Distribution	Andes of Ecuador and S Colombia.
Status	Once common, but now listed by the IUCN as Endangered because of drastic population decline.
Similar species	Several other marsupial frogs live in the Andes and often go under the name of *Gastrotheca marsupiata*, but this is just one of a number of similar species.

The South American marsupial frogs have a remarkable, unique, and very complex method of reproduction. Their name comes from the pouch that the females develop on their back; this is also reflected in the scientific name *Gastrotheca*, which means stomach pouch. In fact, it is a misnomer because the pouches are not on their bellies, unlike those of the "real" marsupials such as kangaroos.

The Riobamba Marsupial Frog breeds throughout the year, and a sample of frogs at any time will contain females with eggs, females carrying tadpoles, and females that are not in a reproductive state at all. Each female, however, breeds only once each year.

The male's call consists of two parts and bears an uncanny resemblance to a clucking chicken. The first part, a croaky "quaaaark," is thought to be territorial and warns off other males. The second part, consisting of two or three explosive "clucks," is thought to attract females. Receptive females make their way toward males and signal their acceptance by touching them with one of their front feet. The pair goes into amplexus, with the male, who is usually smaller, sitting high up on the female's back.

When she is ready to lay her eggs, the female twists her hind legs under her body and, in doing so, lifts her back so that her cloaca is higher than her head. At this time the male produces fluid from his cloaca, presumably containing sperm. He spreads it over the female's lower back, between her cloaca and the small opening of her pouch, using his hind feet. Now the female begins to lay her eggs one at a time. As they appear, the male uses his hind feet to maneuver them into the pouch. During this operation the eggs come into contact with the sperm and are fertilized.

The female carries the eggs, which can number up to 100, for three to four months, by which time they will have grown into well-developed tadpoles. She then moves to a pool or ditch and releases them, helping them out of the pouch with one of the long toes on her hind feet. She also uses this toe to hold open the entrance and, if necessary, to hook out any that are reluctant to

leave. The tadpoles are voracious feeders and grow quickly, leaving the water after another month or two.

⬇ *Riobamba Marsupial Frog, Guaranda, Ecuador. The swollen back of this female shows that tadpoles are developing in her pouch.*

European Tree Frog

Common names	European Tree Frog, Common Tree Frog
Scientific name	*Hyla arborea*
Family	Hylidae
Size	To 1.97 in (50 mm).
Key features	A stocky tree frog with long limbs and adhesive toe pads. Its skin is smooth and usually bright green in color, but sometimes brown or yellowish. A dark stripe runs from the snout through the eye and down each flank to the groin. This stripe has a short upward branch just before it ends.
Habits	Arboreal and mostly nocturnal, although it is active in the evenings and sometimes in the daytime, too.
Breeding	Lays its eggs in still water.
Diet	Invertebrates.
Habitat	Varied, but typically heavily vegetated places with plenty of bushes and trees. Also in reed beds.
Distribution	Most of Europe; absent from the north, including the United Kingdom, although attempts to introduce them have met with some success. Replaced in Italy and parts of Spain and France by related species.
Status	Common in suitable places.
Similar species	There are three other green tree frogs in Europe, but they differ in the length and shape of the side stripe, and they have different calls. Locality is the most reliable means of distinguishing them.

Until recently, this was the one and only tree frog in Europe, but in recent years it has become divided into four similar species, one from southern Spain and parts of France *(Hyla meridionalis)*, another from Italy *(H. intermedia)*, and a third from the islands of Corsica and Sardinia *(H. sardus)*. They differ little from each other, and all have similar lifestyles.

Males have loud raucous calls. They form choruses during the breeding season in spring and early summer but also at other times of the year, especially on warm humid nights.

The European Tree Frog breeds in small shallow pools that warm up quickly in the summer. Males and females migrate toward the breeding sites after rain, and once a male has attracted a mate, they produce up to 50 small clumps of spawn each with a maximum of about 60 eggs. The total number of eggs is about 1,000.

The young metamorphose by the end of the summer, although breeding ponds sometimes dry up before all the young have left the water. They are long-lived, and individuals of up to 22 years have been recorded in captivity.

$\oplus$ *The European Tree Frog lives in a variety of habitats, sometimes several hundred yards away from water, but it is most common in reed beds or in bushes or shrubs around the edges of ponds.*

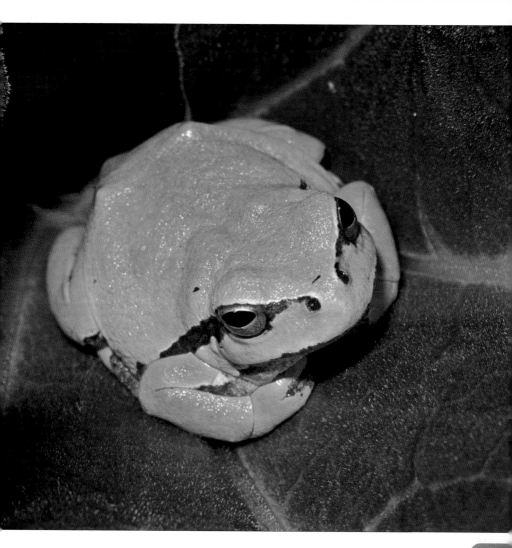

Giant Tree Frog

Common name	Giant Tree Frog
Scientific name	*Hyla boans (Hypsiboas boans)*
Family	Hylidae
Size	3.94–4.52 in (1– 1.15 cm).
Key features	A very large tree frog with large, heavily webbed hands and feet. It has a flattened head and prominently bulging eyeballs. It is typically reddish brown in color, but individuals can change to gray or grayish brown. It sometimes has a thin pale line down the center of its back, and there are usually poorly defined crossbars on the hind legs.
Habits	Arboreal and nocturnal.
Breeding	Lays its eggs in small pools of water constructed by the male.
Diet	Invertebrates.
Habitat	Grasslands and the edges of forests, usually near a river or stream.
Distribution	South America, in the Amazon Basin and on the island of Trinidad.
Status	Not rare, but hard to find.
Similar species	The Gladiator Tree Frog (*H. rosenbergi*) has a similar lifestyle and appearance.

This large tree frog is rarely found far from water. In Trinidad it breeds during the dry season, but breeding occurs throughout the year in other parts of its range.

Males call from trees or bushes, including giant bamboo thickets, near a suitable body of water. Males have a loud cackling call that carries well, even over the sound of running water. Occasionally they will call from the sides of roads if heavy rain has caused water to run across them.

When it is ready to breed, the male moves down to the edge of the water and scoops out a small basin in the sand, mud, or gravel. It fills with water and forms a small pool up to 18 inches (45 cm) in diameter. He calls from the edge to attract a mate. When they are paired in amplexus, the female lays her eggs in the pool, where they float on the surface. The male remains nearby, protecting "his" pool from other males who may try to use it to attract mates of their own. He calls on subsequent nights and may attract additional females, which means that a pool may contain eggs at different stages of development.

When the tadpoles hatch about three days later, the mud walls of the basin begin to disintegrate because of the action of water flowing through it, and the tadpoles are eventually released into the stream. They feed on algae at the edges of the streams, avoiding fast-flowing stretches. Metamorphosis occurs after about eight weeks.

Giant Tree Frog,
Arima Valley, Trinidad.
Unusually for a tree frog,
males of the species
build small mud basins
in which to breed.

Southern Gray Tree Frog

Common names	Southern Gray Tree Frog, Cope's Gray Tree Frog
Scientific name	*Hyla chrysoscelis*
Family	Hylidae
Size	1.26–1.97 in (32–50 mm).
Key features	A heavily built tree frog with relatively short legs and a plump body. Its skin is warty, and the frog is sometimes called a tree "toad." Usually pale gray or greenish gray in color, with a darker marking on its back. The concealed surfaces of its hind legs are orange and visible only when it moves.
Habits	Arboreal and nocturnal.
Breeding	In ponds.
Diet	Invertebrates.
Habitat	Woodlands, usually near water.
Distribution	North America, from S Canada to N Florida. This is a composite range for the Southern Gray Tree Frog and the Gray Tree Frog (see below).
Status	Common.
Similar species	The Southern Gray Tree Frog and the Gray Tree Frog *(H. versicolor)* are almost identical and can be reliably separated only by their chromosome numbers and mating calls.

Until recently the Gray Tree Frog was regarded as a single species, *Hyla versicolor*. But close study of its mating calls, coupled with analysis at the cell level, revealed that there were, in fact, two species involved. The Southern Gray Tree Frog has a call that is higher pitched and faster than that of the Gray Tree Frog. The situation is complicated, however, because the rate of the call is also dependent on the air temperature.

The two species almost certainly started out as one. They have similar genes, and to all intents and purposes are identical in appearance. The Gray Tree Frog, however, has an extra set of chromosomes. This state of affairs is known as "tetraploid," whereas the more usual arrangement of one set of paired chromosomes, as in the Southern Gray Tree Frog, is known as "diploid." The extra set probably developed thousands of generations ago from an abnormality that interfered with the normal process of cell division. Because the two populations were unable to interbreed, they began to evolve in different directions, which resulted in different mating calls.

The Gray Tree Frogs (of both species) are unusual among tree frogs in living on tree trunks rather than in foliage. This explains their slightly rough, gray appearance, which provides them with excellent camouflage. Individuals with greenish coloration are equally well hidden—they resemble tree trunks with lichen growing on them.

Populations from the north of the range, which are *H. versicolor*, experience freezing conditions during hibernation, and survive only because they have glycerol in their blood, which acts as an antifreeze agent.

⬇ *The Southern Gray Tree Frog lives high in the trees but comes down to the water at night to form a chorus and for breeding.*

American Green Tree Frog

Common names	American Green Tree Frog, Green Tree Frog
Scientific name	*Hyla cinerea*
Family	Hylidae
Size	1.26–2.24 in (32–57 mm).
Key features	A streamlined tree frog. Its back is usually bright green but sometimes dull green or slate gray. It has a prominent side stripe of cream or white that runs from the angle of the mouth to the groin, although it may be shorter than this. It often has small scattered specks of yellow or gold on its back.
Habits	A climbing species, mostly nocturnal.
Breeding	In ponds, swamps, and ditches.
Diet	Invertebrates.
Habitat	Reed beds, shrubs, floating vegetation, usually near water. Also found in parks and gardens.
Distribution	North America, in the SE United States.
Status	Common.
Similar species	Other green tree frogs from the region, such as the Squirrel Tree Frog (*H. squirella*) and the Pine Barrens Tree Frog (*H. andersonii*), lack the side stripe and are shorter and plumper.

A very familiar species in the humid southeastern lowlands of the United States, the American Green Tree Frog commonly occurs around picnic sites, garden ponds, and even swimming pools, as well as in more remote situations. It soon learns to visit street and porch lamps to take advantage of the flying insects that are attracted to them and is frequently seen on roads, even in towns, during heavy

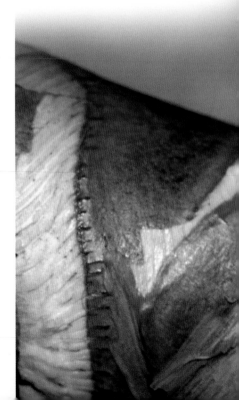

rainstorms. It will also tolerate some degree of salinity in the water in which it breeds.

These frogs are often known as "rain" frogs because they call immediately before rain even if they are not near a breeding site. In fact, certain noises will start them off when it is not raining. Their call is one of the characteristic noises of hot humid nights in the southeastern United States. It consists of a nasal quacking note repeated many times, and large choruses can be heard for several hundred yards.

Breeding takes place throughout the spring and summer, starting as early as March in southern Florida. Females lay about 500 eggs in batches, attached to floating vegetation such as the undersides of the water hyacinth. If there is no suitable vegetation, the eggs are allowed to float on the surface, attached to the surface film. They hatch within a week, and the tadpoles metamorphose in about two months.

⊖ *American Green Tree Frog, Florida. The characteristic white stripe can be seen down the side of its body.*

Map Tree Frog

Common name	Map Tree Frog
Scientific name	*Hyla geographica (Hypsiboas geographicus)*
Family	Hylidae
Size	2.36–3.27 in (60–83 mm).
Key features	A large yellow or brown tree frog with webbed hands and feet, obvious adhesive toe pads, and a small triangular flap of skin on its heels. Its flanks are usually paler than its back and have several dusky transverse bands on them.
Habits	Arboreal and nocturnal.
Breeding	Lays its eggs on the surface of still pools.
Diet	Invertebrates.
Habitat	Grasslands and the edges of forests, usually near a river or stream.
Distribution	South America, in the Amazon Basin and on the island of Trinidad.
Status	Common.
Similar species	The Giant Tree Frog *(Hyla boans/ Hypsiboas boans)* is from the same region, but it is larger and lacks the triangular heel flap.

The Map Tree Frog probably gets its name from the intricate gold reticulations on its lower eyelid, which are obvious when it is sleeping during the day. It is a relatively common species over a wide area in South America, and colonies live near swamps, forest ponds, and the backwaters of streams and rivers.

Adults are not obvious during the day, when they remain hidden, but the tadpoles are very distinctive because they have the habit of forming "balls." Large numbers of them—sometimes as many as 2,000 to 3,000—shoal up together, regardless of whether or not they are from the same batch of eggs. Each individual tries to swim into the center of the ball, with the result that the whole mass appears to be rolling over the bottom of the pond or stream. This is probably an antipredator strategy, using the "safety in numbers" principle, although fish tend to avoid the tadpoles anyway because they are distasteful.

The adults avoid predation by feigning death if they are touched: They pull their limbs in close to their body and release their grip of the surface on which they are resting. The process is known as thanatosis and is found in a variety of other animal groups.

⊖ *The Map Tree Frog is a large frog with variable color and markings. It is found along streams, rivers, and ponds across many parts of South America.*

Barking Tree Frog

Common name	Barking Tree Frog
Scientific name	*Hyla gratiosa*
Family	Hylidae
Size	2–2.6 in (51–66 mm). This is the largest tree frog in North America.
Key features	A stout, rounded tree frog with granular skin. It is usually bright green with a pattern of evenly spaced round spots of brown on its back, head, sides, and limbs. Sometimes brown, in which case the spots are not so obvious, but there are always areas of green visible. A white or cream stripe runs from the angle of the jaw to the groin.
Habits	Nocturnal and arboreal, although it also descends to the ground and may even burrow.
Breeding	Lays its eggs on the bottom of shallow pools.
Diet	Invertebrates, especially crickets.
Habitat	Open woodlands and farmland.
Distribution	North America, in SE United States.
Status	Locally common.
Similar species	None. Its chunky appearance and spotted pattern distinguish this species from others in the region.

Barking Tree Frogs are named for their raucous call, which they repeat nine or 10 times in rapid succession. This is a "treetop" call, made before rain, and it can also be triggered by the calls of other nearby tree frogs, such as the Green Tree Frog (*Hyla cinerea*).

When the male is trying to attract a mate, however, he moves out of the trees and approaches the breeding pond, making single explosive calls. He continues to make these calls when he reaches the edge of the water, until he has attracted a female. The pair chooses shallow ponds that warm up quickly. Although these pools are usually permanent, they occasionally dry out, with the loss of any tadpoles that have not finished their development. Females lay up to 2,000 eggs.

During dry weather, Barking Tree Frogs climb down to the ground and burrow into soft sandy soil at the base of trees to protect themselves from drying out. In cold weather they do the same, spending the winter in hibernation.

⊖ *Barking Tree Frog, Florida. Most populations of this species occur in open country with scattered trees.*

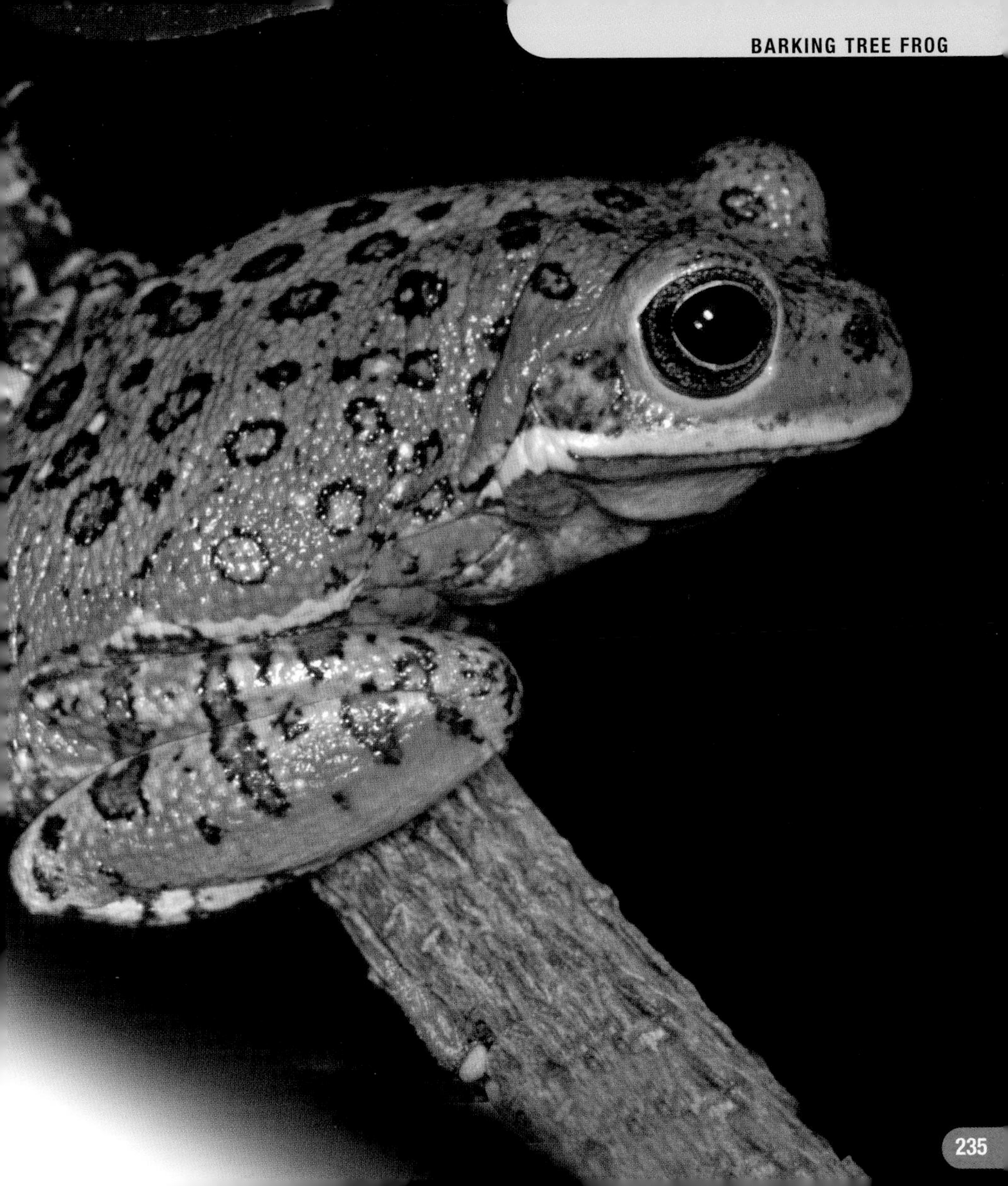

Lancaster's Tree Frog

Common name	Lancaster's Tree Frog
Scientific name	*Hyla lancasteri (Isthmohyla lancasteri)*
Family	Hylidae
Size	1.06–1.5 in (27–38 mm).
Key features	A small tree frog with a snub nose. It is mottled dark green and brown in color and looks almost metallic under certain lights.
Habits	Nocturnal and arboreal.
Breeding	Lays its eggs in streams.
Diet	Invertebrates.
Habitat	Rain forests at moderate altitudes, usually in the vicinity of streams.
Distribution	Costa Rica and W Panama.
Status	Secretive and rarely seen.
Similar species	No other tree frogs from the region have this coloration coupled with the short snout.

This attractive little tree frog lives in tall canopy trees in pristine rain forests. It is seen only during the breeding season, when it comes down from the canopy to congregate alongside small forest streams. This takes place mostly in the dry season when the streams are at their lowest and when small backwater pools form.

Males call from low vegetation and rocks at the edge of the water. The eggs are unusual for tree frogs because they are laid in long sticky strings, each containing about 70 to 80 eggs. The jelly surrounding them breaks down after two or three days, and the eggs sink to the bottom individually. There they rest among the stones and debris until they hatch about one week later.

The tadpoles are brown in color and have a suckerlike mouth with which they can cling to rocks to keep themselves from being swept away when the stream fills with water again. They take about 17 weeks to complete their development.

⊖ *Lancaster's Tree Frog, seen here in Costa Rica, is a secretive little frog that inhabits rain forests.*

Gunther's Costa Rican Tree Frog

Common names	Gunther's Costa Rican Tree Frog, Meadow Tree Frog
Scientific name	*Hyla pseudopuma (Isthmohyla pseudopuma)*
Family	Hylidae
Size	1.5–1.77 in (38–45 mm).
Key features	A very slender tree frog with a narrow waist. It may be brown or yellow in color and usually has a dark stripe running from behind the eye and along each flank. The hands and feet are extensively webbed.
Habits	Nocturnal and arboreal.
Breeding	Lays its eggs in small bodies of water.
Diet	Invertebrates.
Habitat	Rain forests at moderate altitudes, secondary forests, parks, and gardens.
Distribution	Costa Rica and W Panama.
Status	Very common.
Similar species	Could be confused with some other Central American tree frogs, including members of the genus *Smilisca*.

Probably the most common tree frog in the region, Gunther's Costa Rican Tree Frog adapts to a wide variety of situations, including artificial habitats such as fields, meadows, and gardens. It tends to remain near its breeding sites, which range from the tiny bodies of water that collect in foot- and hoofprints, to small ponds, flooded fields, and roadside ditches. During the day it hides between the leaves of forest plants and in bromeliad "vases."

Males have the unusual characteristic of changing color during the breeding season, turning from the normal brown coloration to yellow. They breed during the rainy season and are explosive breeders, with large numbers of males congregating

around the edges of breeding pools. Often all the activity takes place within a day or two, and breeding then stops for a while, only to start up again after more rain.

Each male probably goes to the breeding site at every opportunity, but females have to produce more eggs so they probably visit less frequently, perhaps only once each year. Males scramble for the opportunity to mate with arriving females, and choice by the female appears to play little part in the proceedings.

At Monteverde, Costa Rica, a breeding male Gunther's Costa Rican Tree Frog changes color from brown to yellow.

239

Polka-dot Tree Frog

Common names	Polka-dot Tree Frog, Glass Tree Frog, Spotted Tree Frog
Scientific name	*Hyla punctata (Hypsiboas punctatus)*
Family	Hylidae
Size	1.5 in (38 mm).
Key features	A translucent-looking tree frog with finely granular skin. It is pale green in color with a pale yellow line running from the snout through the eye and to the groin. During the day, this line is picked up below with a fine purple line. At night the frog's back becomes dark red.
Habits	Nocturnal and semiarboreal.
Breeding	Lays its eggs in small ponds, marshes, and flooded fields.
Diet	Invertebrates.
Habitat	Grasslands and other open places, and in sedges and reeds at the edges of water.
Distribution	South America, in the Amazon Basin and on the island of Trinidad.
Status	Common.
Similar species	Other green tree frogs do not undergo the dramatic color change at night.

This frog also goes under the common names of Glass Tree Frog and Spotted Tree Frog, and it is a familiar species throughout much of South America and Trinidad. It is one of only a few species that change color during the night—many species tend to be paler at night than in the day, but this one changes from green to red. The red pigment is contained in cells that shrink during the day. On close examination they appear as tiny flecks that do not influence the overall color. They expand at night to turn the frog's dorsal surface red. The purpose of this is not known.

The Polka-dot Tree Frog is not very arboreal, although it has adhesive toe pads and climbs well. It is nearly always seen on reeds and sedges near water or in long grasses, often at the edges of ponds or emerging from flooded areas in which it breeds.

⊙ *A Polka-dot Tree Frog in Simla, Trinidad, exhibits nighttime coloration.*

Gladiator Tree Frog

Common name	Gladiator Tree Frog
Scientific name	*Hyla rosenbergi (Hypsiboas rosenbergi)*
Family	Hylidae
Size	2.36–3.23 in (60–82 mm).
Key features	A large tree frog with a long snout. It has large, pale-colored eyes and a tan or reddish brown body marked with a network of darker lines. In the day it becomes much paler, and a thin dark line down the center of its back becomes more noticeable. Males have a spur on the insides of their hands.
Habits	Nocturnal and arboreal.
Breeding	Lays its eggs in small pools built in the mud by the male.
Diet	Invertebrates, including large insects.
Habitat	Lowland rain forests.
Distribution	From Costa Rica in Central America S to western Ecuador.
Status	Common in places.
Similar species	Other large brownish tree frogs from the region lack the male's spurs.

Males of the Gladiator Tree Frog and its close relatives build shallow basins in the mud or gravel, which fill with water through seepage. They call to attract females, and the eggs are laid in the basin. They are called Gladiator Frogs because the males defend the pools they have constructed using the spur, or spine, that is present on each hand to injure one another. Normally, however, males space themselves out using their calls as markers, and conflicts are avoided.

Each male returns to his pool every night, having spent the daytime hiding. He will take some time to renovate the walls of the pool and begin calling at dusk. Receptive females approach the males from behind and inspect the nest. If a female dislikes the nest she will leave, and this happens about half the time. If she approves, she bumps the male and they go into amplexus.

Next, the female begins to work on the nest, and egg-laying does not take place until she is satisfied with it several hours later. Her eggs are small and they float on the surface of the pool, probably so that they have better access to oxygen. Once the eggs are laid the female departs, but the male stays near his nest for several days, by which time the eggs have hatched. The tadpoles remain near the surface, gulping air until heavy rain or a general deterioration of the nest results in them being washed into the main stream or pond.

⊕ *Concealed in the palms of this Gladiator Tree Frog from Ecuador are daggerlike spurs, which are used in combat.*

Red-footed Tree Frog

Common name	Red-footed Tree Frog
Scientific name	*Hyla rufitela (Hypsiboas rufitelus)*
Family	Hylidae
Size	1.57–2.17 in (40–55 mm).
Key features	A green frog with large eyes and tan-colored irises. Its back is marked with small patches or light and dark speckles. The webbing on its hands and feet, normally hidden, is bright red.
Habits	Nocturnal and arboreal.
Breeding	Lays its eggs on the surface of small pools.
Diet	Invertebrates.
Habitat	Lowland rain forests.
Distribution	Central America, from Nicaragua to Panama.
Status	Uncommon.
Similar species	There are no other green frogs with red webbing on their feet.

This attractive species leads a secretive life in the forest canopy and is seen only when it descends to remote forest pools to breed. Males have a spur on their hands, as in the Gladiator Frog *(Hyla rosenbergi)*, but breeding is more conventional than in the latter.

Males call from dense vegetation near the breeding ponds and do not go down into the water until joined by a female.

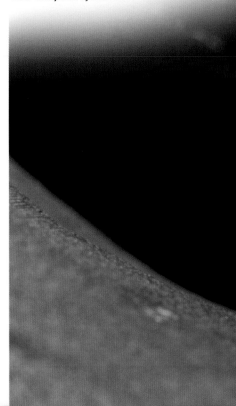

They prefer ponds full of aquatic vegetation or shallow, stagnant, muddy pools. The eggs are attached to the surface film, where there is plenty of oxygen.

The coloration of this frog probably serves to make it hard to spot when resting on leaves covered with mosses and lichens. The red coloring on its feet may be flash markings, designed to confuse predators—they are obvious when the frog jumps, but are hidden as soon as it lands, leaving the predator looking for an image that no longer exists. Many other frogs have flash markings on their flanks (the Red-eyed Leaf Frog, *Agalychnis callidryas,* for instance) or inside their thighs (the Southern Gray Tree Frog, *Hyla chrysoscelis*), which serve the same purpose.

⊙ *A Red-footed Tree Frog, Costa Rica.*

245

Other *Hyla* Species

→ The Pine Barrens Tree Frog (Hyla andersonii) *is native to the southeastern United States. Here a male inflates its vocal sac as it calls to attract a mate.*

← Hyla calcarata (Hypsiboas calcaratus) *makes its home in the branches of tropical rain forest in the Amazon Basin. © Arthur Georges.*

⬇ *In the* cerrado *of central Brazil, a male Pajamas Tree Frog* (Hypsiboas buriti) *perches on a leaf and calls. This species is known only from the type locality, Buritis, in the state of Minas Gerais, Brazil.*

Other *Hyla* Species

⊙ *The Porthole Tree Frog (Hyla taeniopus/Charadrahyla taeniopus) occurs in cloud forests in southeastern Mexico.*

⬆ Hyla lundii (Hypsiboas lundii) *is found in the* cerrado *habitats of central and eastern Brazil.*

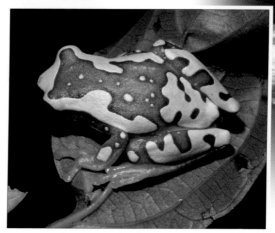

⊙ Hyla ebbraccata (Dendropsophus ebraccatus) *is relatively common in the humid tropical forests of South America including southern Mexico, Costa Rica, and Colombia. It is less common in Ecuador.*

Other *Hyla* Species

↩ *A Brazilian species,* Hyla pseudopseudis (Bokermannohyla pseudopseudis), *prefers to live in rock crevices in streams.*

↩ *The adaptable* Hyla perviridis (Aplastodiscus perviridis) *from Argentina and Brazil lives in forest habitat in the northern parts of its range but will inhabit more open areas in the south.*

↪ *The nocturnal* Hyla marmorata (Dendropsophus marmoratus) *is rarely seen but is native to many South American countries and is common in Surinam.* © Arthur Georges.

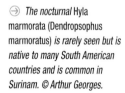

Other *Hyla* Species

⬅ *The Sarayacu Tree Frog (Hyla sarayacuensis / Dendrosophus sarayacuensis) is common in Peru and Ecuador.*

➡ *A male Squirrel Tree Frog* (Hyla squirrella) *from southeastern United States puffs up its vocal sac and calls for a mate.*

⬇ *The Andean Tree Frog* (Hyla pulchella) *is widespread in Brazil, Argentina, Paraguay, and Uruguay.*

White's Tree Frog

Common names	White's Tree Frog. Green Tree Frog, "Dumpy" Frog
Scientific name	*Litoria caerulea*
Family	Hylidae
Size	3.94 in (100 mm).
Key features	A large, heavily built tree frog with large hands and fingers and conspicuous toe pads. Older specimens sometimes become obese and the species is known as the "Dumpy" Frog. It is normally bright green above and paler below, with no markings except an occasional white or yellow spot or two on its back. Captive-raised individuals are often grayish blue.
Habits	Nocturnal.
Breeding	Lays its eggs in any small body of water.
Diet	Invertebrates and small vertebrates.
Habitat	Varied, from rain forests to dry semiarid regions. Often associated with human dwellings such as farms, houses, or drains.
Distribution	Australia and New Guinea (introduced into New Zealand).
Status	Very common.
Similar species	The Australian Red-eyed Tree Frog (*L. chloris*) is similar, with the obvious difference that it has red eyes. *Litoria splendida* is also similar but has orange on the insides of its limbs. The White-lipped Tree Frog (*L. infrafrenata*) has a bold white line along its jawline.

White's Tree Frog, which gets its name from the scientist who first described it (in 1790), not its color, is a popular pet in Australia and elsewhere. This is because of its placid nature and ability to adapt, ensuring that it will thrive and even breed under a number of different conditions. Its main requirement is food, for this is a greedy species that often grows obese and may develop massive parotid glands projecting over its brow.

These frogs live in areas of high humidity but can adapt to drier conditions. Their skin is thick and waxy and this limits the amount of water they lose. In very dry conditions they may bury themselves and form a cocoon of shed skin around their bodies, or they may seek out small sources of permanent water and live nearby. These can include drains, cisterns, lavatories (inside or out), and other vessels. If they are removed by well-meaning humans, they often turn up again after a short time, using an effective homing instinct.

Captive White's Tree Frogs will find a suitable place to rest during the day, such as a leaf or the corner of their cage, and return there at the end of every night—they often appear not to have moved for several weeks. Captive-reared individuals rarely show the bright green coloration of wild frogs. Instead, they are often dull blue green or even blue gray. It seems that lack of a natural diet, or access to sunlight, or both, causes a change in their pigmentation. Captivity has the same effect on green frogs of several other species.

⊙ *Inset: A captive White's Tree Frog exhibits the lack of bright green color of its wild counterpart (main picture).*

Other *Litoria* Species

⬆ *The Red-eyed Tree Frog* (Litoria chloris) *from Australia spends most of its time in the rain forest canopy.*

➡ *The Yule Island Tree Frog* (Litoria congenita) *is native to savanna areas of Indonesia and Papua New Guinea.*

⬇ *The Dainty Tree Frog* (Litoria gracilenta) *is found in a variety of moist woodland habitats in Australia and Papua New Guinea.*

Other *Litoria* Species

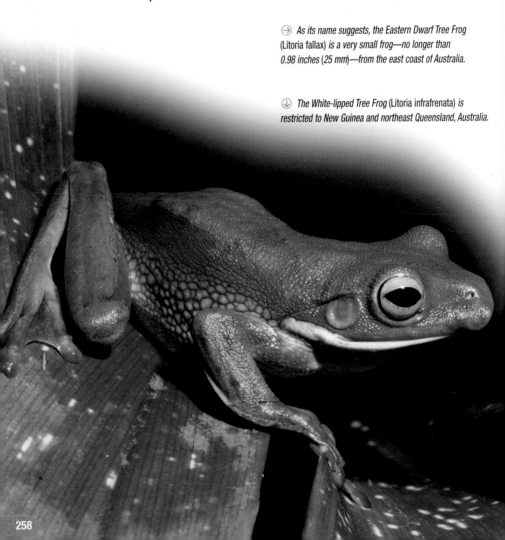

↪ *As its name suggests, the Eastern Dwarf Tree Frog (Litoria fallax) is a very small frog—no longer than 0.98 inches (25 mm)—from the east coast of Australia.*

↓ *The White-lipped Tree Frog (Litoria infrafrenata) is restricted to New Guinea and northeast Queensland, Australia.*

⊖ This medium-sized gray or brown frog is Peron's Tree Frog (Litoria peronii) *from eastern and southeastern Australia.*

Cuban Tree Frog

Common name	Cuban Tree Frog
Scientific name	*Osteopilus septentrionalis*
Family	Hylidae
Size	3.54–4.92 in (90–125 mm). Females are much larger than males.
Key features	A large, stocky tree frog with large toe pads and a warty back. There is a very distinctive fold of skin running from behind the eye, over the top of the eardrum (tympanum), and reaching the base of the front leg. These frogs vary in color and can be pale brown, putty colored, or green, with most shades in between.
Habits	Nocturnal. Arboreal to some degree but also found in most other situations.
Breeding	Lays its eggs in many types of water bodies, including brackish water.
Diet	Invertebrates and small vertebrates.
Habitat	Especially fond of disturbed habitats, including gardens, drains, cisterns, and plant pots.
Distribution	Cuba, the Bahamas, and the Cayman Islands. Introduced into Florida, including the Keys.
Status	Very common.
Similar species	None when fully grown, but young specimens could be confused with a variety of smaller tree frog species.

This is a very successful frog. Not only is it the most common species in Cuba, it has become established over most of Florida, where it can be found in potted plants, in gardens, on the walls and windows of houses, and in many other artificial situations. It was introduced accidentally in about 1930, possibly in shipments of fruit or vegetables, and it spread rapidly throughout the Florida Keys and up the Gulf and Pacific coasts of Florida. It is probably attracted to gardens because they are often watered with sprinklers, maintaining the high humidity that it prefers. Having said this, the Cuban Tree Frog can also tolerate dry conditions for short periods of time, retreating into deep crevices in rocks or down into the folds between the leaves of forest plants to avoid desiccation.

There is some cause for concern, however, because the Cuban Tree Frog is a voracious species that will eat almost any moving thing it can overpower, including other frogs. Since its introduction, some species of native Floridian frogs have become scarce in areas where it lives. In Cuba,

A Cuban Tree Frog emerges from its hiding place inside a bromeliad plant in Soroa, Cuba.

on the other hand, its population is kept in check by competition with other species.

Cuban Tree Frogs breed in most types of water bodies, including drains and cisterns, and will tolerate slightly salty or polluted water. They lay about 130 eggs in a single layer that floats beneath the surface film.

Females probably lay several batches of eggs throughout the breeding season. The eggs hatch within two days, and the tadpoles develop quickly.

Mexican Leaf Frog

Common name	Mexican Leaf Frog
Scientific name	*Pachymedusa dacnicolor*
Family	Hylidae
Size	3.15–3.94 in (80–100 mm). Females are significantly larger than males.
Key features	A heavily built leaf frog with short limbs and large toe pads. The skin on its back is smooth and plain green or green with a few scattered white spots. White spots are also present on the flanks. Individual frogs can change color in minutes from light green to dull dark green.
Habits	Nocturnal and arboreal.
Breeding	Lays its eggs on vegetation overhanging ponds.
Diet	Invertebrates and small vertebrates.
Habitat	In dry deciduous forest in semidesert regions.
Distribution	Mexico, where it is restricted to the Pacific side of the country.
Status	Numerous in places.
Similar species	None in the region. Unmistakable.

The habits of this species are very unusual among the tree frogs. It lives on the edges of the Sonoran Desert, where the dry season lasts for most of the year. Although it hides away during the very hottest times, it can also be found out and about in bushes and even on roads during dry weather. It breeds as soon as the seasonal rains start, usually in June or early July, and hundreds of males congregate around forest pools at this time. Their call is a single, quiet, low-pitched note; males call alternately, repeating the call every few seconds.

Females are attracted to calling males and come out of the forest to mate with them. They go into amplexus then move about in the vegetation until they have found a suitable place for egg-laying—this can take several hours. The eggs are laid in clumps of 100 to 350, usually attached to leaves but sometimes laid on the grassy banks of ponds. The tadpoles escape the egg mass by wriggling and dropping into the water below. If the eggs have been poorly sited, the tadpoles may land on the ground and flip around until they reach the water.

The tadpoles have many predators once they become aquatic, so they hide in dense vegetation when necessary. At other times they hang in the water at an angle of about 45 degrees with their head directed upward. If their pond is a small one, they rely on further rains to keep it topped up— otherwise it may dry out before they metamorphose, which is the fate of many batches.

→ *The Mexican Leaf Frog is a large bulky frog. It avoids desiccation in very hot dry weather by hiding in burrows.*

Milky Tree Frog

Common name	Milky Tree Frog
Scientific name	*Phrynohyas venulosa (Trachycephalus venulosus)*
Family	Hylidae
Size	2.76–4.53 in (70–115 mm). Females are larger than males.
Key features	A big, robust tree frog with wide fingers and toes and large toe pads. The skin on its back is uneven, and that on its flanks and underside is granular. Its color varies from light brown to dark reddish brown, and it usually has a large dark blotch in the center of its back.
Habits	Nocturnal and arboreal.
Breeding	Lays its eggs in temporary ponds.
Diet	Invertebrates and small vertebrates.
Habitat	Lowland rain forests.
Distribution	Central and South America, from Mexico through to the Amazon Basin. Also on Trinidad and Tobago.
Status	Numerous, but rarely seen outside the breeding season.
Similar species	Many large tree frogs could be confused with this species. Its tendency to secrete a milky substance from its skin when handled is a good guide to identification, although there are other, less common, species of *Phrynohyas* that have a similar habit.

The Milky Tree Frog is a large tree frog that can turn up almost anywhere in the lowland forests of the extensive region over which it occurs. Although it is most common during the rainy season, when it breeds, it also hunts at night at other times of the year. During the day or in dry weather it retreats into the centers of bromeliad plants, between the folded leaves of other plants, or in tree holes, where some moisture remains.

This species' common and scientific names refer to a thick milky fluid that it can secrete from the glands in its skin. With very little provocation it will quickly coat itself with this "goo," which is not only poisonous but also sticky and an irritant. The substance is especially painful if it finds its way into an eye or an open wound. There is some evidence that, as well as its defensive function, the secretion may help the frog avoid dehydration during dry periods by reducing the permeability of its skin.

⊖ *The granular underside of the Milky Tree Frog can be seen clearly in this photograph, taken at Shell-Mera, Ecuador.*

Giant Monkey Frog

Common names	Giant Monkey Frog, Two-colored Leaf Frog
Scientific name	*Phyllomedusa bicolor*
Family	Hylidae
Size	3.54–4.72 in (90–120 mm). Females are larger than males.
Key features	A large leaf frog with a slightly rough back, large disks on its toes, and a prominent parotid gland that forms a ridge from the eye to the flanks. Mostly green in color, with brown flanks. Its pupils are vertical.
Habits	Nocturnal and arboreal.
Breeding	Lays its eggs on vegetation overhanging ponds.
Diet	Invertebrates and small vertebrates.
Habitat	Rain forest, secondary forest, and clearings.
Distribution	Amazon Basin, in parts of the Guianas, Venezuela, Colombia, Bolivia, Peru, and Brazil.
Status	Uncommon.
Similar species	None in the region.

This large leaf frog has a limited range in the Amazon Basin and is uncommon. The region has been extensively logged, and much of the frog's natural habitat has disappeared. Although in the short term this may benefit the frog by providing opportunities to breed in temporary pools created by the clearance, its long-term future in some places is not so bright. Like most leaf frogs, this species attaches its eggs to vegetation overhanging pools, usually about 6 feet (1.8 m) above the water's surface, and the tadpoles fall into the water to complete their development.

This species has attracted attention recently thanks to the substances produced in its skin. They contain peptides that have a dramatic effect when introduced into the human bloodstream. Some Amazonian Indians in northern Peru use the dried skin secretions, called "sapo," mixed with human saliva, in rituals designed to improve hunting. When rubbed into a surface wound (usually created by burning the skin), at first the concoction causes gastric and cardiac distress. But this is soon followed by an increase in physical strength, a heightening of the senses, and resistance to hunger and thirst.

⊖ *The Giant Monkey Frog is highly arboreal. Males call from branches 26 feet (8 m) or more off the ground before descending to about 6 feet (1.8 m) to mate above ponds.*

Lemur Leaf Frog

Common name	Lemur Leaf Frog
Scientific name	*Phyllomedusa lemur (Hylomantis lemur)*
Family	Hylidae
Size	1.57–1.97 in (40–50 mm). Females are larger than males.
Key features	A small leaf frog with long legs and smooth skin. Its eyes are large and prominent and its irises are silvery white. It is mainly pale green in color with yellow or orange flanks. The edges of its limbs are white, as are its lips. At night the green color changes to dark reddish brown.
Habits	Nocturnal and arboreal.
Breeding	Lays its eggs on vegetation overhanging ponds.
Diet	Invertebrates.
Habitat	Rain forest at elevations of 2,100–5,250 feet (640–1,600 m).
Distribution	Central America, in Costa Rica and Panama.
Status	Uncommon and listed by the IUCN as Critically Endangered due to drastic population decline partly caused by the disease chytridiomycosis.
Similar species	None in the region.

The story of the Lemur Leaf Frog is becoming a familiar one across many parts of the world. It used to be relatively common in the submontane forests of Costa Rica and neighboring Panama, but its populations have declined dramatically in the last 20 years. It has disappeared completely in at least 50 percent of places; and where it still remains, numbers are down. One cause may be infection by the chytrid fungus, but there are more fundamental problems.

Illegal squatters clear forests to plant crops. This can affect the rainfall and water-holding properties of the soil. Fewer trees and more open spaces lead to rapid

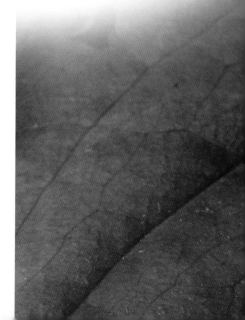

run-off of water, coupled with higher temperatures and more wind because of the lack of cover. This in turn causes the drying up of small pools and water seepages in which the frog's tadpoles live. Like all frogs, the Lemur Leaf Frog cannot move to more suitable places once its habitat is destroyed, so its numbers dwindle. Once numbers fall below a critical level, breeding takes place only infrequently, and the extinction of the colony is inevitable. It seems likely that the Lemur Leaf Frog will go the same way as the Golden Toad *(Bufo periglenes)* from the same part of the world.

⬅ This Lemur Leaf Frog was well camouflaged on a leaf in Costa Rica.

Painted-belly Leaf Frog

Common names	Painted-belly Leaf Frog, Waxy Frog
Scientific name	*Phyllomedusa sauvagii*
Family	Hylidae
Size	To 3.94 in (100 mm). Females are larger than males.
Key features	Fairly heavily built for a leaf frog, with a wide head and large, silvery white irises. Its back is light green in color, with a bold, black-edged white line running along its flanks and a number of rounded white spots on the underside.
Habits	Nocturnal and arboreal.
Breeding	Lays its eggs on vegetation overhanging temporary ponds.
Diet	Invertebrates.
Habitat	The scrubby, semiarid *chaco* region.
Distribution	Eastern Bolivia, N Paraguay, S Brazil, and N Argentina.
Status	Uncommon.
Similar species	None in the region.

Although the Painted-belly Leaf Frog is arboreal, it is not found in the leafy rain forest but in the dry thorny scrub that grows across the *chaco* region of northern Argentina and neighboring countries. This seasonally bone-dry place has a number of frog species, but most estivate in the dry season, burrowing into the mud to escape the worst of the arid weather.

The Painted-belly Leaf Frog has a different strategy: It remains in the open, even exposing itself to baking heat and drying winds, but avoids desiccation by coating its skin in the waxy substance from which it gets one of its common names. The substance is derived from a mixture of lipids (fats) that it secretes from glands in its skin. It smears this over its body with its hind feet, performing contortions in order to reach every part. This gives it almost total protection against evaporation—as much as that of the lizards from the same region, for instance.

The frog further reduces water loss by excreting its waste material in the form of uric acid, a white paste that requires hardly any water to carry it out of the body. The water saved in this way is reabsorbed through the walls of the bladder.

⊙ *Painted-belly Leaf Frog, Argentina.*

Tiger-striped Leaf Frog

Common names	Tiger-striped Leaf Frog, Monkey Frog, Orange-sided Leaf Frog
Scientific name	*Phyllomedusa tomopterna*
Family	Hylidae
Size	To 2.76 in (70 mm).
Key features	A slender leaf frog with a narrow waist and wide head. Its limbs are long and slender and its toes have well-developed adhesive pads. Its back is dark green with orange flanks. The orange areas have bold black lines crossing them. The large eyes have vertical pupils.
Habits	Nocturnal and arboreal.
Breeding	Lays its eggs on vegetation overhanging temporary ponds.
Diet	Invertebrates.
Habitat	Primary lowland rain forest.
Distribution	Amazon Basin.
Status	Uncommon.
Similar species	The orange and black flanks are distinctive.

Like other members of the genus, the Tiger-striped Leaf Frog is also known as the Monkey Frog, because of its opposed thumb and its deliberate way of walking, hand-over-hand, along branches and twigs. This species' brightly colored flanks, which are hidden when it is at rest, are probably a form of flash coloration, designed to confuse predators.

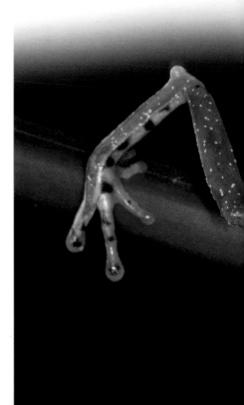

The Tiger-striped Leaf Frog is highly arboreal and never found on the ground. It lives in tall canopy trees. During the breeding season it descends to lower trees, shrubs, and palms growing around the edges of small permanent or temporary forest ponds. The males call from vegetation about 6 feet (1.8 m) above the ground. Females are attracted to the males and make their way to large leaves overhanging the water. As she lays her eggs the female uses her hind feet to roll the edges of a leaf around them so that, by the time egg-laying has been completed, the eggs are held in a tube. They hatch after three to five days, and the movement of the tadpoles causes them to slide down the leaf and into the water, where they complete their development in the normal way.

⊕ *With the long slender limbs typical of the family Hylidae, the Tiger-striped Leaf Frog takes slow, measured steps along a branch in Ecuador.*

Trinidad Leaf Frog

Common name	Trinidad Leaf Frog
Scientific name	*Phyllomedusa trinitatus*
Family	Hylidae
Size	3.15–3.54 in (80–90 mm).
Key features	Well built with long limbs and large toe pads. Its snout is rounded from above but sloping when seen from the side, and the eyes are large and prominent. This species is plain green with some white and bluish speckles on its flanks, and it has golden irises.
Habits	Nocturnal and arboreal.
Breeding	Lays its eggs on vegetation overhanging small ponds.
Diet	Invertebrates.
Habitat	Primary forest including second-growth forests and plantations.
Distribution	Trinidad and the coastal region of N Venezuela.
Status	Locally common.
Similar species	None in Trinidad— its large size, slow, deliberate gait, and vertical pupils make it easy to distinguish.

This leaf frog seems to prefer bushes and small trees at the edges of forests rather than tall canopy forests. During the breeding season, males space themselves out in small bushes at the edges of ponds. They call with a soft chuckling song. If one male encroaches too closely toward another, the rate of calling increases. If this does not have the desired effect, the two individuals interlock arms and wrestle with each other until one is either dislodged or falls.

Females arrive at the pond a few hours after calling has begun and select a male. Once they are in amplexus, they move about in the bush until they find a suitable large leaf overhanging the water. Egg-laying may last well into the early hours of the morning. As she lays the eggs the female uses her hind feet to roll the edges of the leaf around them, forming a tube. Together with the shaded place the frogs usually select, this helps prevent the eggs from drying out during the days to come. Probably for the same reason, the female lays a blob of extra jelly, containing no eggs, at the beginning and end of the spawning sequence, forming a "plug" in the top and bottom of the tube. In spite of these precautions at least one snake, *Leptodeira annulata*, preys heavily on the eggs, moving through the bushes to eat large mouthfuls.

The eggs hatch after about one week, and the tadpoles grow to a large size, hanging tail-down in midwater. They metamorphose about 12 weeks later.

⊖ *A pair of Trinidad Leaf Frogs in amplexus, Arima Valley, Trinidad. Note that the male (above) is significantly smaller than the female.*

Other *Phyllomedusa* Species

⬆ Phyllomedusa camba, *hanging from a branch in an Amazonian forest in Brazil.*

➡ *The Tiger-legged Waxy Monkey Tree Frog* (Phyllomedusa hypochondrialis azurea) *inhabits dry tropical forests of Bolivia, northern Argentina, and Paraguay.*

Known only from the cerrado of central Brazil, Phyllomedusa oreades lives among short shrubs and breeds in small streams.

277

Spring Peeper

Common name	Spring Peeper
Scientific name	Pseudacris crucifer
Family	Hylidae
Size	0.75–1.26 in (19–32 mm).
Key features	A small brown, gray or olive tree frog with a distinctive cross-shaped darker marking on its back (hence the scientific name crucifer). Its fingers and toes have little or no webbing and its toes are only slightly expanded at the tips.
Habits	Partially arboreal but also found in low vegetation or on the ground. Nocturnal.
Breeding	In spring, when they breed in small ponds or swamps.
Diet	Small insects.
Habitat	Sparse woodlands in damp places, such as swamps, meadows with ponds and streams, and around the edges of permanent ponds.
Distribution	North America, in SE United States.
Status	Common.
Similar species	The Southern Gray Tree Frog (Hyla chrysoscelis) has a warty back and lacks the cross-shaped marking. Several other tree frogs in the region may also have similar coloration but the cross, or lack of it, is usually a good way of separating them.

The Spring Peeper owes its common name to its breeding habits—it makes a high piping call, repeated many times. It often sings in large choruses that can be heard for several hundred yards. In the south, breeding may begin in winter and continue through until March, whereas in the north it may not start until March and continue into July. After the breeding season, males may call from trees during rain or humid weather.

They usually choose small ponds in which to breed, often surrounded by dense vegetation. The females lay about 900 eggs in small clusters, and the tadpoles take about three months to develop fully. They rarely migrate far from the breeding pond when they metamorphose, and most populations live within a short distance of a suitable breeding pond.

Spring Peepers hibernate on land, and in northern parts of their range their body fluids may partially freeze without any permanent damage thanks to the

presence of glycerol in their cells during winter. Glycerol is absent from their bodies during summer, however. These frogs are declining in numbers over much of their range, probably as woodlands are cleared and small ponds are drained. They were formerly placed in the genus *Hyla* but have been moved to *Pseudacris* because of their reduced toe pads.

⊖ *A Spring Peeper on vegetation beside a forest river in South Carolina. Unlike most other hylids, frogs in the genus Pseudacris do not have conspicuous expanded toe pads.*

Pacific Tree Frog

Common names	Pacific Tree Frog, Pacific Chorus Frog
Scientific name	*Pseudacris regilla*
Family	Hylidae
Size	0.75–1.97 in (19–50 mm).
Key features	A small brown, gray, or green tree frog with a black stripe running through its eye. Its back is rough and slightly warty and sometimes has darker spots and blotches. Its fingers are not webbed and its toes are webbed only at their bases.
Habits	Partially arboreal but usually found in low vegetation, among rocks, or on the ground. Nocturnal.
Breeding	In winter or spring, depending on locality. Eggs are laid in small ponds.
Diet	Small insects.
Habitat	Varied: grasslands, scrub, sparse woodlands, rocky canyons, marshes, etc.
Distribution	North America, along the west coast, from British Columbia, Canada, to the tip of Baja California.
Status	Common.
Similar species	In the same region the Mountain Tree Frog *(Hyla eximia)* has an eye stripe that continues to the groin. The Canyon Tree Frog *(H. arenicolor)* and the California Tree Frog *(Pseudacris cadaverina)* lack the eye stripe altogether.

This is a very adaptable little frog that occurs in a wide variety of situations and modifies its life cycle according to the conditions. It is equally at home among shrubs, grasses, and swamp vegetation in the cool habitats of inland California or British Columbia as it is in the rocky scrub surrounding small permanent water holes in the deserts of Baja California. In arid parts of its range colonies have become isolated as the land around them has gradually dried out over tens of thousands of years, leaving populations stranded around small ponds and shallow rivers in shaded gorges.

In the southern parts of its range it breeds in the winter from November onward, but in the north it waits until spring. It hibernates in the north for several months but may estivate in the south, becoming largely inactive and resting in cool, shaded rock crevices. Where conditions are favorable, it occurs in high densities, and the tadpoles often crowd together in small shrinking pools.

This species was previously included in the genus *Hyla* before being moved, together with several of its closest relatives, into *Pseudacris*, a genus that previously contained only the chorus frogs.

⊖ *A Pacific Tree Frog, Baja California. This species can lighten or darken its body color in a few minutes in response to the temperature and the amount of moisture in the air. This ability gives it enhanced camouflage protection as it moves about on different surfaces in its varied habitat.*

Red-snouted Tree Frog

Common name	Red-snouted Tree Frog
Scientific name	*Scinax ruber*
Family	Hylidae
Size	1.3–1.54 in (33–39 mm).
Key features	A small brown tree frog with a pointed snout, little or no webbing between its fingers and toes, and wide toe pads. It is light to mid brown in color, with two wide dark brown stripes down its back.
Habits	Arboreal and nocturnal.
Breeding	Eggs laid in ditches and small ponds.
Diet	Insects.
Habitat	Grasslands, forest edges and clearings, and disturbed habitats.
Distribution	Panama to the Amazon Basin in Brazil. Also Trinidad and Tobago.
Status	Common.
Similar species	Various species of *Scinax* are extremely difficult to identify with certainty unless they are from a region where only one or two species occur.

This is one of the few frogs that may have benefited from human activities in rain forest regions. It appears to prefer cleared open land rather than dense forest, and it has been able to expand its range, especially in South America, as a direct result of logging, road-building, and agricultural development. In some regions it is hardly ever found away from farms, villages, and towns, and it frequently enters buildings.

It breeds in roadside ditches and pools, often with dense aquatic vegetation. The male has a pleasant but monotonous "chuck-chuck-chuck" call, and breeding lasts throughout the rainy season.

Because of its tendency to live near humans, this species is frequently transported around the world, especially in bananas, and it is not unusual for two or three to be found in one crate after they have presumably hidden among the fruit during the day.

The genus *Scinax* contains 91 species of mostly small, fairly nondescript tree frogs from tropical America. Many of them were previously included within the genera *Hyla* and *Ololygon*. They are separated on account of their reduced webbing and several skeletal differences that are not obvious in living specimens.

⬅ *Red-snouted Tree Frog, Trinidad.*

Central American Smilisca

Common name	Central American Smilisca
Scientific name	Smilisca phaeota
Family	Hylidae
Size	1.57–2.6 in (40–66 mm).
Key features	A stout tree frog with well-developed toe pads. Its back is bronzy brown, green, or a combination of both colors. It has a white line running along its outer jaw.
Habits	Arboreal and nocturnal.
Breeding	Eggs laid in ditches and small ponds.
Diet	Insects.
Habitat	Lowland forests, secondary forests, and disturbed areas.
Distribution	Honduras to Ecuador.
Status	Common.
Similar species	Male Smiliscas have paired vocal sacs, which separates them from other tree frogs, but females and juveniles are more difficult to distinguish.

Smiliscas are generalist frogs, living in a variety of habitats rather than specializing in one particular type. They are active throughout the wet season, which can vary according to locality, and they will breed whenever it rains.

Males call from the edges of breeding ponds, usually from hidden places under or between leaves. When the male's vocal sac is inflated it forms a two-lobed structure with one lobe on either side. This is common to all *Smilisca* species, but it serves to separate them from *Hyla* species, to which they are otherwise very similar.

Roadside ditches are favorite places for breeding. The females lay up to 2,000 eggs, which float to the surface and form a raft. The tadpoles are also generalists and feed mainly on algae and, as they grow, tougher plant material. They can apparently survive for up to 24 hours out of water.

⊖ *A pair of Central American Smiliscas in amplexus, Turrialba, Costa Rica.*

Orinoco Lime Tree Frog

Common name	Orinoco Lime Tree Frog
Scientific name	*Sphaenorhynchus lacteus*
Family	Hylidae
Size	1.26–1.57 in (32–40 mm).
Key features	A slender tree frog with a noticeably pointed snout. Its body is translucent pale green in color with a white stripe running from the snout through the eye and fading on the flanks. The edges of the hind limbs also have a white stripe.
Habits	Arboreal and nocturnal.
Breeding	Eggs laid in ditches and small ponds.
Diet	Insects.
Habitat	Grasslands, forest edges, and reed beds.
Distribution	Amazon Basin and Trinidad.
Status	Probably common, but easily overlooked.
Similar species	The Polka-dot Tree Frog *(Hyla punctata)* is similar when in its daytime coloration, but it lacks the distinctive pointed snout of the Orinoco Lime Tree Frog.

This attractive tree frog is rarely seen except during rain. It lives in open places, such as grasslands and open woodlands, and breeds in small bodies of water or at the edges of larger ponds or flooded fields. Males call from vegetation 6 inches (15 cm) to 2 feet (61 cm) above the water, often hidden among tall grasses or reeds that grow up out of the pond.

Alternatively, they may call from floating vegetation, such as Water Hyacinth (*Eichhornia* species). Their call is a sudden croak with long intervals between calls. They do not form choruses, but between three and 20 males may call from the same pond.

The Orinoco Lime Tree Frogs are just one small group of dozens of species of hylids in Central and South America, a region where speciation within this family has run riot. The extensive rain forests in this part of the world have provided a stable environment over thousands of generations, allowing frogs to explore many evolutionary avenues. An abundance of hiding places, prey, and breeding situations make this the ideal region to live if you are a frog.

⊖ *Orinoco Lime Tree Frog, Trinidad.*

Other Hylids

↑ *This relatively uncommon frog from the Amazon Basin is* Osteocephalus buckleyi. *© Arthur Georges.*

→ Osteocephalus taurinus *is a nocturnal frog from the Orinoco Amazon basins. Its preferred habitat is primary and secondary rain forest. © Arthur Georges.*

Other Hylids

→ Scinax elaeochraoa *is found in lowland rain forests of the Caribbean. It has dark green bones that are visible through the skin beneath its hind legs. Here it is attached to the eggs of the Red-eyed Tree Frog.*

← *Another common species,* Scinax fuscovarius *occurs in open habitats across Brazil, Paraguay, northern Argentina, and northern Uruguay.*

↓ *The arboreal* Trachycephalus venulosus *from Central America is highly adaptable and can even be seen in disturbed habitats and human dwellings.*

Paradoxical Frog

Common name	Paradoxical Frog
Scientific name	*Pseudis paradoxa*
Family	Pseudidae
Size	1.77–2.76 in (45–70 mm). Females are larger than males.
Key features	This frog has a rounded snout, large eyes positioned on top of the head, horizontal pupils, long powerful hind legs, and extensively webbed toes. It is usually bright or dull green in color, merging into brown on the flanks.
Habits	Very aquatic.
Breeding	Females lay frothy masses of eggs among aquatic vegetation.
Diet	Aquatic invertebrates and their larvae, and small frogs.
Habitat	Permanent water bodies such as swamps, marshes, and large ponds.
Distribution	South America east of the Andes, from Venezuela to Paraguay and including the island of Trinidad.
Status	Common.
Similar species	Six other species of *Pseudis* are similar to the Paradoxical Frog, but their ranges do not all overlap. Paradoxical Frogs bear a superficial resemblance to ranid frogs which are, however, very limited in number in South America.

The Paradoxical Frog is so named because, unlike other frogs, its immense tadpole is much larger than the adult form. Because of this, early scientists thought they were dealing with two different species. Later it was thought that, in a reversal of the usual sequence of events, the frog turned into the tadpole, hence "paradoxical." In fact, tadpole size tends to vary from one part of the species' range to another, but they can measure more than 8.6 inches (22 cm), compared with a maximum adult size of 2.75 inches (70 mm). The largest tadpoles occur in the Guianas in northern South America, and the smallest are from Paraguay and Bolivia.

Most populations of Paradoxical Frogs live in permanently wet swamps and marshes, typically staying on the water's surface with their forelegs resting on submerged or emergent vegetation. Males call from the same position, with just their head and paired vocal sacs showing. Amplexus is axillary, and the eggs are laid in

frothy masses attached to vegetation in the shallower parts of the water, usually around the edges. The eggs are greenish in color, and the newly hatched tadpoles have a greenish tinge to their undersides for the first few days.

⊖ *A Paradoxical Frog resting at the surface in the Nariva Swamp, Trinidad.*

Midas Glass Frog

Common name	Midas Glass Frog
Scientific name	*Cochranella midas*
Family	Centrolenidae
Size	0.77–0.98 in (19.5–25 mm).
Key features	A small, delicate, green frog with large eyes and adhesive tips to its toes. Like many members of its family, its internal organs can be seen when viewed from the underside, hence the common name of glass frog. This species is plain green with a few yellowish spots on its back.
Habits	Nocturnal and arboreal.
Breeding	It breeds alongside forest streams, laying its eggs on leaves hanging over the water.
Diet	Small invertebrates such as flies.
Habitat	Forest streams passing through lowland and montane rain forests.
Distribution	South America, in Amazonian Ecuador and Peru.
Status	Widespread and probably common in undisturbed habitat, but extremely hard to find.
Similar species	Most other members of its family are superficially similar in appearance.

All glass frogs (family Centrolenidae) are small, delicate in appearance, and have large eyes situated on top of their slightly flattened heads, directed forward at about 45 degrees.

The family contains 138 species in four genera. The Midas Glass Frog belongs to the largest genus, *Cochranella*, which has 67 species. Many of them are unusual in having green bones, caused by the green pigment biliverdin that is also present in most other parts of their bodies. It is even evident in their eggs, which have a greenish tinge.

Male glass frogs are highly territorial and call from their favorite leaves on trees overhanging forest streams. They use the leaves for feeding as well as breeding. Other males approaching an occupied leaf are subjected to vigorous calling, followed by an attack if they do not retreat immediately. The male calls until he attracts a female, who will also lay her eggs on leaves overhanging the stream, at heights ranging from a few inches to several feet.

The female deposits her small clutch of greenish eggs in a single layer, firmly stuck to the underside of the leaf, and then withdraws. The male stays with the eggs, sitting on them at night and keeping them moist by emptying the contents of his bladder if necessary. During the day he moves to one side but faces the eggs, with one hand resting on the edge of the clutch so he can protect them from parasites, such as flies and wasps, that may try to lay their eggs on them. When they hatch, the tadpoles drop into the water.

→ *The Midas Glass Frog* (Cochranella midas) *is plain green with yellow spots on its back.* © Arthur Georges.

Fleischmann's Glass Frog

Common name	Fleischmann's Glass Frog
Scientific name	*Hyalinobatrachium fleischmanni*
Family	Centrolenidae
Size	0.75–1.26 in (19–32 mm). Females are slightly bigger than males, but there is some overlap.
Key features	A small, semitransparent, green frog in which areas of white pigment covering the liver and other internal organs are visible. It has long slender limbs and expanded toe pads. The only markings on the green back and limbs are small spots of yellow.
Habits	Nocturnal and arboreal.
Breeding	Eggs are laid on leaves overhanging forest streams.
Diet	Small invertebrates, mostly small flies.
Habitat	Rain forest in lowlands and foothills.
Distribution	Central and S America, from Mexico to Ecuador.
Status	Very common.
Similar species	All centrolenid frogs are similar, but the regular yellow spots on this one are a good aid to identification.

These frogs live in large colonies in trees and shrubs bordering small streams that run through rain forests. Males remain near the stream throughout the year, but females disperse into the surrounding forest after breeding. The male calls from the underside of a leaf that can be up to 8 feet (2.4 m) above the stream. The call serves to keep them spaced out, as well as to attract females.

The female approaches a male, and he climbs onto her back. She moves about in the leaves, looking for a suitable egg-laying site. She lays a clutch of 10 to 50 greenish eggs in a gelatinous mass on the underside of a leaf, 2 feet (0.6 m) or more above the water. She leaves immediately after, but the male stays nearby, visiting the eggs every few nights and sitting over them. He may wet them with the contents of his bladder to keep them from drying out. In dry weather he visits more often than in wet weather, and the function of "guarding" the eggs against predators does not seem to occur in this species.

The tadpoles, which are pink, hatch after about 14 days, but they may remain on the leaf for another 10 days until heavy rains wash them off into the stream below. They immediately burrow down into the debris on the bottom of the stream.

⊙ *Fleischmann's Glass Frog seen resting in the daytime in a Panamanian cloud forest.*

The main predators of the eggs are frog flies, which lay their eggs on the egg mass so that their maggots can feed on it. Glass frogs are thought to be their only food source. The frogs' eggs may also be infested with a fungus—it is unclear whether the fungus or the flies get to the eggs first, or if one causes infestation by the other. Studies show that 21 to 88 percent of eggs and larvae perish through infestation by flies or fungus (or both).

Cape River Frog

Common name	Cape River Frog
Scientific name	*Afrana fuscigula*
Family	Ranidae
Size	2.95–4.92 in (75–125 mm).
Key features	Large and stocky with strong legs and plenty of webbing between the fingers and the toes. Brown or greenish brown in color, with an indistinct pattern of darker areas on its back. There is sometimes a thin plain line down the center of the back.
Habits	Semiaquatic and nocturnal.
Breeding	In pools and the edges of larger water bodies.
Diet	Mainly insects but also small vertebrates.
Habitat	Large permanent ponds, reservoirs, and lakes.
Distribution	South Africa and Namibia.
Status	Common.
Similar species	Other *Afrana* species, but the Cape River Frog can be differentiated by its very wide head.

The Cape River Frog is a very large, powerful water frog found in a variety of habitats but always near permanent water. It may wander away from the edge of its lake or pond at night looking for food, but it is never more than a few long jumps from safety. It is a voracious predator and eats almost anything it can get into its mouth, including freshwater crabs, other frogs, and small rodents, as well as insects, which form the bulk of its diet.

It breeds in the wettest time of the year, which differs from place to place. The male takes up a position in aquatic vegetation, often in very deep water, and calls during the day as well as at nighttime throughout the breeding season. Males space themselves out, and if the numbers are large they call in a chorus. Choruses start slowly and build up to a crescendo before fading away again after about three minutes. The eggs are laid on the bottom of quiet stretches of water, attached to plants or stones. Females produce about 1,000 eggs in a single night and may spawn more than once on successive nights.

The *Afrana* species used to be included in the large genus *Rana*. Recently, however, it has been moved to a new genus, *Amietia*, although this is not widely used at present.

Cape River Frog at Cape Peninsula, South Africa.

Van Dijk's River Frog

Common name	Van Dijk's River Frog
Scientific name	*Afrana vandijki*
Family	Ranidae
Size	2.17 in (55 mm).
Key features	A stout frog with long, powerful hind legs and almost fully webbed fingers and toes. It has a conspicuous fold of skin running from the eye to the top of the arm and this partially hides the eardrum (tympanum). It is brown or greenish in color with a complicated pattern of mottled dark brown patches.
Habits	Terrestrial and mainly nocturnal.
Breeding	In streams.
Diet	Invertebrates.
Habitat	Alongside rocky streams in heavily vegetated or wooded gullies.
Distribution	South Africa.
Status	Probably common in a few localized places.
Similar species	None of the other stout ranids from the region have the prominent fold of skin above the tympanum.

This frog was only discovered in 1997. It lives in heavily vegetated valleys or gullies, known locally as *kloof*s, where fast-flowing streams run over a substrate of rocks, forming cascades and waterfalls. The frogs are not found far from the water and often sit on rocky ledges behind or next to small waterfalls. They probably escaped the attention of scientists for so long because these gullies are difficult to explore, and the only accessible parts of the habitat are where a few mountain roads cross them. Van Dijk's River Frogs share their specialized habitat with a couple of species of ghost frogs *(Heleophryne)*.

They breed in the dry season, when the streams have subsided and slowed down. Males call from the edge of the stream, and the eggs are laid among the stones and gravel on the bottom. Details of the tadpoles are lacking, but they probably live in small backwaters where they are not subjected to the full force of the flow.

The *Afrana* species of frogs used to be placed in the large genus *Rana* but have recently been moved to *Amietia*, although this is not widely used at present.

⊖ *Van Dijk's River Frog at Tradouw's Pass, South Africa.*

Larut Hills Torrent Frog

Common name	Larut Hills Torrent Frog
Scientific name	*Amolops larutensis*
Family	Ranidae
Size	1.3–2.09 in (33–53 mm). Females are larger than males.
Key features	A long-legged ranid with a granular skin and toes that end in large pads. The hind feet are heavily webbed. Its back is green or yellowish, with many small black markings and several yellow spots. The limbs have black bars. Juveniles and males are less colorful than females but the large toe pads are always obvious.
Habits	Nocturnal and semiaquatic.
Breeding	In fast-flowing rivers and streams.
Diet	Invertebrates.
Habitat	Alongside rivers and streams that run through forests.
Distribution	Malaysian Peninsula.
Status	Very common in suitable habitat.
Similar species	There are no similar species in the region.

The Larut Hills Torrent Frog is named for the place it was first discovered in the state of Perak, Malaysia. It is a specialized ranid, never found far from fast-flowing rivers and streams in forests. In suitable places many individuals can be seen clinging to wet rocks surrounded by the torrent, using their large pads to cling to the surface and often facing head-down. They also live on the rocks at the base of and behind large waterfalls. They occasionally leap into the water, only to reappear a few seconds later, usually in the same place—their powerful hind legs and webbed feet enable them to swim against the current.

This species breeds in the rivers and streams in which it lives. There is no information on its eggs or egg-laying, which probably takes place at the edges of the river where the water is quieter.

The tadpoles are very distinctive. They have a large head with small eyes positioned on the top, and a small tail. They are grayish with scattered spots of dark and light pigment. The underside of their body consists of a grazing mouth in the center of a large sucker, which they use to cling to the wet rocks in the rushing water, or on the rock faces of waterfalls. They

graze on the layer of algae and bacterial slime that grows at the waterline and are often visible above the surface as the river surges and recedes.

↑ *The dark blotchy pattern can be seen on the back of this Larut Hills Torrent Frog from the Gombak Forest, Malaysia.*

Solomon Islands Leaf Frog

Common names	Solomon Islands Leaf Frog, Triangle Frog
Scientific name	*Ceratobatrachus guentheri*
Family	Ranidae
Size	To 3 in (76 mm).
Key features	Unmistakable. It has a sharply pointed snout and another point over each eye. Its back is marked with false "veins," and its limbs have frilly margins, all designed to make it look like a leaf. Brown or yellowish brown in color.
Habits	Terrestrial and nocturnal.
Breeding	Direct development.
Diet	Invertebrates and small vertebrates.
Habitat	Forests.
Distribution	Solomon Islands and Bougainville Island, Papua New Guinea.
Status	Unknown.
Similar species	There are no similar species.

Superficially similar to the Asian Horned Toad *(Megophrys nasuta)*, although not related to it, the Solomon Islands Leaf Frog is a remarkable species. Its color and shape provide almost perfect camouflage among the dead forest leaves of its habitat. There is a brown form and a rare yellow form, both equally effective. Also like the Asian Horned Frog, this species has a wide gape and can tackle relatively large prey, including other frogs.

Like many frogs from this part of the world, it undergoes direct development. Males call from the forest floor at night with a loud, barklike call, and the females lay small clusters of pea-sized eggs in damp places, especially among mosses or in shallow depressions in the leaf litter. The tadpoles remain inside the egg capsule, feeding off their yolk supply, until they are fully formed. Young froglets break out of the egg capsule and become independent at about 0.25 inches (6 mm) in length.

The species, along with the members of five other genera from the same part of the world, have recently been moved to a separate family, the Ceratobatrachidae, but this change has not yet been widely adopted.

⊙ *Shaped just like a leaf, the Solomon Islands Leaf Frog is a master of camouflage.*

Rice Paddy Frog

Common names	Rice Paddy Frog, Grass Frog, Cricket Frog, Field Frog
Scientific name	*Fejervarya limnocharis*
Family	Ranidae
Size	1.26–2.28 in (32–58 mm).
Key features	A small frog with a narrow head and pointed snout. It has long limbs, and its hind feet are partially webbed, but the front feet are not webbed. Its back has several short ridges running down it, each broken into short lengths. It is gray or brown in color with darker markings scattered across its back, head, and limbs. There is also a white line running down the center of its back, although this is sometimes missing.
Habits	Terrestrial and nocturnal.
Breeding	In small bodies of permanent and temporary water.
Diet	Invertebrates.
Habitat	Disturbed habitats, including rice paddies, fields, roadsides, and gardens.
Distribution	Tropical Asia.
Status	Very common.
Similar species	There are several similar species in the region, but this is the one most likely to be seen around towns and villages.

This frog is hardly, if ever, seen in natural habitats. It lives around villages and emerges from its daytime hiding places during humid and rainy nights. Males call from almost any body of water, including potholes in main roads, ditches, flooded gardens and playing fields, and rice fields. Its total population must number hundreds of millions. It has a rapid, frenetic call consisting of rapidly repeated chirps that fill the air on warm rainy nights.

Females lay small clumps of eggs in temporary pools, and the tadpoles develop quickly in the warm water, metamorphosing in one to two months, provided the pool does not dry out first. Frogs that

⊕ *This juvenile Rice Paddy Frog was found in Thailand.*

lay their eggs in temporary pools run the risk of losing whole batches of offspring. They avoid predation from fish, however, and in regions with high rainfall, subsequent rains keep the pools topped up long enough for development to take place.

⊕ *An adult Rice Paddy Frog, photographed at Marang, Terengganu, west Malaysia.*

This species has been known under a variety of different names, including *Rana limnocharis* and *Limnonectes limnocharis*.

Sri Lankan Wart Frog

Common names	Sri Lankan Wart Frog, Corrugated Water Frog
Scientific name	*Lankanectes corrugatus*
Family	Ranidae
Size	1.38–2.76 in (35–70 mm).
Key features	A stocky frog with its widest part just behind the head, across the shoulder region. It is brown or gray in color with irregular dark spots and blotches and, usually, dark crossbars on its limbs. Its back has a series of ridges or corrugations running across it, like an old-fashioned washboard.
Habits	Semiaquatic and nocturnal.
Breeding	In small bodies of water.
Diet	Invertebrates.
Habitat	Small streams running through lowland rain forests.
Distribution	Sri Lanka.
Status	Uncommon.
Similar species	The corrugations on its back make identification easy.

The Sri Lankan Wart Frog is an uncommon species that lives only along slow-moving streams and among tussocky marshes in Sri Lanka. Little is known of its lifestyle. The purpose of the unusual folds of skin that cross its back, forming the corrugations that give the frog its name, is also a mystery.

On the face of it, species such as the Sri Lankan Water Frog have a massive area of suitable habitat in which to live and breed: Sri Lanka has very large areas of marshes, rice paddies, and shallow reservoirs known as "tanks." While this may have been the case up until 20 or 30 years ago, rice paddies are now liberally sprayed with insecticides. This reduces or eliminates the insects that water frogs rely on as a food supply and also pollutes the water in which they live and breed. As a result, large areas of seemingly suitable habitat contain only one or two of the commoner, more robust species that can withstand the conditions, whereas the more sensitive species are restricted to small areas that have escaped the worst of the pollution.

⊖ *The Sri Lankan Wart Frog is rarely seen, and suitable habitat in which it can live and breed is diminishing.*

Kuhl's Creek Frog

Common names	Kuhl's Creek Frog, Large-headed Frog
Scientific name	*Limnonectes kuhlii*
Family	Ranidae
Size	1.73–2.64 in (44–67 mm).
Key features	Very thickset, with a wide head and body and powerful limbs. Males have a broader head than females. The eardrums are not visible, and the back is covered in many small lumps, ridges, and raised reticulations. The hind feet are fully webbed but the hands are not. The frog is brown or gray in color with a vague pattern of darker areas on its back and limbs.
Habits	Semiaquatic and nocturnal.
Breeding	In streams.
Diet	Invertebrates.
Habitat	Streams running through upland forests.
Distribution	Southeast Asia.
Status	Common.
Similar species	Although there are many similar species in the region, the swollen head of this one, coupled with an absence of distinct markings, should serve to identify it. The Rivulet Frog *(L. laticeps)* is smaller.

This frog occurs from sea level to 5,250 feet (1,600 m) in primary rain forests. It is never found far from water and typically rests on rocks at the edge of forest streams or surrounded by the stream. If disturbed, it slips into the water and rests with just its head above the surface. It prefers streams with a reasonably fast flow of clear water, but not cascades or waterfalls. Males do not have vocal sacs, so this species is sometimes included in the so-called voiceless frogs. Strangely enough, males living on the slopes of Mount Kinabalu in Borneo do call, whereas those from lower elevations apparently do not.

They breed in the streams where they live, and the tadpoles live in quiet backwaters or, in dry weather, in small pools formed by the drying stream.

⊙ *Kuhl's Creek Frog, Mount Kinabalu National Park, Sabah, Borneo.*

Malaysian Bullfrog

Common names	Malaysian Bullfrog, Fanged River Frog, Malaga Wart Frog, Stone Creek Frog
Scientific name	*Limnonectes macrodon*
Family	Ranidae
Size	2.76–5.91 in (70–150 mm).
Key features	A large, bulky frog with powerful limbs and webbed feet. The head is broad, and the eardrums are obvious. It is brown, tan, or reddish brown in color, with a few scattered darker markings. There is usually a thin white or yellow line running from the tip of the snout down the center of the back and a similar line on the front of the hind legs.
Habits	Semiaquatic and nocturnal.
Breeding	In water.
Diet	Invertebrates and small vertebrates.
Habitat	Slow-moving rivers running through lowland forests.
Distribution	Burma, Thailand, Malaysian Peninsula, Sumatra, and Java.
Status	Locally common, but Javan and Sumatran populations listed by the IUCN as Vulnerable because of fragmented and declining habitat.
Similar species	Similar large species include the Peat Swamp Frog *(L. malesiana)* and Blyth's Frog *(L. blythii)*, and a combination of characteristics is sometimes needed to separate them.

The Malaysian Bullfrog is a large powerful frog that is capable of making huge leaps. It is a formidable predator, taking small frogs, lizards, and young snakes as well as large insects and spiders. This species and those closely related to it are sometimes known as voiceless frogs because they have no vocal sacs. However, they do call, using the whole of their body to amplify the sound.

The breeding habits of this species have not been recorded but are probably similar to those of the closely related *Limnonectes malesiana*. Males of this

species create a shallow basin in the sand or fine gravel at the edges of a river or stream. When a male has attracted a female to his nest by calling, she may also share in the building of the nest by scraping more material away. The eggs are laid in this small pool, which gives them protection from aquatic predators and prevents them from being swept downstream.

The males of *L. macrodon* and *L. malesiana* have a pair of enlarged teeth on the lower jaw, and these may be used as weapons to drive away other males from the nest, in the same way that the South American Gladiator Frog *(Hyla rosenbergi)* defends its nest, but evidence for this is lacking at present.

Malaysian Giant Bullfrog, Cameron Highlands, Malaysia.

Penang Wart Frog

Common names	Penang Wart Frog, Rhinoceros Frog
Scientific name	Limnonectes plicatellus
Family	Ranidae
Size	1.34–1.69 in (34–43 mm).
Key features	A heavily built frog with a broad head and body and powerful limbs. Males have a bony knob, angled backward, on the top of the head. The eardrums are not visible, and the back is covered in many small lumps and ridges. It is grayish brown with faint darker markings on its back and limbs, and it sometimes has a pale yellow line running down the center of its back.
Habits	Semiaquatic and nocturnal.
Breeding	In streams and seepages.
Diet	Invertebrates.
Habitat	Shallow streams running through lowland forests.
Distribution	Southern Thailand and the Malaysian Peninsula.
Status	Common.
Similar species	There are many similar species in the region, such as the Rivulet Frog (L. laticeps), but male Penang Wart Frogs can be distinguished by the bony knob on their head.

The Penang Wart Frog is also known as the Rhinoceros Frog because the males have a backward-pointing bony projection on top of the head. Its function is unknown, although it is presumed to be connected to breeding behavior, since it is not found in females.

This frog lives along overgrown streams that run through lowland rain forests. They are often muddy, and their banks partially covered with dead forest leaves, beneath which the frogs hide. They may also lay their eggs in small depressions in the mud, under large leaves, but this is yet to be confirmed.

All Limnonectes were previously included in the genus Rana, and are still sometimes listed as such. Limnonectes, however, have warty or ridged backs, whereas in Rana species the back tends to be smooth, sometimes with a pair of fleshy folds running along the edges.

⊝ Penang Wart Frog from the Gombak Forest in Malaysia. The bony knob on its head indicates that this is a male.

Other *Limnonectes* Species

⬅ Blyth's Frog (Limnonectes blythii) *in a Thai rain forest at night. This species occurs widely in Southeast Asia, but some populations are in decline.*

➡ Doria's Frog (Limnonectes doriae) *is a terrestrial species found in primary tropical forests of Southeast Asia. This frog was photographed at Bukit Fraser, Perak, west Malaysia.*

⬇ A Rivulet Frog (Limnonectes laticeps) *in the Gombak Forest, Malaysia. This species occurs in northeastern India, Myanmar, Thailand, Borneo, and Sumatra.*

Mascarene Grass Frog

Common names	Mascarene Grass Frog, Mascarene Ridged Frog, Rocket Frog
Scientific name	Ptychadena mascareniensis
Family	Ranidae
Size	1.57–2.17 in (40–55 mm).
Key features	A typical ranid, with a pointed snout, pear-shaped body, and long hind legs. Its skin is smooth, but there are 6–8 folds of skin running down its back, broken up into short lengths. It may be brown or green and has darker blotches on its back and bars on its limbs. There is often a lighter line running down the center of its back.
Habits	Mostly nocturnal, but sometimes active by day. Terrestrial.
Breeding	In shallow water.
Diet	Invertebrates.
Habitat	Still water in exposed situations, including rice paddies.
Distribution	Madagascar, Seychelles, and eastern parts of the African mainland.
Status	Very common.
Similar species	In Madagascar the introduced Hoplobatrachus tigerinus is the only other typical ranid. In Africa there are other similar Ptychadena species, such as P. oxyrhynchus, but they are smaller.

The Mascarene Grass Frog is hugely successful in places, occurring in large numbers in practically every body of shallow water, including irrigation ditches and rice fields. This species is sometimes known locally as the Rocket Frog, a name that gives a good indication of its leaping ability. All grass frogs have long powerful hind legs that can propel them for enormous distances.

Males form calling choruses from shallow water, and they call during the day as well as at night. Choruses are mostly heard at the beginning of the rainy season, but they tail off as the season progresses and stop almost completely in the dry season. Females lay their eggs in batches of 20 to 30 in shallow water, often attached to aquatic vegetation or submerged grasses. The tadpoles reach a length of about 1.8 inches (45 mm) and feed on algae and plants.

The only other ranid in Madagascar is the Indian Bullfrog (*Hoplobatrachus tigerinus*), which was introduced deliberately as a food source. This species is very large and has a limited range in the north of the country.

⊕ *Mascarene Grass Frog, Maroantsetra, Madagascar.*

Sharp-nosed Grass Frog

Common names	Sharp-nosed Grass Frog, Sharp-nosed Ridge Frog
Scientific name	*Ptychadena oxyrhynchus*
Family	Ranidae
Size	2.44–3.35 in (62–85 mm).
Key features	Triangular in outline when seen from above, with a noticeably pointed snout, long hind legs, and fully webbed hind feet. It has several wavy ridges of skin running down its back, some of them interrupted. It is brown or olive with scattered darker spots and may have a pale line down its back. One or two of the ridges of skin may also be yellow or dirty white in color.
Habits	Mostly nocturnal, but sometimes active by day. Terrestrial.
Breeding	In shallow water.
Diet	Invertebrates.
Habitat	Flooded grasslands, pools, and isolated river backwaters.
Distribution	East and southern Africa.
Status	Very common.
Similar species	Other grass frogs are similar but none is as common or widespread.

The longest frog jump recorded—33 feet 5.5 inches (10.2 m)—was made by a Sharp-nosed Grass Frog in South Africa in 1977.

These frogs usually take off again as soon as they land, putting together two or three jumps that cover huge distances. They are preyed on by various snakes, the Nile Monitor *(Varanus niloticus)*, and, in places, humans.

The Sharp-nosed Grass Frog lives in open grasslands and along the borders of wide rivers. It breeds at the edges of the rivers, in shallow pools formed from floods or storms or in rock pools. Breeding takes place during the rainy season (the summer). The female lays her eggs in short strings that quickly fall apart, allowing the eggs to float away independently. Clutches consisting of up to 3,500 eggs have been recorded.

The tadpoles are thought to eat insects, along with algae and plant material. The tadpoles grow quickly, as do the young frogs, which can reach breeding size in less than a year.

In the height of the breeding season males call sporadically during the afternoon and evening. The choruses build as the night progresses until they become incessant after midnight. The chorus, a loud, high-pitched trill, is a characteristic sound of the African bush.

⊙ *Sharp-nosed Grass Frog, Masai Mara National Park, Kenya. Like all members of its genus, it is very agile and can cover enormous distances in just a few jumps.*

Giant Bullfrog

Common names	Giant Bullfrog, African Bullfrog
Scientific name	*Pyxicephalus adspersus*
Family	Ranidae
Size	To 9.06 in (23 cm). Males are larger than females.
Key features	A potentially gigantic frog, whose width almost equals its length.Its limbs are short and stubby. Its back is olive green and has several skin folds arranged roughly into longitudinal lines. Males have a pair of tusklike projections on the lower jaw. Juveniles are different: bright green with mottled black markings and a pale line down their back.
Habits	Active by day and night. Terrestrial.
Breeding	In temporary pools that appear after heavy rain.
Diet	Anything, including invertebrates, frogs, lizards, snakes, and rodents.
Habitat	Grasslands.
Distribution	Southern Africa.
Status	Common, but only conspicuous after heavy rain.
Similar species	The Edible Bullfrog *(Pyxicephalus edulis)* is similar but not so big. It is not as brightly colored and occurs farther north.

This frog is the African counterpart of the South American horned frogs (*Ceratophrys* species) and Budgett's frogs (*Lepidobatrachus* species). Large examples can weigh in excess of 2 pounds (1.2 kg) and easily tackle prey such as rats.

The breeding behavior of these frogs is very interesting. After spending the dry season in a cocoon *(continued over)*

A Giant Bullfrog at night in savanna in South Africa. This hardy frog can tolerate drought and soaring temperatures.

Giant Bullfrog (cont'd.)

of hardened mud, they emerge from estivation after heavy rain and make for shallow flooded pans. The male calls from the edge of pools and makes a low "whoop" sound. Large males hold the central territory, surrounded by smaller males. Females are attracted to the large calling males but swim under the surface as they approach so that they are not intercepted by the smaller "satellite" males.

The eggs are laid at the edge of the pond by the female, who arches her back until her vent is out of the water. As the eggs are forced out, the male fertilizes them, before they fall into the water. After laying, the female leaves the breeding site, but the male often stays near the eggs.

When they hatch, the male guards the tadpoles and, if they become isolated in a small, drying pool, he will dig a channel to a deeper part of the pond and encourage them to swim along it. Channels of up to nearly 50 feet (15 m) long have been found.

When the tadpoles metamorphose, the emerging froglets are voracious, eating every moving thing they encounter, including each other. The population of newly metamorphosed frogs is thus decimated, and the survivors get off to a head start.

→ Partially submerged, a Giant Bullfrog swims in a seasonal pond in the Okavango Delta, Botswana. These large, powerful frogs are formidable predators and aggressive defenders of their young.

American Bullfrog

Common name	American Bullfrog
Scientific name	*Rana catesbeiana*
Family	Ranidae
Size	3.54–7.87 in (9–20 cm).
Key features	A large frog (the largest in North America) with long, powerful hind legs and heavily webbed feet. It has prominent eardrums, which are larger in males than in females. The frog is mottled olive, brown, or green above and lighter green on the head. Its legs are banded or spotted with dark brown or black, and its chin and throat also have dark markings. Its bellowing call is loud and distinctive.
Habits	Semiaquatic, rarely seen far from water.
Breeding	Lays its eggs in water in the spring and summer.
Diet	Large invertebrates and small vertebrates, including other frogs.
Habitat	Large ponds and lakes, where it usually stays near the water's edge or rests among floating vegetation.
Distribution	Eastern and central North America. Introduced to western United States and other regions.
Status	Common.
Similar species	Adults are distinctive on account of their size. Juveniles could be confused with several other medium-sized ranids from the region.

Large, powerful hind legs launch the American Bullfrog on a long, arching trajectory when it makes its enormous leaps. They also propel it through the water at great speed when it swims.

The American Bullfrog is a thoroughly aquatic species, with heavily webbed hind feet. It is often seen basking at the water's edge, usually facing the water, or floating just below the surface with only the top of its head and its eyes visible. It is wary, though, and if disturbed on land it jumps into the water, making a considerable splash before swimming rapidly away. With one or two kicks, it covers several feet and may dive to the bottom.

These bullfrogs are voracious predators, taking small mammals, lizards, snakes, and other frogs, including smaller members of their own species. In places where they have been introduced (California and several other western states, Mexico, Cuba, Puerto Rico, Hispaniola, and Jamaica in the Americas; the Netherlands, France, Spain, and Italy in Europe; and Java, Japan, Thailand, and Taiwan in Asia) they are often implicated in the *(continued over)*

→ *American Bullfrog, North America. Adult bullfrogs are large and robust with big golden eyes. Both sexes have a pronounced tympanum just behind and below the eye.*

American Bullfrog (cont'd.)

disappearance or reduction in numbers of native species living in similar habitats. They are one of the causes of the decline of the Red-legged Frog *(Rana aurora)* in California, for instance.

Males produce the famous bellowing call and defend territories from other males, fighting if necessary to drive them away. Males have much larger tympanums than females, but nobody knows why. Both sexes apparently hear equally well. Territory holders puff up their body and raise themselves up out of the water.

Females are attracted to males with "good" territories even though they often swim off to another part of the pond to lay their eggs once they have paired up. Females lay huge masses of spawn, averaging more than 11,000 eggs, which float near the surface in a foamy film; the record is 47,840 eggs—more than any other frog or toad.

⊙ *With its tongue extended, an adult American Bullfrog in North America leaps out of the water to catch its prey.*

White-lipped Frog

Common name	White-lipped Frog
Scientific name	*Rana chalconota*
Family	Ranidae
Size	1.3–2.36 in (33–60 mm).
Key features	A gracefully shaped frog with a slender body and pointed head. Its legs are relatively long, and its hind feet are fully webbed. Its front limbs have enlarged tips. Green or brown in color with a pearly white line along the upper jaw.
Habits	Nocturnal and terrestrial.
Breeding	In quiet pools.
Diet	Invertebrates.
Habitat	Forests, parks, and gardens.
Distribution	Southeast Asia.
Status	Common.
Similar species	Hose's Frog *(R. hosii)*, is brighter green, and Paddy Frog *(R. erythraea)* has a pair of bold white stripes down its back.

A forest species, the White-lipped frog forages among leaf litter and may climb into low bushes at night looking for food. It tolerates disturbed places and occurs around plantations and in the grounds of houses and parks. This agile and alert species sometimes goes under the names of *Hylarana chalconota* and *Hydrophylax chalconotus*.

Males call from the edges of permanent ponds and streams. Isolated pools at the edges of streams, formed from backwaters when the water level recedes, are favored places for breeding. There is no record of how the eggs are laid, but the tadpoles live in still water, hiding among the leaf litter that collects on the bottom. They have an attractive pattern of light and dark markings on the head.

⊙ *White-lipped Frog, Templer Park, Malaysia. The expanded tips on its front limbs help it climb over forest leaves.*

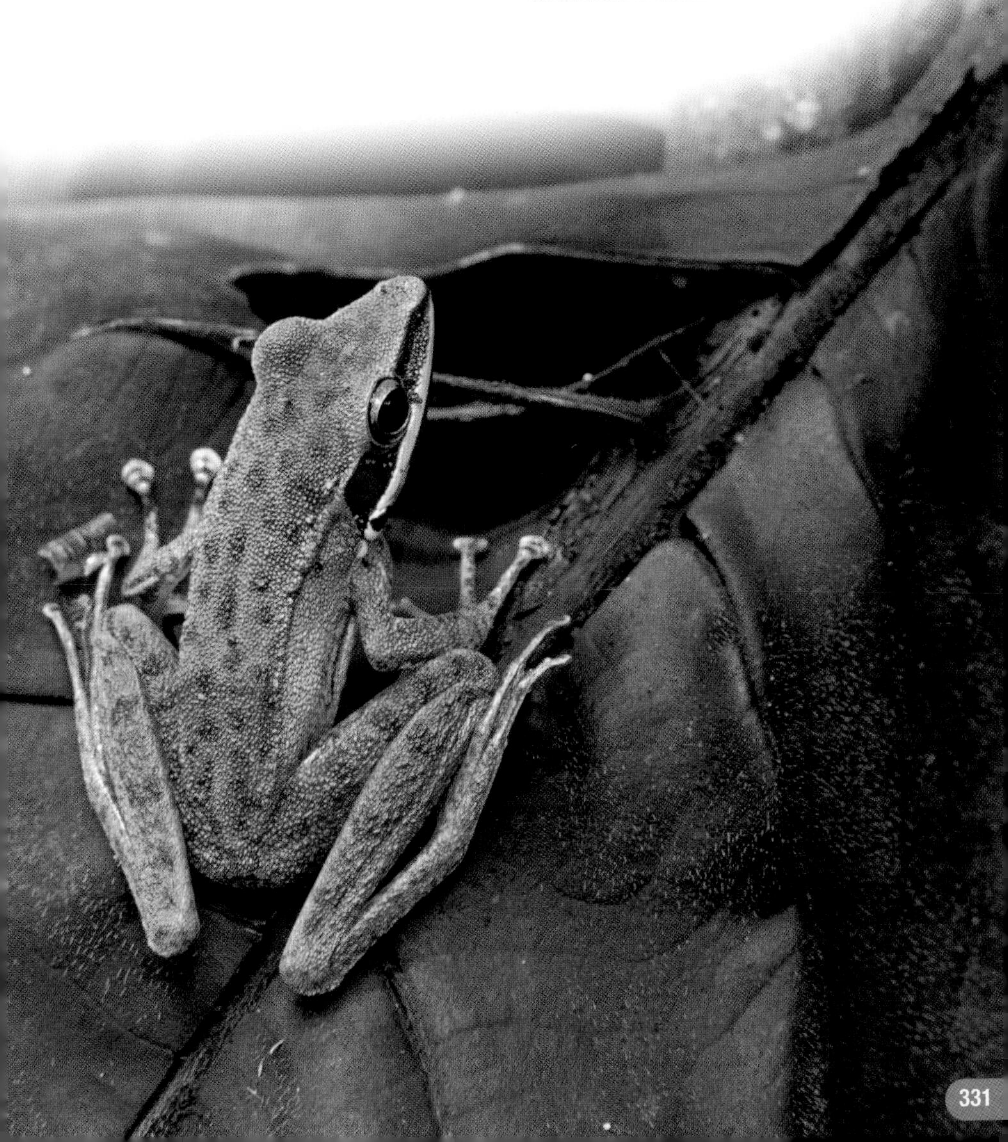

Agile Frog

Common name	Agile Frog
Scientific name	*Rana dalmatina*
Family	Ranidae
Size	To 3.54 in (90 mm).
Key features	A typical ranid, but with very long legs. Its back feet are fully webbed, and the toes are long. It has a black "mask" across its eyes, and its body is pale pinkish brown—there is little variation.
Habits	Mostly nocturnal. Terrestrial.
Breeding	In quiet pools and swamps.
Diet	Invertebrates.
Habitat	Lightly wooded areas.
Distribution	Central and E Europe.
Status	Common.
Similar species	Other brown frogs in the region include the Italian Agile Frog *(R. latastei)*, the Balkan Stream Frog *(R. graeca)*, and the Iberian Frog *(R. iberica)*, but all these have dark markings on their throat and smaller eardrums.

This frog has a wide distribution throughout much of Europe but it is not often seen. It lives in woodlands, especially oak woods, where its coloration makes it difficult to see against the dead leaves. It also occurs in meadows, especially in damp places. It is a poor swimmer, however, and is more likely to leap into cover than into water when it is disturbed. It is at its most active from the evening onward, but it also hunts during the day, especially in wet or misty weather.

In breeds close to its preferred habitat, usually in still pools in swamps, but also in streams, ditches, and ponds very early in the year. Females lay up to 1,800 eggs in a single large clump, wrapped around dead twigs or aquatic plants. As they swell, the eggs float to the surface and are often covered in green algae. They take about three weeks to hatch, and the tadpoles metamorphose at the end of summer. They reach breeding size in another two or three years.

⊖ *Agile Frog, Austria. The wide masklike black bands running from the nose through the eyes, and its large eardrums are characteristic of the species.*

Green Paddy Frog

Common names	Green Paddy Frog, Common Green Frog
Scientific name	*Rana erythraea*
Family	Ranidae
Size	1.26–2.95 in (32–75 mm). Females are larger than males.
Key features	A streamlined ranid, with a pointed head and very long legs. Its back feet are almost fully webbed, and the toes have slightly expanded tips. It has a green back, bordered on each side by a dark-edged white line. Its flanks are also green, and a second pair of white lines borders these green areas. The limbs are brown.
Habits	Mostly nocturnal and terrestrial.
Breeding	In still water.
Diet	Invertebrates.
Habitat	Disturbed areas, especially paddy fields.
Distribution	Southeast Asia, including Indo-China and the Philippines.
Status	Very common.
Similar species	Other ranids in the area lack the green and white coloration.

The Green Paddy Frog is a ubiquitous species that is often seen and heard around villages, farms, irrigation ditches, and cultivated fields of rice. It is rarely seen in undisturbed habitats and is one of the species that has benefited from human activity. Its toe pads enable it to cling to the leaves and stems of plants growing alongside or emerging from standing water. It is active by day and by night, stalking small insects such as flies and grasshoppers. In places it also lives among the large mats of the introduced water hyacinth plant, basking on the leaves and quickly disappearing into the water below if it is disturbed. This is a very wary and elusive frog, hard to approach, and even harder to catch.

Males call from vegetation near water, and they breed throughout the year provided there is water. The eggs are laid in still, shallow water and may be attached to aquatic vegetation. The tadpoles feed on algae at first, later progressing to tougher plants. They grow quickly in the warm shallow water and metamorphose after about a month. The young frogs reach sexual maturity in about nine months (males) and 11 months (females).

⊖ *A Green Paddy Frog in rain forest in Thailand, seen at night.*

Edible Frog

Common name	Edible Frog
Scientific name	*Rana* kl. *esculenta* (This is a naturally occurring hybrid species.)
Family	Ranidae
Size	4.72 in (12 cm).
Key features	Plump for a ranid, with a triangular head and pointed snout. Its hind legs are muscular (and tasty, apparently!) but not obviously long, as in some other species. It is usually green in color, with a lighter stripe running down the center of its back. The back of its thighs are often yellow. There is a low fleshy ridge running down each side of its back.
Habits	Very aquatic. Active at night and during the day.
Breeding	Lays large numbers of eggs in water.
Diet	Invertebrates. It can feed underwater.
Habitat	Almost any body of water, from small muddy pools to the edges of lakes; also found in brackish water.
Distribution	Central and E Europe. Small colonies in S England may be introduced.
Status	Common in suitable habitats.
Similar species	The two parent species (see text and following pages), the Marsh or Laughing Frog (*R. ridibunda*) and the Pool Frog (*R. lessonae*) are very similar.

The Edible Frog is common throughout much of central and eastern Europe in ditches, canals, ponds, and lakes. It is a hybrid between the Pool Frog *(Rana lessonae)* and the Marsh or Laughing Frog *(R. ridibunda)*, hence the addition of the "kl." in the species name.

All three species are active in the day, even in bright, warm weather. They emerge onto banks, often sitting under clumps of grass or other vegetation. When disturbed, they jump into the water and swim to the bottom but quickly reappear on the surface, scanning for danger. If satisfied they are safe, they swim back to the shore to continue basking. They call throughout the year, but most loudly in the spring and summer, and in large choruses.

Where Edible Frogs occur with either the Pool Frogs or the Marsh Frogs (or both), they breed with one or other of the parent species, maintaining their hybrid state. On rare occasions, however, Edible Frogs live in colonies without either parent, even though they owe their existence to them. It appears, very unusually, that they are able to maintain themselves as a pure population without either of the parent species being present. This seems to be because in addition to the normal diploid Edible Frogs (with two sets of chromosomes), there are triploid ones (with three sets, in which the additional set is inherited from one or other of the parent species). The result of interbreeding involving triploid forms maintains the hybrid state.

⊖ *Edible Frog, France. These hybrid frogs are active during the day even in warm sunny weather.*

Edible Frog (cont'd.)

⤊ *The Pool Frog* (Rana lessonae) *is a European species, seen here in France.*

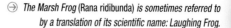

⤳ *The Marsh Frog* (Rana ridibunda) *is sometimes referred to by a translation of its scientific name: Laughing Frog.*

Forrer's Grass Frog

Common name	Forrer's Grass Frog
Scientific name	*Rana forreri*
Family	Ranidae
Size	2.56–4.49 in (65–114 mm).
Key features	Large and heavily built, with a pair of skin folds running down either side of the back. Brown or olive, with several large oval brown blotches on its back and sides, and a black line from the nostrils to the eyes. Its feet are fully webbed.
Habits	Diurnal and nocturnal. Terrestrial.
Breeding	In quiet pools and swamps.
Diet	Invertebrates.
Habitat	Ponds and marshes.
Distribution	Mexico to Costa Rica.
Status	Common.
Similar species	The combination of webbed feet and the skin folds down its back serve to identify this species.

This large frog is rarely seen far from water. It lives in shallow pools and marshes and typically sits in a few inches of water or on mud or rocks at its edge. If disturbed, it makes a single long leap into the water and dives to the bottom, where it hides among the mud, dead leaves, or other debris.

Males have a pair of vocal sacs, one on each side of the mouth, which they inflate when they are calling. They normally do this while floating on the surface of the water. They breed during the wet season, often in temporary pools or in small pools that swell after rainfall. The eggs are black

and white and are laid in clumps of about 1,000, attached to submerged plants or debris.

These frogs have been introduced into Baja California, where they live in a ranch pond surrounded by desert. They share their home with other introduced animals, including a mud turtle, freshwater shrimp, and various tropical fish. The motive for the introduction is not known but may have been to provide an extra food source.

⊕ *Forrer's Grass Frog, Baja California, Mexico.*

Hose's Frog

Common names	Hose's Frog, Poisonous Rock Frog
Scientific name	*Rana hosii*
Family	Ranidae
Size	1.77–3.94 in (45–100 mm). Males are smaller than females.
Key features	This frog has an elongated body and head with a pointed snout. The hind limbs are very long and the fingers and toes are also long and end in expanded toe pads. The head and back are bright green and the limbs are brown.
Habits	Active mainly at night. Terrestrial and semiarboreal.
Breeding	In streams.
Diet	Invertebrates.
Habitat	Alongside fast-flowing streams.
Distribution	West Malaysia, Sumatra, and Borneo.
Status	Common in suitable habitats.
Similar species	The bright green coloration and specialized habitat are distinctive.

Hose's Frog, sometimes called the Poisonous Rock Frog, is only found close to rivers and streams. It uses its long digits and sticky toe pads to cling to wet rocks at the water's edge and also climbs into trees and shrubs at night while foraging. During the day it often clings to vertical surfaces, especially rock faces at the side of or behind waterfalls. If disturbed, it jumps into the water and swims upstream for a short distance before climbing back out onto the rocks.

Males have a high-pitched chirping call that can be heard above the noise of the rushing water, and they call throughout the year. Females lay clumps of 500 to 2,000 white eggs in the water, where they lodge between rocks and debris. The newly hatched tadpoles are also white but gradually turn gray. When they metamorphose they are dark gray, and it takes several weeks for the distinctive green color to appear.

⊖ *Hose's Frog, Gombak River, Malaysia.*

Iberian Frog

Common name	Iberian Frog
Scientific name	*Rana iberica*
Family	Ranidae
Size	2.17–2.76 in (55–70 mm).
Key features	A small brown frog with a pair of folds down its back, spaced well apart. Its hind feet are fully webbed, with the webbing reaching the tips of its toes. Its back is brown, pale brown, or reddish brown and it sometimes has indistinct darker markings.
Habits	Active by day and night. Terrestrial.
Breeding	In streams or bogs.
Diet	Invertebrates.
Habitat	Near cool mountain streams, glacial pools, and boggy places.
Distribution	Portugal and NW and C Spain.
Status	Common in suitable habitats, but listed by the IUCN as Near Threatened as a result of significant population decline.
Similar species	The Common Frog *(Rana temporaria)* has webbing that comes only part of the way up its toes.

The Iberian Frog is a small brown frog from a specialized habitat. It lives in mountains and can occur at nearly 8,000 feet (2,400 m) above sea level, well above the tree line and usually close to moorland streams or pools, where it is usually the only frog present. At lower elevations its habitat is less extreme, and it can occur in lightly wooded areas and meadows, sometimes in company with Midwife Toads (family Discoglossidae) and other species. It tends to stay close to water, into which it leaps when disturbed.

Depending on the local conditions, it may start breeding in November, whereas in exposed montane

situations breeding is delayed until the following April. The females lay 100 to 450 eggs in small clumps, attached to stones on the bottom of the pool or stream or stuck to aquatic vegetation. It seems likely that tadpoles from cold environments overwinter and metamorphose in their second year.

The Italian Stream Frog *(Rana italica)* lives in similar habitats in Italy, and there is another frog, the Balkan Stream Frog *(R. graeca)* in the Balkan Peninsula. These frogs are clearly closely related. They probably arose from populations that were isolated from each other in mountain ranges as the ice cap receded and Europe became warmer.

⊕ *The Iberian Frog is found in northwestern parts of the Iberian Peninsula.*

345

Iberian Water Frog

Common names	Iberian Water Frog, Perez's Frog
Scientific name	*Rana perezi*
Family	Ranidae
Size	To 3.94 in (100 mm).
Key features	Slender and agile, with an acutely pointed snout. Its hind legs are long and fully webbed. There is a pair of raised folds of skin down its back, which can be lighter in color than the rest of the back. Overall it can be green, gray, or brown, with a pattern of fairly regular dark blotches on its body and limbs.
Habits	Active by day and night. Semiaquatic.
Breeding	In ponds and backwaters.
Diet	Invertebrates and small vertebrates.
Habitat	All kinds of running and still water.
Distribution	Southern France, Spain, and Portugal.
Status	Common.
Similar species	There are no other large water frogs in the region.

This species can occur in huge numbers in suitable habitats. It often congregates to bask in the sun around the edges of large lakes and reservoirs, rice fields, irrigation ditches, or along the banks of wide shallow rivers. It tolerates polluted and brackish water. It has a loud call, and choruses can start up at any time. If it is disturbed, it makes its way into deep water and dives to the bottom, where it disappears among vegetation or in the mud.

The breeding season lasts all spring and summer, and the Iberian Water Frog is very prolific. Females lay up to 10,000 eggs in a single season. The tadpoles can survive in small bodies of water, tolerating high temperatures and low oxygen levels, and they metamorphose in two to four months. In stagnant water that is likely to dry up they can accelerate their development and leave the water at a smaller size. Tadpoles resulting from eggs laid at the end of summer may overwinter and metamorphose the following spring.

⊙ *Iberian Water Frog, Andalucia, Spain.*

Northern Leopard Frog

Common names	Northern Leopard Frog, Leopard Frog
Scientific name	*Rana pipiens*
Family	Ranidae
Size	4.33 in (1.1 cm). Females are larger than males.
Key features	Essentially a heavily spotted frog with a pointed snout, long hind limbs, and fully webbed feet. It may be green, bronze, or brown in color with evenly spaced, rounded spots of dark brown, each edged with a thin white line. There is a pair of folds down each side of its back, and these are usually lighter in color than the rest of the frog.
Habits	Active by day and night. Semiaquatic.
Breeding	In ponds.
Diet	Invertebrates and small vertebrates.
Habitat	Pools and streams in forests and open areas, and bogs.
Distribution	North America, from Canada to central United States.
Status	Common in suitable habitats.
Similar species	The Southern Leopard Frog (*R. sphenocephala*) is similar but its spots lack the white edges.

Northern Leopard Frogs tolerate cold conditions and are among the first frogs to emerge and start breeding in the spring, often while there is still snow on the ground. Males have a rasping, snorelike call but they do not call in choruses, and their presence can therefore be overlooked. The eggs are laid in a round clump, containing several thousand eggs, in shallow ponds with plenty of vegetation.

Although it is a common and widespread species, populations in some parts of its range are declining. In northern California, which represents the southwestern edge of its range, several populations were started or increased in former times by the introduction of small groups—perhaps leftovers from biology classes—and so its range increased. Water diversions and irrigation schemes helped it spread farther.

In recent years, however, numbers have declined again, and the frogs have disappeared entirely from some places. The cause is thought to be a combination of habitat change—by grazing, for instance—and introduced predators such as the American Bullfrog (*Rana catesbeiana*) and various exotic fish. In other places, particularly parts of Canada, population declines are thought to be caused by the effects of acid rain, which makes ponds unsuitable for tadpoles.

The scientific name *pipiens* means "piping" and was given in error. The scientist who named the frog mistook the calls of the Spring Peeper *(Pseudacris crucifer)* for those of this species.

⊕ *The Northern Leopard Frog is found in a wide range of habitats, including permanent ponds, swamps, marshes, and slow-moving streams.*

Striped Stream Frog

Common names	Striped Stream Frog, Matang Frog
Scientific name	*Rana signata*
Family	Ranidae
Size	1.3–2.68 in (33–68 mm). Females are larger than males.
Key features	A small frog with a wide head and large eyes. Its fingers and toes have slightly expanded tips, and its hind feet are partially webbed. It is dark brown in color with cream markings in the form of a pair of stripes that run from the snout over each eye and continue to the groin. There are also other, smaller markings. The limbs are heavily marked with cream.
Habits	Mainly nocturnal and semiaquatic.
Breeding	In streams.
Diet	Invertebrates.
Habitat	Streams running through rain forests.
Distribution	Borneo.
Status	Locally common.
Similar species	The Spotted Stream Frog *(R. picturata)* is similar in shape and habits but its markings take the form of spots rather than stripes.

These pretty frogs live in colonies along the banks of streams running through primary rain forests below about 2,500 feet (760 m). Males perch on exposed roots and twigs that project out from the bank, and call most nights—their call is a drawn-out "waak." Although they usually call singly, an

occasional chorus will form, and this attracts females. There is no information on egg-laying, but related species lay small clumps of eggs on the bottom of small pools that form at the side of the main stream. The tadpoles live in these pools, which become filled with dead leaves and other forest debris. When they metamorphose, they apparently leave the stream and live on the forest floor, returning to the stream only when they reach breeding size.

The closely related Spotted Stream Frog *(Rana picturata)* occurs alongside the Striped Stream Frog in Borneo and is also found in Peninsula Malaysia and Sumatra. Where they occur together, their calls are sufficiently different to prevent hybridization.

⤓ *The Striped Stream Frog, seen here in Borneo.*

Southern Leopard Frog

Common name	Southern Leopard Frog
Scientific name	*Rana sphenocephala*
Family	Ranidae
Size	1.97–3.54 in (50–90 mm).
Key features	Similar in general outline to the Northern Leopard Frog *(R. pipiens)*, but the spots on the back of the Southern Leopard Frog lack the pale outline, and this species has a light area in the center of each eardrum that is lacking in the Northern Leopard Frog.
Habits	Active during the day and night. Semiaquatic.
Breeding	In still or slow-moving water.
Diet	Invertebrates.
Habitat	Almost any damp place, including ditches, bogs, pond and stream edges, and flooded fields and meadows.
Distribution	Southeastern United States.
Status	Very common.
Similar species	The Northern Leopard Frog *(R. pipiens)*.

Although it is not as widespread as its northern relative *Rana pipiens*, with which it is often confused), the Southern Leopard Frog is the most common frog in the states in which it occurs. It lives in any type of damp habitat, including large and small bodies of still water, ditches, swamps, and coastal

brackish pools. It typically rests near the edge of the water or on the bank, ready to leap into deep water if it is disturbed. Walking along the edge of such a pond or ditch will result in a succession of plops as numerous frogs take to the water one after the other. Once in the water the frog dives to the bottom and turns sharply under the cover of disturbed mud before surfacing unexpectedly in a different location. In the summer it wanders away from the breeding sites, living among damp vegetation, leaf litter, and under logs and rubbish.

It breeds during the winter and spring, and the male makes a rasping call, similar but not identical to that of the Northern Leopard Frog. Males often congregate to breed, forming calling choruses. The eggs are laid in spherical clumps of more than 1,000 in shallow water, attached to the stems of aquatic vegetation and submerged grasses and reeds. The tadpoles feed on algae and grow quickly, emerging from the water in late spring or summer.

← *As seen here, the Southern Leopard Frog's spots lack the pale outline present on those of its northern counterpart.*

Bronze Frog

Common names	Bronze Frog, Kerala Frog
Scientific name	*Rana temporalis*
Family	Ranidae
Size	To 1.97 in (50 mm).
Key features	Graceful, with a streamlined body, pointed snout, and long hind legs. There is a pair of distinctive skin folds running down the back. Brown or reddish brown on the back, with lighter flanks. It has a black "mask" marking under its eyes and indistinct dark markings on its limbs.
Habits	Mainly nocturnal and terrestrial.
Breeding	In streams.
Diet	Invertebrates.
Habitat	Small streams running through rain forests.
Distribution	Southwestern India; parts of Sri Lanka.
Status	Locally common, but listed by the IUCN as Near Threatened because of the probable shrinking of its relatively small distribution.
Similar species	Gravenhorst's Frog *(Rana gracilis)*, which can be differentiated easily by a white line along its flanks.

The Bronze Frog is primarily a forest species. It lives among rocks and pools along the small streams that drain hilly country. If disturbed, it is quick to dive into the water (usually a muddy backwater or pool). It also climbs into low vegetation at night. Males call from the water's edge, but the process of breeding is unknown. Tadpoles live between stones and dead leaves in backwaters and isolated pools along the streams.

This type of habitat is plentiful in untouched forests in Sri Lanka and the hilly parts of southern India, and provides a home for a variety of frogs. Some prefer fast-flowing stretches or waterfalls, while others prefer sluggish stretches where the water is held up behind rocks or fallen tree trunks.

Unfortunately, these habitats are disappearing because of the conversion of forested hillsides for growing tea, cardamom, and rubber. Timber extraction is also a problem. These activities result in the banks of the streams becoming opened out, eliminating shade. In addition, silt gets washed into the water, clogging the spaces between stones and making the water turbid. Insecticides, which often go hand in hand with agricultural development, kill the insects on which the frogs prey, and run-off also pollutes the water in which the tadpoles live.

↑ *A close relative, Gravenhorst's Frog* (Rana gracilis), *seen in Nilgara Fire Savanna, Sri Lanka. It is similar to the Bronze Frog but has a white line along its sides.*

← *Bronze Frog, Gampola, Sri Lanka.*

Common Frog

Common names	Common Frog, European Common Frog, Grass Frog
Scientific name	*Rana temporaria*
Family	Ranidae
Size	1.97–3.94 in (50–100 mm).
Key features	Highly variable. Brown, greenish, pinkish, yellowish, or tan in color, with dark "mask" markings behind its eyes. The back legs have dark bars across them. Adults have a rounded snout, but juveniles have an altogether more streamlined shape. Its skin is smooth except for a pair of raised fleshy ridges running down either side of its back.
Habits	Diurnal and nocturnal; terrestrial.
Breeding	In water in the spring, with large masses of spawn.
Diet	Invertebrates.
Habitat	Highly varied. Woods, hedges, bogs, fields, meadows, ditches, ponds, streams, and sluggish rivers.
Distribution	Central and N Europe, eastward across Siberia.
Status	The commonest species over much of its range.
Similar species	Similar to several other frogs in the region, especially the Agile Frog (*Rana dalmatina*).

This frog is the most abundant frog across much of Europe and central Asia. It is likely to be present wherever there is suitable habitat, but it is one of the least aquatic of its genus. In many places it returns to water only in early spring to breed, spending the rest of the year in damp meadows, hedgerows, woodland edges, and gardens. In drier regions, however, it often remains near permanent water throughout the year.

The Common Frog is very tolerant of cold and lives in harsh habitats up to 9,000 feet (2,740 m) in the Pyrenees and only slightly lower in the Alps. Here it breeds well above the tree line in isolated glacial ponds with little or no aquatic vegetation. Farther north it occurs in mountains and moorlands, and breeds in almost any body of water, including wheel ruts and cattle tanks. The Common Frog occurs well inside the Arctic Circle in Norway, Sweden, Finland, and Russia and is the most northerly occurring European frog. A very similar species, the Wood Frog *(Rana sylvatica)*, occurs inside the Arctic Circle in North America.

After breeding, the frogs usually leave the ponds and return to the summer feeding grounds, but some stay in the water. Males may even hibernate *(continued over)*

⊕ *The Common Frog occupies a variety of habitats across its wide range but always returns to water to breed.*

Common Frog (cont'd.)

in the mud at the bottom of the pond. When the ponds freeze over, the frogs breathe entirely through the skin— as their metabolism slows down they need much less oxygen, and the cold water is well oxygenated. Under extreme circumstances, though, when ponds freeze over for long periods, the water's oxygen may be depleted and frogs can suffocate.

The Common Frog is an explosive breeder, and large numbers migrate from the surrounding countryside in early spring to breeding ponds. Some travel several miles to get there, and in built-up areas hundreds are killed by traffic. In some years the frogs reach the ponds just before a cold spell and then they can be seen moving around under the ice. They wait in the ponds until the weather warms up again before spawning.

↑ *Common Frogs gather in ponds to breed in early spring. This spawning pair was seen in northern England.*

→ *A newly metamorphosed juvenile Common Frog, found in a garden at the same locality.*

Females produce large clumps of spawn, containing 700 to 4,500 eggs, in shallow water. Since there may be hundreds of spawning frogs in the same part of the pond, the sperm of a number of males may contribute to the fertilization of each clump, although most are fertilized by the mate of the female that lays them. The clumps float just under the surface and can cover several square yards. This strategy seems to have evolved in cold climates to help the eggs retain heat and develop more quickly.

Vaillant's Frog

Common names	Vaillant's Frog, Central American River Frog
Scientific name	*Rana vaillanti*
Family	Ranidae
Size	2.64–4.92 in (67–125 mm). Females are larger than males.
Key features	Large, with a pointed snout and a pair of skin folds down its back. The skin between the folds has a rough texture and is brown at the base, becoming green on the nape of the neck and the head. There are scattered indistinct dark markings on the flanks and limbs.
Habits	Active by day and night. Semiaquatic.
Breeding	In ponds.
Diet	Invertebrates and small vertebrates.
Habitat	Pools within rain forests.
Distribution	Central and S America, from Mexico to Ecuador.
Status	Common in suitable habitats.
Similar species	This species is one of about seven similar ranids from Central and South America, all of which used to go under the name *Rana palmipes*. Vaillant's Frog is the most common species, and its green head is a good means of identification.

Vaillant's Frog is the most common "pond" frog from Central and South America. It is typically seen floating just below the water's surface, surrounded by aquatic plants, with just the top of its head and its eyes showing. It lies in wait for prey to blunder past and quickly snaps up any flying insects, small fishes, and frogs that come within striking distance. It has also been known to eat small birds and mammals.

Males are territorial and call from the water's surface or the edge of the pond during the day or night, with a grunting call. Apart from attracting females, this enables them to keep themselves spaced out. Breeding probably takes place throughout the year, especially in wetter regions, and the eggs are laid in clumps. The tadpoles grow very large—up to 3.15 in (80 mm)—before metamorphosing.

Vaillant's Frogs, together with seven other closely related and similar species, are the only ranids in Central and South America—a part of the world in which other species, notably members of the Leptodactylidae, have evolved to fill their niche.

⊕ *Vaillant's Frog, Selva Verde, Costa Rica.*

Other *Rana* Species

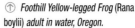

⬆ *Foothill Yellow-legged Frog* (Rana boylii) *adult in water, Oregon.*

⬅ *The Pig Frog* (Rana grylio) *is endemic to southern and southeastern coastal regions of the United States.*

➡ *This slender frog is the Pickerel Frog* (Rana palustris) *from North America.*

Other *Rana* Species

The Wood Frog (Rana sylvatica) *is the North American counterpart of the European Common Frog* (R. temporaria).

A Carpenter Frog (Rana virgatipes), *from North America, feeding. This frog preys on insects and small vertebrates.*

Other *Rana* Species

↑ *A mating pair of Moor Frogs (Rana arvalis) from Europe. During the breeding season male Moor Frogs take on light blue coloration.*

→ *Seen here leaping out of the water is a Black-spotted Frog (Rana nigromaculata). It is found over much of East Asia, including Japan, Korea, China, and parts of Russia.*

Short-headed Burrowing Frog

Common names	Short-headed Burrowing Frog, Banded Sand Frog
Scientific name	Sphaerotheca breviceps
Family	Ranidae
Size	To 1.97 in (50 mm).
Key features	Short and stout, with a wide head and short hind limbs. The back feet have a spade-shaped tubercle, used in burrowing. Its back is mainly brown or olive, with extensive ocher-colored markings. A thin dark line runs down the center of its back.
Habits	Nocturnal and terrestrial.
Breeding	At the edges of ponds.
Diet	Small vertebrates.
Habitat	Desert edges, foothills, and lightly wooded places.
Distribution	Asia (Bangladesh, Myanmar, Pakistan, India, and Sri Lanka).
Status	Common in suitable habitats.
Similar species	There are four other species in the genus, all similar, but the others have limited ranges. The large ocher patches on the back distinguish this species from the others.

This is one of the few ranid frogs that live in dry habitats, and its body shape reflects that ability. Rounded shapes have a smaller surface area to weight ratio, so stout frogs do not lose moisture through their skin as quickly as other frogs. Most burrowing frogs are rotund, therefore, including the African pixie frogs (*Tomopterna* species). The Short-headed Burrowing Frog bears a close resemblance to these frogs and was once placed in the same genus.

In common with other burrowing frogs, the Short-headed Burrowing Frog has a sharp-edged projection on the heel of its feet, which it uses to shuffle backward into the sandy soil where it lives. In this way, it can avoid the heat of the day and emerge to forage at night. In addition, it can remain underground for extended periods during droughts. On wet and humid nights large numbers emerge to forage on the ground for insects, millipedes, and other invertebrates.

It breeds at the beginning of monsoon rains, when males gather at the edges of extensive shallow ponds, formed or enlarged as a result of flooding. The resultant choruses are loud and can be heard hundreds of yards away, mingled with the calls of several other species of frogs that breed at the same time.

The eggs are large and laid in small clumps that stick to the stalks of submerged grasses and other plants. The tadpoles grow quickly in the warm water and reach a length of nearly 1.5 inches (38 mm) before metamorphosing and dispersing.

⊙ *The Sri Lanka Burrowing Frog* (Sphaerotheca rolandae), *seen here at Nilgara Fire Savanna, Sri Lanka, is a close relative of the Short-headed Burrowing Frog.*

⊙ *Short-headed, or Banded Sand Frog, photographed at Puttulam, Sri Lanka*

Green-spotted Semaphore Frog

Common name	Green-spotted Semaphore Frog
Scientific name	*Staurois tuberilinguis*
Family	Ranidae
Size	0.91–1.42 in (23–36 mm). Females are larger than males.
Key features	A slender ranid with long legs, webbed hind feet, and large pads at the tips of its digits. Its back is granular and is greenish brown with indistinct markings. It is light green or bluish green on the flanks and underside. Males are less colorful than females.
Habits	Nocturnal and semiaquatic.
Breeding	In fast-flowing rivers and streams.
Diet	Invertebrates.
Habitat	Alongside rivers and streams that run through forests.
Distribution	Borneo (Sabah and Sarawak).
Status	Uncommon.
Similar species	The Rock Skipper *(S. latopalmatus)* is darker, and the Black-spotted Semaphore Frog *(S. natator)* is green with black spots. Hose's Frog *(Rana hosii)* is larger and bright green. Otherwise, there are no similar species in Borneo.

The Green-spotted Semaphore Frog lives near highland streams and rivers. Its typical resting places are rocks surrounded by torrents of small plants, especially ferns, that grow on such rocks. Groups of frogs of different sizes can sometimes be seen clinging to a single plant stem. The fast-flowing, clear water is essential to them, and they are never found in other types of habitat. Their tadpoles are unknown, but those of related species live on the bottom of quiet backwaters among dead leaves that have collected there.

This frog breeds in the rivers and streams in which it lives. Males call with sharp, high-pitched squeaks but they have a more important means of communication, which is unique to this genus. The webbing on their back feet is bright blue, and the frogs communicate visually with each other by slowly extending the hind legs one at a time and spreading their toes, so that the webbing shows up like a flag. This behavior is thought to have evolved because in the cascades and waterfalls near where they live, audible communication is difficult.

⊙ *The Green-spotted Semaphore Frog from Borneo has a characteristic pointed snout, long legs, and webbed hind feet.*

Clicking Stream Frog

Common names	Clicking Stream Frog, Gray's Stream Frog
Scientific name	*Strongylopus grayii*
Family	Ranidae
Size	1.38–2.52 in (35–64 mm).
Key features	A pointed head and snout and very long toes, which are not fully webbed. Variable in color but usually gray or brown with a series of regular darker spots. There is often a pale stripe down its back, which may be narrow or wide, and white, yellow, or orange in color.
Habits	Active by day and night. Semiaquatic.
Breeding	Eggs laid above the water, on plants or mud.
Diet	Small vertebrates.
Habitat	Streams and ponds, including brackish pools in the spray zone.
Distribution	Southern Africa.
Status	Common.
Similar species	All *Strongylopus* species have long toes. This species is the most common; otherwise identification is best achieved by locality.

The Clicking Stream Frog is found almost everywhere within the southern part of South Africa, in streams but also in natural and artificial ponds (including stagnant ones), flooded pits, and brackish pools within dune systems. It is very tolerant and very adaptable. It is polymorphic, showing a great deal of variation in its markings, even within a single colony. This is often a strategy to prevent predators from forming a "prey image." In addition, its skin contains substances called bradykinins, which cause illness in small mammalian predators.

Males start calling in the winter, just before the start of the rains, and their call is a short click

or tap, repeated two or three times a second. Large choruses combine to produce a crackling sound.

The 250 to 350 eggs are laid singly or in small clusters, just above the water level in damp places, under rocks, or beneath leaves lying on the ground. If the weather turns dry, the eggs can remain in this state for up to 50 days. As soon as rain causes the water level to rise again and cover the

eggs, they hatch. After hatching, the tadpoles continue to develop in the usual way.

⊕ *Clicking Stream Frog, Clanwilliam, South Africa.*

Cape Sand Frog

Common names	Cape Sand Frog, Cape Pixie Frog, Delalande's Sand Frog
Scientific name	*Tomopterna delalandii*
Family	Ranidae
Size	To 1.97 in (50 mm).
Key features	Short and stout, with a wide head and short but powerful limbs. The back feet have a hardened flange, used in burrowing. Gray, with lighter and darker patches. There is often a thin pale line down the center of its back.
Habits	Nocturnal and terrestrial.
Breeding	In temporary and permanent ponds.
Diet	Small vertebrates.
Habitat	Flat, sandy places.
Distribution	South Africa.
Status	Common in suitable habitats.
Similar species	There are eight other *Tomopterna* species, all varying slightly in coloration. The Cape Sand Frog is the only one in its area.

Sand frogs are small and stout, with spadelike adaptations on the hind feet with which they burrow into the sand or soil. The Cape Sand Frog lives along the southwest coast of South Africa and into Namaqualand, an area that includes some of the driest areas in the region. It lives around permanent ponds, often those that have been created for cattle or drinking water, but also survives in areas that flood temporarily after heavy rains. A favorite location for this species is the sandy, dried-out riverbeds, in which it burrows down to a level where some moisture is retained even in the drier parts of the year.

With the coming of rain, which varies from place to place, it emerges from the ground. Males call from the shallow edges of ponds, typically less than 3 feet (1 m) from the bank. Females lay up to 2,500 eggs in a slimy egg mass that is said to have an unpleasant odor. The tadpoles grow and develop quickly so that they can metamorphose before the water dries up.

This species has met with mixed success as a result of agricultural development in the region. On the one hand, irrigation, the damming of rivers, and artificial water holes that are kept topped up for cattle have provided a reliable source of breeding sites. On the other hand, the changes in land usage have led to the drainage of some areas and urban development, which has reduced the frog's available habitat.

⊖ *The stout little Cape Sand Frog, photographed at Kamieskroon, Namaqualand, South Africa.*

Squeakers

Common name	Squeakers
Scientific name	*Arthroleptis* species
Family	Arthroleptidae
Size	1.34 in (34 mm).
Key features	Small frogs with long hind limbs and slightly expanded toe pads. Males have elongated third fingers. The back is brown with indistinct markings in a darker shade.
Habits	Nocturnal and terrestrial.
Breeding	Direct development.
Diet	Small invertebrates.
Habitat	Evergreen montane forests.
Distribution	Central and E Africa.
Status	Probably common in suitable habitat but easily overlooked.
Similar species	All *Arthroleptis* species are similar.

The squeakers, genus *Arthroleptis,* are sometimes placed in the Ranidae, but it is more accurate to deal with them as a family of their own, the Arthroleptidae. There are about 35 species altogether, although some of them are disputed. These are not well-known frogs, being inconspicuous and living as they do in some of the least explored parts of Africa.

They are leaf-litter species, restricted to forested slopes in mountainous regions and the few remaining lowland forests. The natural history of many species is still unknown, but they are all believed to

have similar lifestyles. Males call during the night and day from hidden places under living and dead vegetation. The call is a short whistle or squeak, hence the collective common name, and several males sometimes form a chorus. The eggs are laid in hollows under the leaf litter or in burrows in the soil, in secluded places. The eggs are creamy white and laid in groups of up to 80. The young develop entirely within the egg capsule and there is no free-living tadpole.

⊕ *A Common Squeaker* (Arthroleptis stenodactylus) *rests on leaf litter on the forest floor in the Shimba Hills, Kenya.*

Marbled Pig-snouted Frog

Common names	Marbled Pig-snouted Frog, Marbled Snout-burrower
Scientific name	Hemisus marmoratus
Family	Hemisotidae
Size	1.38–2.17 in (35–55 mm). Females are much larger than males.
Key features	This frog has a globular body and a small pointed head. Its eyes are tiny, and there is a fold of skin between them. Its snout is pointed and hardened, and its legs are muscular. Usually gray in color with extensive darker marbling and some random lighter spots.
Habits	Burrowing and nocturnal.
Breeding	Underground, in chambers.
Diet	Small vertebrates, mainly termites.
Habitat	Grasslands and arid places.
Distribution	Sub-Saharan Africa.
Status	Numerous but rarely seen.
Similar species	All the pig-snouted frogs, of which there are eight species, have similar body shapes and habitats. Colors and markings differentiate the species. Rain frogs (in the genus Breviceps) have similar body shapes but have blunt snouts.

The eight species of pig-snouted frogs all belong to the genus *Hemisus* and they are so different from other frogs that they are placed in a family of their own, the Hemisotidae. They are all burrowing species and unusual in that they burrow nose-first. Nearly all the other burrowing frogs, of which there are many, burrow back-first, using "spades" on the hind feet to move down through the soil. Pig-snouted frogs use their pointed cartilaginous snout to drive through the sandy soil, and their back legs to push them along. Using this method, they can disappear from the surface twice as quickly as backward burrowers.

They also have an unusual breeding system. Males call from hidden places at the edge of muddy pools. Females approach the male, and they go into amplexus. The larger female then begins to burrow down into the mud, dragging the male with her. When they reach a suitable place, often under a log or rock, the female lays about 150 to 200 eggs in a small chamber. Although the nest is created above the waterline, subsequent rains raise the water level until it floods the nest, causing the eggs to hatch and releasing the tadpoles into the pool. In the event of no rain falling, the eggs hatch and the tadpoles develop in the moist surroundings of the nest.

→ *The mottled appearance of the Marbled Pig-snouted Frog, seen here in South Africa, provides excellent camouflage against its grassy habitat.*

Forasini's Spiny Reed Frog

Common names	Forasini's Spiny Reed Frog, Common Bird-dropping Frog
Scientific name	*Afrixalus forasini*
Family	Hyperoliidae
Size	1.5–1.57 in (38–40 mm).
Key features	A small frog with small black spines covering its back. Its back is brown and white, with a dark brown stripe starting between the eyes and continuing down the center of the back. Either side of this are wide white bands; these in turn are bordered by wide brown bands. When seen from above it resembles a bird dropping, hence the alternative common name for the frog.
Habits	Semiarboreal and nocturnal.
Breeding	On leaves overhanging water.
Diet	Small invertebrates and frogs' eggs.
Habitat	Reedy ponds.
Distribution	Southern and E Africa.
Status	Numerous in suitable places.
Similar species	Several other spiny reed frogs occur in the region, but the bold dorsal stripes of Forasini's are distinctive.

Spiny reed frogs belonging to the genus *Afrixalus* are closely related to the *Hyperolius* reed frogs but differ in having small spines on their back. Fornasini's Spiny Reed Frogs inhabit thick reed beds growing in deep ponds, and live most of their life among the dense vegetation. They are rarely seen, but their calls are distinctive.

Males call from vegetation overhanging the water, making a series of clacking sounds following a short, soft buzz. Neighboring males call in response to each other, and the chorus builds up to a crescendo and can be heard over long distances.

The female lays her eggs attached to leaves, usually about 3 feet (1 m) above the surface of the water. She starts to lay at the tip of the reed and rolls

the edges over the eggs as she goes, sticking them in place with the jelly. As they hatch, the elongated tadpoles slide down the leaf and into the water.

This species has the unusual habit—perhaps unique among frogs—of eating the eggs of another species. If it finds a foam nest of the African Foam-nesting Tree Frog *(Chiromantis xerampelina)* it thrusts its head into the foam mass and engulfs large mouthfuls of the eggs.

⊙ *Protected by its resemblance to bird feces, the closely related Pygmy Bird-dropping Frog* (Afrixalus pygmaeus) *sits on a leaf in Kenya in full view and during daylight.*

⊙ *A pair of Forasini's Spiny Reed Frogs at rest in Kenya, mimicking bird droppings.*

Betsileo Reed Frog

Common name	Betsileo Reed Frog
Scientific name	*Heterixalus betsileo*
Family	Hyperoliidae
Size	0.71–1.14 in (18–29 mm).
Key features	A small reed frog with webbed hands and feet and expanded pads at the tips of its fingers and toes. Its back is greenish or dirty yellow, with yellow bands running down its flanks. The hidden surfaces of its hands, feet, and limbs are orange.
Habits	Arboreal and mainly nocturnal.
Breeding	In small pools.
Diet	Small vertebrates.
Habitat	Open grasslands and forest clearings.
Distribution	Madagascar.
Status	Common.
Similar species	Other Madagascan frogs can be similar, but the yellow stripes down the side help identify this species.

The reed frogs are the African and Madagascan counterparts to the tree frogs in the family Hylidae that are found in many other parts of the world. They have sticky pads at the ends of their digits, which they use to climb about in vegetation, and long hind limbs that they use for jumping. Many of them have colorful markings.

The Betsileo Reed Frog is very common in suitable habitats, which include open grassy places such as roadsides, overgrown plots of agricultural land, and open spaces surrounded by forests. They are not found in rain forests, however, and are one of the few Madagascan species that may have benefited from the large-scale deforestation that has taken place over the last century. Females often sit on the leaves of low shrubs during the day, exposed to sunlight.

They breed in flooded fields, rice paddies, and small pools, often in stagnant water. The tadpoles develop quickly in the warm water and metamorphose in a few weeks. The young frogs can reach adult breeding size within four months, which may be the shortest time in which any frog species can mature.

⊖ *The Betsileo Reed Frog, seen here at Andasibe, Madagascar, has well-developed pads and extensive webbing to its hands and feet.*

Madagascan Reed Frog

Common name	Madagascan Reed Frog
Scientific name	Heterixalus madagascariensis
Family	Hyperoliidae
Size	To 1.57 in (40 mm), although usually smaller.
Key features	A large reed frog with webbed hands and feet and expanded pads at the tips of its fingers and toes. Highly variable in color, its back may be white, yellow, or blue. Some have fine speckling overlying the main color. The undersides of its feet and the hidden surfaces of its limbs are orange.
Habits	Arboreal and mainly nocturnal.
Breeding	In small pools.
Diet	Small vertebrates.
Habitat	Dunes, grasslands, and forest clearings.
Distribution	Eastern Madagascar.
Status	Very common.
Similar species	The Spotted Reed Frog (Heterixalus punctatus) is similar but has distinct black spots on its back and is smaller.

This is the predominant species of reed frog occurring along the east coast of Madagascar. It often lives in close proximity to villages and farms. It is not always obvious, however, especially during the day, when it hides near pools and disappears into the water if disturbed. In the evening it starts to appear on the leaves of shrubs and small trees around

⊕ *The black spots on its back identify this Madagascan reed frog as* Heterixalus punctatus.

the edges of pools, and the males begin to call. They have a quiet, chirping call, repeated rapidly—up to 10 times per second. They appear to call throughout the year, and breeding probably takes place continuously. The tadpoles and young frogs grow rapidly and can reach breeding size within six months of the eggs being laid.

The Madagascan Reed Frog is highly variable, and there is some debate as to whether it consists of more

⬆ *The Madagascan Reed Frog, photographed at Andasibe, Madagascar, is restricted to the eastern part of the island.*

than one species. Even within the same population individuals may be blue, white (especially in the daytime), or yellow. The existence of populations with different calls also points to the possibility that new species are being "hidden" within a single name.

Argus Reed Frog

Common name	Argus Reed Frog
Scientific name	*Hyperolius argus*
Family	Hyperoliidae
Size	To 1.34 in (34 mm).
Key features	A small reed frog with males and females of different colors. The male is light green or gray with small black spots on his back, whereas the female is brown with a horseshoe-shaped cream mark that runs around the top of the snout from eye to eye.
Habits	Arboreal and mainly nocturnal.
Breeding	In shallow pools.
Diet	Small vertebrates.
Habitat	Around the edges of ponds, especially where there are water lilies.
Distribution	Southern Africa, from Mozambique to NE South Africa.
Status	Common.
Similar species	The female is unmistakable, but the male is similar to several other species, such as the Water Lily Reed Frog *(Hyperolius pusillus)* which, however, is much smaller.

Male and female Argus Reed Frogs differ so widely that anyone could be forgiven for thinking they are different species. Such marked sexual dimorphism is unusual among frogs, and the reasons for it are unclear. Juveniles are green, like the adult males, and females gain their adult colors as they mature.

These frogs live in large numbers in and around small pools formed in depressions in flooded pans. They are strongly associated with water lilies, and males call from the floating leaves. The eggs are

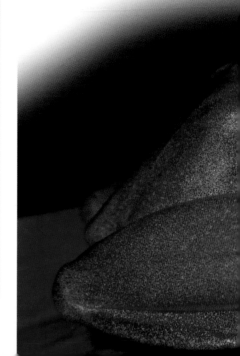

tiny—only 0.04 inches (1 mm) in diameter—and they are laid in small clusters of about 200 that stick firmly to submerged leaves, often from overhanging vegetation.

Hyperolius species are the mainland counterparts of the Madagascan *Heterixalus*, which are also known as reed frogs. The most notable difference, however, is in the shape of their pupils, which are vertically elliptical in the Madagascan genus but horizontal in the African species.

⤓ *The horseshoe-shaped markings of the female Argus Reed Frog make it easily distinguishable from the male.*

Marbled Reed Frog

Common name	Marbled Reed Frog
Scientific name	*Hyperolius marmoratus* complex
Family	Hyperoliidae
Size	To 1.69 in (43 mm).
Key features	A very difficult frog to describe because it can occur in up to 10 distinct pattern forms. These include spotted, striped, and plain forms. Juveniles are also variable and may change when they mature or they may remain the same. Scientists are undecided as to whether this "species" in fact represents a number of closely related species.
Habits	Arboreal and nocturnal.
Breeding	Small clumps of eggs are attached to submerged vegetation.
Diet	Small vertebrates.
Habitat	Along streams and rivers and in small temporary or permanent pools. Also in gardens and the grounds of hotels, etc.
Distribution	Most of Sub-Saharan Africa, where there is suitable habitat.
Status	Very common.
Similar species	Many of the color forms bear similarities to other species of reed frogs. Positive identification in areas where more than one species occurs is often difficult.

The Marbled Reed Frog appears to be a polymorphic species. In other words, in occurs in a wide range of colors and patterns. The most common types include a striped form, which has five cream bands and four dark brown ones, all of roughly equal width, and a mottled form, which has a black or dark brown back sprinkled with many small light spots. Juveniles are often pale brown or beige with small scattered flecks, and some retain this pattern into maturity, whereas others change.

The frequency of the various types varies from place to place, and the mottled form described above is most common in (but not unique to) the Cape region of South Africa. In other localities different forms predominate. This creates a problem for scientists, who have to decide whether or not some of the color forms are separate species. In the case of some other frogs, for example, the American Gray Tree Frogs (*Hyla chrysoscelis* and *H. versicolor),* these studies have been helped by analyzing the males' calls—different calls indicate different species. In the Marbled Reed Frog, however, the call is a short "wheep" that does not provide enough material for analysis. A number of males calling together produce a sound like a squeaky wheelbarrow.

The eggs of this (or these) species are laid in small clusters of about 20, attached to submerged plants. The tadpoles metamorphose in 60 to 100 days, and the young grow quickly, maturing in less than a year. Females spawn repeatedly, laying eggs every two weeks of so when conditions are suitable.

⬆ One of the many different color forms of Marbled Reed Frog; this one is from South Africa. (More forms are shown on the following pages.)

Marbled Reed Frog (cont'd.)

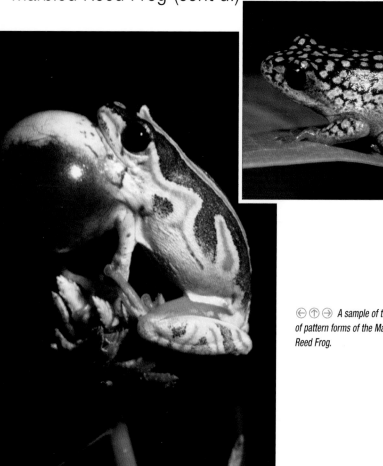

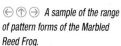

⬅ ⬆ ➡ *A sample of the range of pattern forms of the Marbled Reed Frog.*

Spotted Running Frog

Common name	Spotted Running Frog
Scientific name	*Kassina maculata*
Family	Hyperoliidae
Size	To 2.68 in (68 mm).
Key features	A heavily built tree frog with large, bulging eyes. Its hind feet are partially webbed, and all its digits have expanded toe pads. It is grayish brown with large black spots, each bordered by a thin white line. The back legs have red bars alternating with black ones on their hidden surfaces.
Habits	Arboreal and nocturnal.
Breeding	In pools.
Diet	Invertebrates and small vertebrates.
Habitat	Around the edges of ponds.
Distribution	East and southern Africa, from Kenya to NE South Africa.
Status	Common but not easily observed.
Similar species	The spotted body and red leg markings easily identify this species.

This large frog is the only member of the genus *Kassina* that climbs, and it used to be in a separate genus, *Hylambates*. It breeds in deep temporary pools and hides in leaf axils during the day. The male calls from the edge of the water or from emergent vegetation, and the eggs are laid in small groups attached to submerged plants.

This frog produces toxins in glands in its skin, which have been well studied. They contain at least three types of peptides: one that stimulates the large intestine; another group, known as tachykinins, that lower blood pressure and increase the heart rate; and a third type that stimulates the gallbladder and pancreas. The combined effect of these substances is to cause violent illness in any animal that attempts to swallow the frog. Their purpose is to make the predator drop the frog before it has killed it and, hopefully, resist the temptation to tackle it another time.

The red patches on its legs may serve to warn predators that the frog is toxic and tastes bad. Despite these defenses, the frog is widely eaten by at least one species of egret and by the Bird Snake (*Thelotornis kirtlandii*).

→ *Red markings can be glimpsed on this Spotted Running Frog's hind legs.*

Senegal Running Frog

Common names	Senegal Running Frog, Bubbling Kassina
Scientific name	*Kassina senegalensis*
Family	Hyperoliidae
Size	To 1.93 in (49 mm).
Key features	This species has an elongated body and bulging eyes. It is beige or yellowish brown (sometimes gray) in color with a series of well-defined black or dark brown lines running down its back. These lines, one down the center and one to each side, are often pale-edged, and there are spots of a similar color on the sides and limbs.
Habits	Nocturnal and terrestrial.
Breeding	Eggs are laid in shallow water.
Diet	Small vertebrates.
Habitat	Flat grasslands, including arid regions.
Distribution	Most of Sub-Saharan Africa, where there is suitable habitat.
Status	Common.
Similar species	Weale's Running Frog *(Semnodactylus wealii)* has pale centers to the stripes on its body.

This species is rarely seen except when it is breeding. At other times of the year it remains hidden underground, and has been found in the burrows of a large lizard, *Cordylus giganteus*, and in termite mounds. Like many savanna species, it is galvanized into activity by heavy rains, when thousands of Senegal Running Frogs may be active in a small area, and their calling fills the air, along with that of several other species that breed opportunistically in response to rain.

This species is sometimes known as the Bubbling Kassina because it has a strange but attractive call that sounds like someone blowing across the top of a bottle—"whooop, whooop"—and, when many males are calling together, the songs combine to produce a melodious bubbling sound.

The male calls away from water and attracts a female. Once she has approached, they go into amplexus, and the female carries the male to the breeding site, which is the shallow edge of a flooded pan. Each female lays from 250 to 400 eggs. She scatters them singly or in small batches, diving to the bottom of the water and attaching them to a piece of underwater plant or debris by pressing her vent against it while the eggs are expelled. The tadpoles metamorphose in 60 to 90 days.

⊖ *The diminutive Senegal Running Frog is widely distributed in the savanna regions of tropical Africa.*

Natal Bush Frog

Common name	Natal Bush Frog
Scientific name	*Leptopelis natalensis*
Family	Hyperoliidae
Size	To 2.56 in (65 mm).
Key features	A chunky tree frog that typically sits with an upright posture. Its eyes are large, and the irises may be reddish or golden. The frog's color and pattern are variable—it may be plain green, plain brown, or bronze with bright green blotches, some of which may have narrow black edges.
Habits	Nocturnal and arboreal.
Breeding	On land near water.
Diet	Small vertebrates.
Habitat	Coastal forests.
Distribution	South Africa, in the province of Natal.
Status	Uncommon.
Similar species	Variation makes this species difficult to identify, but it is the most southerly occurring of the bush frogs. Other species occur in neighboring countries and into Central and West Africa.

The Natal Bush Frog is a semiarboreal species that hides itself in trees and bushes or among forest debris during the day. The mottled form of this frog is stunningly beautiful.

Related species, such as the Long-toed Tree Frog *(Leptopelis stenodactylus)*, live in highlands where trees are sparse. They live in burrows on the ground and hunt among tussock grass, and they lack the expanded toe disks found in the climbing species.

The Natal Bush Frog lays its eggs in small depressions in the ground, in mud or leaf litter. The eggs take two weeks to hatch, but hatching may be delayed if the weather is dry.

When the tadpoles eventually hatch, they are elongated and have long whiplike tails that help them wriggle across the ground and into the water. The tail also enables the tadpole to flip itself forward. Its instinct to make its way to water is so strong that it can work its way up the side of a plastic container. It takes about six weeks to complete its development and can survive dry spells by absorbing water through a network of capillaries on its underside.

⊖ *This Natal Bush Frog was found in forest in South Africa at nighttime.*

Other Hyperoliids

⊕ The Red-spotted Reed Frog (Hyperolius rubrovermiculatus) *is known only from the Shimba Hills, south of Mombasa, Kenya. Its preferred habitat is forest and savanna, and it breeds in temporary pools and marshes.*

⊙ Boettger's Reed Frog (Heterixalus boettgeri), *Fort Dauphin, Madagascar. This species lives in and around forests as well as among crops and close to human settlements. It breeds in still water.*

Other Hyperoliids

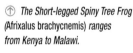

⤴ *The Short-legged Spiny Tree Frog (Afrixalus brachycnemis) ranges from Kenya to Malawi.*

↪ *Opposite: Aptly named, the Big-eyed Tree Frog (Leptopelis vermiculatus) is from the forests of Tanzania.*

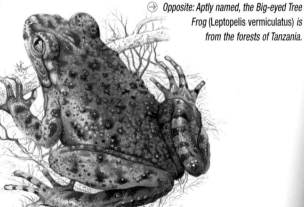

↪ *The Tinker Reed Frog (Hyperolius tuberilinguis) is found in the lowlands of eastern and southern Africa.*

African Foam-nesting Tree Frog

Common names	African Foam-nesting Tree Frog, Gray Tree Frog, Gray Foam-nest Tree Frog
Scientific name	*Chiromantis xerampelina*
Family	Rhacophoridae
Size	2.76–3.35 in (70–85 mm). Females are larger than males.
Key features	A stocky tree frog with large eyes and horizontally elliptical pupils. Its hands and feet are webbed, the toes have large adhesive pads, and it has opposable toes, allowing it to grip thin twigs. Its back has a rough texture and is usually gray but can be almost white or brown with darker markings, even in the same animal.
Habits	Arboreal and active at night, though resting in exposed positions in the day.
Breeding	Lays its eggs in foam nests.
Diet	Invertebrates.
Habitat	Wooded grasslands, including seasonally dry areas.
Distribution	Southern and East Africa, and an apparently isolated population in Angola.
Status	Common.
Similar species	There are three other species of *Chiromantis* in Africa, but none of them occurs alongside this species.

This species is an expert at surviving the hot, dry conditions of the African grasslands and has several tricks to keep itself from drying out. Like the Painted-belly Leaf Frog *(Phyllomedusa sauvagii)*, the African Foam-nesting Tree Frog sits in fully exposed positions during the day, seemingly oblivious to the heat and drying effect of the African sun. By tucking its limbs under its body it reduces the amount of skin exposed to the dry air. In addition, it secretes fluid under its outer layer of skin during the dry season, forming a waterproof cocoon around itself. Finally, it gets rid of its nitrogenous waste in the form of uric acid, a whitish paste that requires very little water to carry it out of the body. Reptiles typically produce uric acid, but amphibians normally produce ammonia or urea, both of which require large volumes of water to dilute them.

Males call from a branch or a rock hanging over a pool. Other males are soon attracted, until there is a group of up to eight by the time the female arrives. One of the males grips the female in amplexus, and she secretes a substance that she whips into a foam *(continued over)*

⊙ *In typical pose, an African Foam-nesting Tree Frog sits fully exposed to the fierce African sun.*

⊖ *Another, similar, foam-nesting tree frog,* Chiromantis petersi, *lives in Kenya and Tanzania.*

African Foam-nesting Tree Frog (cont'd.)

by paddling with her hind legs. Then she lays her eggs into this mass while the male fertilizes them. Often, however, one or more of the other males also gets in on the act, clasping the amplectant pair and adding its sperm to that of the primary male. The mass of eggs and the subsequent offspring therefore have more than one male parent.

The female may run out of fluid before the nest is complete, in which case she climbs down to the water and absorbs some more through the thin skin on her underside. She may make three or four trips to the water altogether and may mate with the same male or with different males each time she returns.

A nest contains between 500 and 1,200 eggs, and the female sometimes returns to the nest the following night to add more foam, but no more eggs. The foam on the outside of the nest dries to a hard crust, like a meringue, and the developing tadpoles rely on the foam in the center for their moisture and oxygen. After three to five days the bottom of the nest breaks down, probably as a result of enzymes produced by the developing tadpoles, and also because of the disturbance caused by their movements. The whole mass then drops into the water below.

→ *Large amounts of foam are whipped up around the eggs. The foam prevents the tadpoles from the drying effects of the sun, and the next rains wash the tadpoles into the water below. This picture was taken at night in savanna in South Africa.*

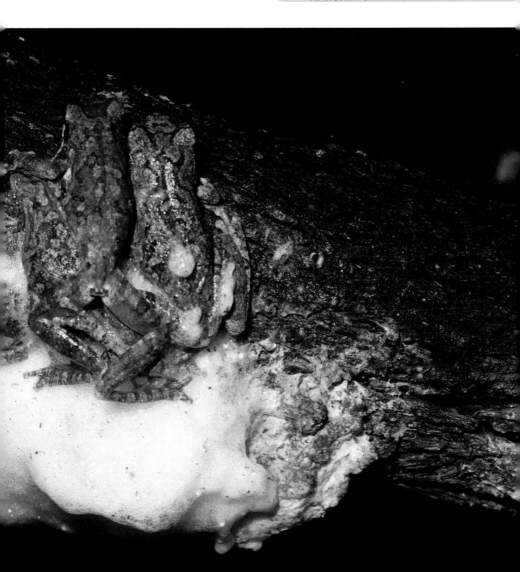

Cinnamon Frog

Common name	Cinnamon Frog
Scientific name	*Nyctixalus pictus*
Family	Rhacophoridae
Size	1.18–1.34 in (30–34 mm).
Key features	A small frog with a triangular head and pointed snout. The tips of its fingers and toes are expanded into disks, for climbing, and the toes (but not the fingers) are partially webbed. Cinnamon brown or russet in color, sprinkled with small white spots. There is also a row of white spots from the snout to each eye.
Habits	Nocturnal and arboreal.
Breeding	In holes in trees or logs.
Diet	Small vertebrates.
Habitat	Rain forests.
Distribution	Malaysia, Sumatra, and Borneo.
Status	Rare and listed by the IUCN as Near Threatened because of a decline in the extent and quality of its habitat.
Similar species	There are no similar species in the region. The coloration is unique.

The habits of this pretty tree frog are poorly known. It belongs to a genus of four species—one of the other species comes from China, one from the Philippines, and one from Java. The Chinese and Philippines species are covered in short spines, and all have the same distinctive rich brown coloration.

The Cinnamon Frog is rarely seen because it lives in dense forests and remains hidden in the canopy. It sometimes moves down to lower levels, however, and can occasionally be found resting on the leaves of shrubs and small trees, possibly as a prelude to breeding.

It breeds in the small pools of water that collect in tree holes or in cavities in logs, or in the pools that form between the buttresses of large rain forest trees. Tadpoles have also been found in the hollow husks of large rain forest fruits.

Several males gather around suitable egg-laying sites and call to attract females. Details of egg-laying and clutch size are lacking. The tadpoles develop in these small transient bodies of water, where they are largely free from predators and from competition.

⊙ *This newly metamorphosed juvenile Cinnamon Frog is from the Danum Valley, Sabah, Borneo.*

Bubble-nest Frog

Common name	Bubble-nest Frog (no specific common name)
Scientific name	*Philautus cuspis*
Family	Rhacophoridae
Size	To about 1.5 in (38 mm).
Key features	A small stocky frog with adhesive toe pads. It has a pointed snout and large eyes. Its back is brown with a faint hourglass marking, and it has a black line running from its snout over each eye and onto the shoulder.
Habits	Nocturnal and arboreal.
Breeding	Eggs laid on land.
Diet	Small invertebrates.
Habitat	Rain forests.
Distribution	Sri Lanka.
Status	Uncommon and listed by the IUCN as Endangered because of a decline in the extent and quality of its very restricted and fragmented habitat.
Similar species	Identifying *Philautus* species can be difficult, but this one's sharply pointed snout makes it distinctive.

The 85 or so species of *Philautus* are distributed throughout South and Southeast Asia and live in wet tropical forests from sea level to nearly 10,000 feet (3,000 m). Many, including *P. cuspis*, are new to science: It was described only in 2005.

These little frogs present zoologists with something of a problem: Because they are small, secretive, and highly variable, they are very difficult to study and classify. Many species look similar, and some are so variable that they have been described two or three times under different names. Some species have very limited ranges and are known from a small number of individuals, while others are more common and widespread.

All the species have adhesive toe pads, and most have webbing to their fingers and toes, although this is reduced in some species and absent in a few. They vary in color, even among members of the same species living in the same area, but most are mottled in brown or green, sometimes with yellow markings and often with brighter colors on their thighs. These thigh markings are known as flash markings. They are visible only when the frog jumps and they serve to confuse predators.

As far as anyone knows, however, all *Philautus* species lay small clutches of relatively large unpigmented eggs. They get their collective common name of bubble-nest frogs from the appearance of the small clusters of eggs, which look like bubbles. Most species lay their eggs under dead leaves or among moss, where they develop directly into small frogs before breaking out of the egg capsule (in the same way as the American *Eleutherodactylus* species).

Philautus eggs have also been found inside the pitchers of pitcher plants (*Nepenthes* species), which are numerous in parts of Southeast Asia, especially Borneo. Tree-hole breeders, and probably pitcher breeders too, attach their eggs to the sides of the hole or pitcher, just above the water level, so that they slide down into the water when they hatch. The tadpoles are nonfeeding and quickly develop into adult frogs.

⬇ *Bubble-nest Frog, Gampola, Sri Lanka.*

Perak Bubble-nest Frog

Common names	Perak Bubble-Nest Frog, Vermiculate Bush Frog
Scientific name	*Philautus vermiculatus*
Family	Rhacophoridae
Size	1.3 in (33 mm).
Key features	A small, stocky frog with a blunt snout and large eyes. Its toe pads are relatively large and obvious, and the toes on its back feet are webbed to half their length. Its markings are variable; it may be green or pale brown with or without intricate vermiculations over its back. The hidden surfaces of its body and limbs are yellow.
Habits	Nocturnal and arboreal.
Breeding	Eggs laid on land.
Diet	Small invertebrates.
Habitat	Rain forests.
Distribution	Malaysian Peninsula, including S Thailand.
Status	Locally common.
Similar species	Within the region this is one of the more distinctive bush frogs.

This attractive little frog is common in the cool and damp hill country of Malaysia, and individuals appear to be widely scattered throughout the forest. Males certainly do not congregate together when they call. Instead, they find a perch on a leaf, a mossy tree trunk, or a vine, usually 3 to 6 feet (0.9–1.8 m) above the ground, and make a repetitive tinkling call that can be hard to locate.

Details of the mating process have not been observed, but it is safe to assume that females are attracted to calling males and approach them; the pair then goes into amplexus. The eggs are laid among moss and they hatch directly into small froglets without passing through a free-living tadpole stage. During the daytime the adults hide in hollow bamboo stems, leaf axils, and among moss and epiphytic plants that cover tree trunks and branches.

The similarities in appearance and behavior between these frogs and their South American counterparts, the litter frogs (*Eleutherodactylus* species), is striking. Like the litter frogs, the bush frogs form a very large genus.

⊖ *Like many bush frogs, the Perak Bubble-nest Frog has mottled skin and expanded toe pads.*

Barred Tree Frog

Common names	Barred Tree Frog, Spurred Frog
Scientific name	*Polypedates eques*
Family	Rhacophoridae
Size	1.97 in (50 mm).
Key features	A narrow-bodied tree frog with an angular head and pointed snout. It has a small flap of skin on each heel, and its fingers and toes are long and have large adhesive pads at their tips. Its back is brown with a darker hour-glass marking, and its flanks are yellow. The upper margin of its mouth is white.
Habits	Nocturnal and arboreal.
Breeding	Eggs laid in a foam nest.
Diet	Invertebrates.
Habitat	Hill forests.
Distribution	Central Sri Lanka.
Status	Rare and listed by the IUCN as Endangered because of a decline in the extent and quality of its very restricted and fragmented habitat.
Similar species	Only likely to be confused with the Four-lined Tree Frog *(P. leucomystax)*, which is much more common but lacks the triangular flaps of skin on its heels.

The Barred Tree Frog is one of several endangered species in the hill country of central Sri Lanka. Its habitat has been greatly degraded and reduced by agricultural development in the region, which is important for the production of vegetables and, especially, tea. Not only does this reduce the amount of suitable habitat, but the associated use of insecticides and herbicides causes pollution in the small bodies of water in which the frog breeds. Conversion to organic tea production has greatly helped frogs reestablish themselves locally and is a step in the right direction.

In other areas logging for the timber trade has a similar effect and can lead to drought and fire. Tourism is a small but additional pressure. The Barred Tree Frog lives in a few protected parks and gardens, and these are probably the most important reservoirs for the population. Happily, the fungal disease chytridiomycosis, which is heavily implicated in the decline of amphibian populations in other parts of the world is not—as far as anyone knows—a threat to this species at present.

The natural history and breeding biology of the Barred Tree Frog follows the

same pattern as that of other *Polypedates* and related frogs, such as the Four-lined Tree Frog *(P. leucomystax).*

⤓ *The Barred Tree Frog is also known as the Spurred Frog because of the skin flaps on its heels.*

Four-lined Tree Frog

Common names	Four-lined Tree Frog, Brown Tree Frog, White-lipped Tree Frog
Scientific name	*Polypedates leucomystax*
Family	Rhacophoridae
Size	1.46–2.95 in (37–75 mm).
Key features	A medium-sized tree frog with a narrow body and long limbs. Its fingers and toes are also long and they end in well-developed toe pads. It usually has a black area passing over the lower half of its eyes and four faint dark lines on its back. Some individuals, however, are plain, and others are spotted.
Habits	Nocturnal and semiarboreal.
Breeding	Eggs laid in a foam nest.
Diet	Invertebrates.
Habitat	Varied, from forest edges to gardens, plantations, and villages, at low altitudes.
Distribution	South and Southeast Asia, from Nepal to Borneo and the Philippines.
Status	Very common.
Similar species	There are several other brown tree frogs of this type. The four lines, if present, are a good feature for identification.

Very happy to associate with human activities, this tree frog is found around villages, ditches, gardens, plantations, and parks. It also occurs in forests but only in clearings and along roadsides. It is an arboreal species but not as strictly tree-dwelling as most other *Polypedates* species, and it can be found in low vegetation and even on the ground.

Like all *Polypedates* it builds a foam nest for its eggs, sometimes on leaves overhanging water but often on grassy banks, tree trunks, and even on the sides of cisterns, walls, and bridge structures. Each nest is about the size of an orange and is produced by the action of the female. As she lays her eggs, she uses her hind feet to whip up the jelly surrounding them into a single mass of froth.

The male, who is much smaller, does not contribute to the task, but fertilizes the eggs as they are laid. The foam remains in place until the eggs are ready to hatch and then gradually disintegrates, allowing the tadpoles to fall into the water. The frogs frequently choose a poor site, and the tadpoles come to grief as they fall on the ground several yards from the water.

⊙ *Four-lined Tree Frog, Malaysia.*

File-eared Tree Frog

Common names	File-eared Tree Frog
Scientific name	*Polypedates otilophus*
Family	Rhacophoridae
Size	2.52–3.82 in (64–97 mm).
Key features	A large tree frog with a distinctive serrated ridge that runs from the eye, above the eardrum, and down toward the flanks. Its head is angular and its limbs are long, ending in long fingers and toes with well-developed pads. It is brown or tan by day but becomes yellow at night. There is a series of thin wavy lines running down the back, and the limbs have dark bars.
Habits	Nocturnal and arboreal.
Breeding	Eggs laid in a foam nest.
Diet	Invertebrates.
Habitat	Primary rain forests, secondary forests, and plantations.
Distribution	Borneo and Sumatra.
Status	Locally common.
Similar species	There are several other brown tree frogs, but the bony ridge is unique.

This impressive tree frog is common in certain areas, especially when breeding. It moves toward small forest pools on rainy and humid nights, which occur throughout most of the year in the places where it lives. Males perch in tall bushes and shrubs and characteristically sit across a stem or branch. Their call is loud and raucous and consists of a series of "chuck, chuck, chuck," followed by a pause of several minutes. Males tend to time their calls so that they do not overlap, and they sometimes seem to be answering one another. It is likely that all the mature males in an area visit the breeding site on every suitable night, but that females only visit when they are ready to lay eggs. Nobody knows if they lay more than one clutch per year, but it seems likely.

When a pair is in amplexus, they climb up into a tree overhanging the water to make their foam nest. The tadpoles of this species are especially large, growing to more than 2 inches (50 mm) long. They are often visible near the surface of their pond, diving into the murky water if disturbed.

⊖ *The File-eared Tree Frog has a strange sawlike ridge behind each ear.*

Masked Tree Frog

Common name	Masked Tree Frog
Scientific name	*Rhacophorus angulirostris*
Family	Rhacophoridae
Size	1.22–2 in (31–51 mm).
Key features	A small tree frog with a sharply pointed, but short, snout. Its eyes are large and its hands and feet are extensively webbed. It is usually brown in color, sometimes greenish, with indistinct markings on the back and dark bars on the limbs.
Habits	Nocturnal and arboreal.
Breeding	Eggs laid in a foam nest.
Diet	Invertebrates.
Habitat	Highland rain forests.
Distribution	Borneo and Sumatra.
Status	Rare and listed by the IUCN as Endangered, since all individuals are in fewer than five locations, and its favored habitat is in decline.
Similar species	The shape of the snout identifies this species.

The most noticeable features of this small tree frog are its eyes, which are large and reddish brown with a narrow pale blue border. It lives in the forests of western Sabah on the flanks of Mount Kinabalu and other mountains, and is most easily found alongside the small, rocky, fast-flowing streams that run through the forest.

Males climb into tall trees and shrubs several feet above the water to call. There are no details of mating and egg-laying, but the tadpoles live in the spaces between gravel and rocks on the bottom of the streams. The borders of their mouth are wide and form a cup-shaped structure, which they probably use to attach themselves to stones in the fast-flowing streams.

All *Rhacophorus* species differ from *Polypedates* in that their front feet as well as their back feet are webbed, although the amount of webbing varies slightly. The tadpoles of the two genera also differ—those of *Polypedates* species have eyes on the sides of the head, whereas those of *Rhacophorus* species have them positioned on top of the head. All the *Polypedates* species were formerly included in the *Rhacophorus*.

⊕ *Masked Tree Frog, Mount Kinabalu National Park, Sabah, Borneo.*

Frilled Tree Frog

Common names	Frilled Tree Frog, Rough-armed Tree Frog
Scientific name	*Rhacophorus appendiculatus*
Family	Rhacophoridae
Size	1.18–1.97 in (30–50 mm).
Key features	A small tree frog with a pointed snout. Its eyes are large and its head and back are covered with small ridges and bumps. The outer edges of its lower jaw and limbs have wavy-edged frills of skin, although the extent of these varies. Coloration is also variable and may be brown, green, or a combination of both.
Habits	Nocturnal and arboreal.
Breeding	Eggs laid in a foam nest.
Diet	Invertebrates.
Habitat	Lowland rain forests.
Distribution	Peninsular Malaysia, Borneo, Sumatra, and the Philippines.
Status	Locally common.
Similar species	The frilly flaps of skin help identify this species.

The rough skin and frills around the edges of its limbs and head effectively camouflage this small frog when it is resting on mossy or lichen-encrusted branches and tree trunks. The Frilled Tree Frog is easily overlooked unless it is disturbed, in which case it may leap and give itself away.

This species lives throughout the forest, and males congregate around small depressions in the forest floor to call in advance of rain. When they fill with water these depressions turn into ideal places for the tadpoles to live, since they are free from aquatic predators. The eggs are laid in small foam nests attached to twigs and vegetation 3 to 10 feet (1–3 m) from the ground. The tadpoles either fall or are washed into the temporary pools as they hatch.

The rough texture and frilly edges of this frog help break up its outline and eliminate shadows when it is resting during the day. This is known as disruptive coloration and is relatively common in tropical frogs, snakes, and lizards. The leaf-tailed geckos *(Uroplatus)* of Madagascar are the experts in this field—they are almost invisible when they are motionless in the day. There are also several other "mossy" frogs in Southeast Asia and in other parts of the world.

⊖ *Frilled Tree Frog, Sukau River, Sabah, Borneo. The frog's body is almost perfectly disguised against the mossy background.*

Jade Tree Frog

Common name	Jade Tree Frog
Scientific name	*Rhacophorus dulitensis*
Family	Rhacophoridae
Size	1.3–1.97 in (33–50 mm).
Key features	An attractive small tree frog with a pointed snout and heavily webbed front and hind feet. Its most notable feature, however, is its bright green coloration, which is translucent over parts of its body. Apart from this, it has reddish eyes and a thin white line running from the tip of its snout to each eye.
Habits	Nocturnal and arboreal.
Breeding	Eggs laid in a foam nest.
Diet	Invertebrates.
Habitat	Lowland rain forests.
Distribution	Sabah and Sarawak in E Borneo, and Sumatra.
Status	Secretive and rarely seen. Listed by the IUCN as Near Threatened because of forest loss within its range.
Similar species	Its coloration is unmistakable.

The skeleton of this spectacular frog consists of green bones, easily visible in places through its semitransparent skin. In this respect it parallels some of the glass frogs in the family Centrolenidae from Central and South America, even though it is not closely (or even distantly) related to them.

Unfortunately, it is rarely seen because it appears to live among the tops of the tallest rain forest trees and comes down to ground level only to breed. Its heavily webbed hands and feet appear to give it the option of gliding down should it so wish, but there is no evidence that this happens. Like other members of its genus, it congregates around small pools in the forest, presumably in response to heavy rain, although its appearances do not appear to form a pattern. The tadpoles live in these ponds, but their natural history has not been studied.

Jade Tree Frog, Danum Valley, Sabah, Borneo. As its name suggests, this little frog is a beautiful shade of pale green.

Wallace's Flying Frog

Common name	Wallace's Flying Frog
Scientific name	*Rhacophorus nigropalmatus*
Family	Rhacophoridae
Size	3.15–3.94 in (80–100 mm).
Key features	This frog is large with enormous hands and feet, all fully webbed and all with digits ending in large toe pads. The outer edges of the limbs have narrow flaps of skin. The back is green with a few scattered white spots, and the flanks and the hidden surfaces of the limbs are yellow. The webbing of the feet is black toward the base of the digits, becoming yellow.
Habits	Nocturnal and arboreal.
Breeding	Eggs laid in a foam nest.
Diet	Invertebrates.
Habitat	Primary rain forests at low elevations.
Distribution	Peninsular Malaysia, S Thailand, Borneo, and Sumatra.
Status	Rarely seen except at breeding time. Listed by the IUCN as Near Threatened because of forest loss within its range.
Similar species	Unmistakable due to its large size and bright coloration.

This is the most famous of the so-called flying frogs. Its enormous hands and feet are fully webbed, and when it leaps from high branches it spreads its fingers and toes, stretching the skin below them to form four effective little parachutes. In this way it can glide over long distances, and the webbing parachutes also break its fall. The similarity in appearance and lifestyle to the Central and South American leaf frogs belonging to the genus *Agalychnis* is remarkable, even though they belong to an entirely different family.

Wallace's Flying Frog is hardly ever seen except when it descends from the forest canopy to breed. Breeding activity is stimulated by heavy rain that creates small muddy pools in animal wallows or rutted paths and tracks. The large foam nests are attached to the muddy banks of these pools or to leaves hanging over them, and the tadpoles develop in the nests. Juveniles and immature frogs are hardly ever seen, presumably because they climb into the canopy as soon as they metamorphose and remain there until they reach breeding size.

⊕ *The huge, fully webbed feet and toes that end in large pads provide clues to the lifestyle and habits of Wallace's Flying Frog, seen here in the Danum Valley, Sabah, Borneo.*

Harlequin Flying Frog

Common name	Harlequin Flying Frog
Scientific name	*Rhacophorus pardalis*
Family	Rhacophoridae
Size	1.54–2.79 in (39–71 mm).
Key features	A narrow-waisted tree frog with a broad triangular head and large eyes. Its limbs are long and its fingers and toes are fully webbed. The head and body are brown and there are sometimes small red markings on the back. The webbing between the digits is bright red.
Habits	Nocturnal and arboreal.
Breeding	Eggs laid in a foam nest.
Diet	Invertebrates.
Habitat	Primary and disturbed lowland rain forests.
Distribution	Borneo, Sumatra, and the southern Philippine islands.
Status	Rarely seen except at breeding time but apparently quite common.
Similar species	The red webbing separates this species from other frogs in the area..

Although smaller than the more famous "flying frogs," this species is equally spectacular. The webs between its fingers and toes are bright red and extensive, forming a strong contrast with its otherwise light brown coloration. It is an excellent glider and lives in a variety of habitats, including secondary forests and tree plantations. It descends to small forest pools to breed and is sometimes present in large numbers. The tadpoles develop in still water.

Of 13 species of *Rhacophorus* in Borneo at least three species are known to glide *(R. nigropalmatus, R. pardalis, and R. reinwardti)*. Others probably also glide because they have heavily webbed feet and, since they do not enter the water to breed, they seem to have no other use for them.

There are some other flying *Rhacophorus* species on the Malaysian Peninsula and in other parts of Southeast Asia, including southern China. Although generally thought to be tropical frogs, three species from Japan (which are not fliers) descend to the ground and hibernate in the earth or among moss.

⊕ *Harlequin Flying Frog, Danum Valley, Sabah, Borneo. The red webbing on all four limbs allows it to glide from tree to tree.*

Harlequin Flying Frog (cont'd.)

⊖ *In Borneo a Harlequin Flying Frog glides gently down toward a leaf, using its webbing to break its fall. The flight is not very controlled, and its trajectory is usually less than 45 degrees. For example, a frog that launches itself from a height of about 15 feet (4.6 m) would land about 12 horizontal feet (3.6 m) away.*

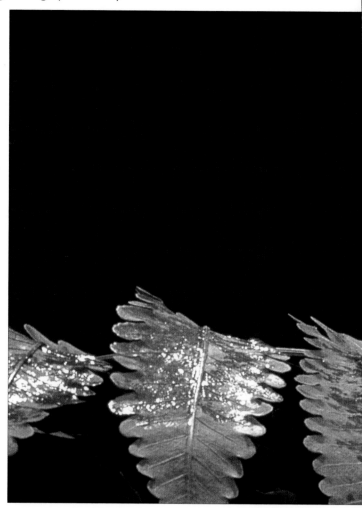

Reinwardt's Flying Frog

Common names	Reinwardt's Flying Frog, Black-webbed Tree Frog, Green Flying Frog
Scientific name	*Rhacophorus reinwardtii*
Family	Rhacophoridae
Size	1.77–2.56 in (45–65 mm). Females tend to be bigger than males.
Key features	A medium-sized tree frog with a wide head, large eyes, and horizontal pupils. It has huge hands and feet, all completely webbed, and large adhesive toe pads. Its forearms have a fringe of loose skin, and there are flaps of skin on its lower legs. It is bright or dark green in color and sometimes yellow on the flanks. The webbing between its toes is yellow and blue or black and blue.
Habits	Arboreal and nocturnal.
Breeding	Eggs are laid in a foam nest.
Diet	Insects.
Habitat	Primary rain forests at low elevations.
Distribution	Southeast Asia (Malaysian Peninsula, Sumatra, Java, and Borneo).
Status	Probably common in suitable habitat but hard to observe.
Similar species	Several other *Rhacophorus* species from the region are green and of a similar size.

Reinwardt's Flying Frogs are rain forest canopy specialists, rarely coming down to ground level except to breed or if they are chased by predators. At such times they may jump from high branches, hold their limbs out to the side, and spread their large webbed feet to break their fall. By adjusting the position of their limbs they have a certain amount of control over their "flight" (which is really a glide) and usually land among foliage lower down.

Their convergence with the Central American *Agalychnis* species, which look and behave in a similar manner, is obvious, even though they are not closely related. Furthermore, they have similar breeding habits: Both groups of flying frogs attach their eggs to leaves hanging over water, and the tadpoles drop down into the water when they hatch.

This particular species breeds in forest ponds, often using wallows that have been made by wild pigs or rhinoceroses. Their tadpoles are typical pond dwellers, with a globular body and high fins—this type of tadpole is common to many other *Rhacophorus* species. Others, though, such as the Masked Tree Frog

(*R. angulirostris*), lay their eggs over flowing streams. Their tadpoles live either in the crevices between rocks and stones or end up in quiet streamside pools where dead leaves and other forest debris collects. The Brown Tree Frog *(R. harrissoni)* attaches its eggs to tree trunks above water-filled cavities or the pools formed between the buttress roots of large forest trees.

Reinwardt's Flying Frog, Southeast Asia. This frog has black and blue webbing between its digits, but some individuals have yellow and blue webs.

Other Rhacophorids

⬅ ⬆ *These* Philautus *species, seen at Nuwara Eliya in Sri Lanka in 2005, may be undescribed frogs. Research in remote parts of Sri Lanka has resulted in the discovery of more than 100 new frogs, making this one of the world's richest regions. Many of them are small leaf-litter frogs belonging to the genus* Philautus, *collectively known as bush frogs, and are still waiting to be officially named.*

➡ *Collett's Tree Frog* (Polypedates colletti) *is distributed in Borneo, Sumatra, Indonesia, Peninsular Malaysia, and southern Thailand.*

Madagascar Jumping Frog

Common name	Madagascar Jumping Frog
Scientific name	Aglyptodactylus madagascariensis
Family	Mantellidae
Size	1.77–3.54 in (45–90 mm). Females are significantly larger than males.
Key features	The angular shape of the head is accentuated by the dark patch in front of the eye. The eyes are large, their upper halves pale, and their lower halves dark. Brown in color, with darker markings on the back and dark mottling on the inside of the thighs. There is a pair of dark spots on each side of the lower back, normally hidden when the legs are folded.
Habits	Mostly nocturnal and terrestrial.
Breeding	Eggs laid in forest pools.
Diet	Invertebrates.
Habitat	Primary and secondary forests.
Distribution	Madagascar.
Status	Secretive but quite common.
Similar species	Several brown forest frogs are similar, but a combination of features, such as the eye color, relative size of the male and the female, and the presence of the spots on the back, will help.

Apart from the fact that in the breeding season males of the species turn bright yellow, especially on the flanks, this is a rather nondescript little frog. The explanation for this transformation is unknown, but seasonal color change among frogs is very rare. The Madagascar Jumping Frog spends its time foraging on the forest floor among leaf litter, mostly at night but sometimes in the daytime, too. It is a good jumper but may also defend itself by inflating its body and pressing itself to the ground. This is possibly a method of deterring small snakes, which need to engulf their food whole.

Breeding takes place explosively. Large numbers of males migrate to the breeding ponds after heavy rain and call from the edge of the water. Females join them, and most breeding activity takes place over a short period of about two to three days. The female lays between 1,000 and 2,000 eggs that are scattered in the water. They do not clump together nor are they attached to anything. They are laid in still, often stagnant, pools that are exposed to the sun. The tadpoles develop quickly, leaving the water about three months later.

→ Seen here in Maroantsetra, the Madagascar Jumping Frog is found in the forests of the northern and eastern parts of the island.

Central Bright-eyed Frog

Common names	Central Bright-eyed Frog, Red Boophis
Scientific name	Boophis rappiodes
Family	Mantellidae
Size	0.91–1.34 in (23–34 mm). Females are larger than males.
Key features	A small tree frog with a slender body and large eyes. Its feet are fully webbed and its hands are partially webbed. Its fingers and toes end in toe pads. It is yellowish green with red spots on its head, back, and flanks; most heavily spotted on the upper surfaces.
Habits	Nocturnal and arboreal.
Breeding	Eggs laid in streams.
Diet	Invertebrates.
Habitat	Forests.
Distribution	Madagascar.
Status	Fairly common.
Similar species	The red pigmentation is distinctive. Other Boophis species of similar size are mostly green.

This small frog lives near forest streams. It hides during the day in places such as leaf axils and hollow stems and emerges at night to feed on small insects and to breed. Males call from leaves of plants near small, slow-running streams. Ginger plants seem to be a common choice because they grow in thickets along the edges of streams and have robust leaves that can easily support a small calling frog.

Calling males make a short double-click note, which differs from the call they make in response to rain or to advertise territory. Once the female has been attracted, the pair makes its way into the stream, where the female deposits 200 to 300 light green or yellowish eggs. The tadpoles live at the edges of the streams, where overhanging vegetation provides shade. They are black with small bright green spots.

A similar species, *Boophis erythrodactylus*, which has more widely spaced red spots on its back, secretes a strong-smelling fluid if it is touched; some scientists suggest that it helps the frog identify others of the same species.

⊕ *Central Bright-eyed Frog, Andasibe, Madagascar.*

Dumeril's Bright-eyed Frog

Common name	Dumeril's Bright-eyed Frog
Scientific name	*Boophis tephraeomystax*
Family	Mantellidae
Size	1.38–1.97 in (35–50 mm). Females are larger than males.
Key features	A medium-sized tree frog with toe pads but very little webbing between its toes. It is brown or beige in color with a darker area on each side of the face and a row of yellowish spots, sometimes forming a continuous line, on each flank.
Habits	Nocturnal and arboreal.
Breeding	Eggs laid in ponds.
Diet	Invertebrates.
Habitat	Forests, fields, villages, and houses.
Distribution	Madagascar.
Status	Common.
Similar species	Several other brown tree frogs are similar. The pale line down the flanks is a useful field mark.

Together with seven or eight close relatives, this species differs from other *Boophis* species in having little, if any, webbing on its front feet. Dumeril's Bright-eyed Frog is the most common of this group because it has adapted to disturbed habitats and it ventures into fields, shrubs in villages and gardens, and frequently enters houses and hotels. It also tolerates dry conditions better than most

related species, retreating deep into leaf axils to avoid the worst of any drought.

Males call from vegetation 0.5 to 2 feet (15–60 cm) above the surface of water. They choose small, still, often stagnant, bodies of water such as pools, swamps, or rice fields. The tadpoles are yellowish with beige spots but turn greenish toward the end of their development.

⬇ *Dumeril's Bright-eyed Frog is one of several medium-sized tree frogs that are endemic to Madagascar.*

Green Bright-eyed Frog

Common name	Green Bright-eyed Frog
Scientific name	*Boophis viridis*
Family	Mantellidae
Size	1.14 in (29 mm).
Key features	A small tree frog with toe pads and webbing between its fingers and toes. Light green in color with some small red speckles, sometimes extensive, over its head, back, and the outer surfaces of its limbs.
Habits	Nocturnal and arboreal.
Breeding	Eggs laid in streams.
Diet	Invertebrates.
Habitat	Forests.
Distribution	Madagascar.
Status	Very localized.
Similar species	Other similar green *Boophis* are smaller and have eyes of a different color.

This species is known only from one locality—the forests around Andasibe on the east of Madagascar, about 3,000 feet (900 m) above sea level. It is distinguished by the color of its large eyes, which have a brown iris surrounded by first a black and then a blue ring. Iris color is an important characteristic in identifying the small *Boophis* species, of which there are many that resemble each other superficially. In practice, however the calls of the frogs are different, which is why the species are isolated from each other.

The Green Bright-eyed Frog has a short chirping call, made from leaves 3 to 6 feet (0.9–1.8 m) above streams. The eggs and tadpoles of this species have not been found, but they probably resemble those of related species, which are known to lay them among stones and pebbles on the bottom of streams, where the tadpoles live and feed.

The parallels between these small *Boophis* species and the Central and South American glass frogs in the family Centrolenidae are interesting. Both groups contain small, green, semitransparent frogs

that call from vegetation
overhanging forest streams. They
differ in their egg-laying habits, however.
Whereas the glass frogs lay their eggs on leaves and
their tadpoles drop into the water, the *Boophis* frogs, as
far as is known, all lay their eggs directly into the water.

⊕ *A male Green Bright-eyed Frog sits on a leaf and
calls to attract a mate; Andasibe, Madagascar.*

441

Other *Boophis* Species

⊕ A pair of Green Cascade Frogs (Boophis luteus) *in amplexus by a stream in a Madagascan rain forest.*

⬆ With its camouflage coloration this Dead-leaf Tree Frog (Boophis madagascariensis) *is barely noticeable on the floor of a rain forest in Madagascar.*

⬇ Boophis reticulatus *in cryptic daytime resting pose in a Madagascan rain forest.*

Madagascan Bullfrog

Common name	Madagascan Bullfrog
Scientific name	*Laliostoma labrosum*
Family	Mantellidae
Size	1.65–2.52 in (42–64 mm).
Key features	A stocky frog with short limbs and a wide head. Its back feet are partially webbed but there is no webbing on its front feet, nor do any of the digits end in an expanded disk. Overall brown, with a light-colored patch just below the eyes and various darker blotches over its back and limbs.
Habits	Nocturnal and terrestrial.
Breeding	Eggs laid in temporary swamps and ponds.
Diet	Invertebrates.
Habitat	Dry forests, grasslands, and cultivated areas.
Distribution	Madagascar.
Status	Common.
Similar species	Some *Mantidactylus* species are superficially similar, but the body shape and the light mark on the face should identify this species.

The Madagascan Bullfrog was originally placed in the African pixie frog genus *(Tomopterna)* because its shape, coloration, and habits are similar to theirs. For many years this convergence was regarded as evidence for continental drift, the process whereby the various large landmasses broke free from each other and moved to different parts of the world. As it turns out, *Laliostoma* is not very closely related to the African pixie frogs, and it is now placed in a separate genus and family.

The Madagascan Bullfrog lives in some of the drier, more open forests toward the east of the island. Here it can avoid the driest part of the year by burrowing backward into the soil, using its hind feet to scoop away the earth. It breeds explosively after the first heavy rains, congregating around the edges of large, shallow expanses of temporary pools.

The tadpoles form large shoals and develop quickly in the warm water so they can metamorphose and leave the water before it dries up. They are often found in the company of tadpoles belonging to other species, notably those of the Mascarene Grass Frog *(Ptychadena madagascariensis)*.

⊖ *A Madagascan Bullfrog, seen at Ampijoroa, Madagascar.*

Golden Mantella

Common names	Golden Mantella, Golden Frog
Scientific name	*Mantella aurantiaca*
Family	Mantellidae
Size	0.79–1.02 in (20–26 mm). Females are larger than males.
Key features	A tiny orange frog with an "orange peel" texture over its skin. Its eyes are black, and there are occasionally red patches on its underside. There are no other markings—this species is unmistakable.
Habits	Diurnal and terrestrial.
Breeding	Eggs laid on land.
Diet	Small invertebrates.
Habitat	Humid forests.
Distribution	Eastern Madagascar.
Status	Common over a small area of less than 4 sq. mi (10 sq. km). Because its habitat is declining, it is listed by the IUCN as Critically Endangered.
Similar species	Can be confused only with a black-eared form *(M. milotympanum)*, which is sometimes regarded as a subspecies *(M. aurantiaca milotympanum)*.

This charismatic little frog is the most recognizable of Madagascar's extensive range of frog species. Like its counterparts in Central and South America—the poison dart frogs in the family Dendrobatidae—it flaunts its bright colors by being active during the day and by moving around on the dimly lit forest floor where, despite its small size, it glows like a beacon.

The Golden Mantella is found in a small area of southeastern Madagascar at about 3,000 feet (900 m) above sea level, in a region that is especially rich in frog species. It prefers wet pandanus forests and spends most of its time on the ground, although it sometimes climbs into the lower leaves of the forest understory. It lays its eggs on the forest floor in small clutches of 20 to 60. They hatch in about 14 days and are washed into small pools by rain. When they first metamorphose the tadpoles are greenish brown, and the orange coloration develops slowly over the next few months.

A similar species, possibly a subspecies, is the Black-eared Mantella *(Mantella milotympanum)*. It differs in that it is less brightly colored and has a dark mark over its eardrum. It is also slightly smaller, has a more nervous disposition, and is active in the evening rather than the middle of the day.

⊖ *With its bright orange coloring and jet black eyes, the tiny Golden Mantella is unmistakable.*

Bronze Mantella

Common name	Bronze Mantella
Scientific name	*Mantella betsileo*
Family	Mantellidae
Size	0.79–1.1 in (20–28 mm).
Key features	One of the less colorful mantellas, with a yellowish or bronze-brown back and a few indistinct darker markings. Its flanks are black and there is a sharp contrast between this and the color of the back. It is black underneath with scattered blue spots.
Habits	Diurnal and terrestrial.
Breeding	Eggs laid in small pools or puddles.
Diet	Small invertebrates.
Habitat	Humid forests.
Distribution	Coastal Madagascar.
Status	Locally common.
Similar species	Other frogs with similar markings include the Green Mantella (*M. viridis*), but this species lacks the jet black flanks, which are a good means of identifying the Bronze Mantella.

The Bronze Mantella and a group of its close relatives occur in lowland coastal areas and are not restricted to forest habitats. Among other characteristics, they have light-colored markings on their throat and, when the males inflate their throat during calling, the markings become conspicuous visual "flags."

Males of the Bronze Mantella call from large stones where they can be seen easily. Females lay their eggs in small puddles of water, sometimes

under stones. In heavy rains the eggs are washed into streams, where they continue their development.

These frogs eat very small insect prey and must, therefore, eat a large number of separate items. If they find a trail of ants they will position themselves next to it and flick up the individual ants as they pass by, as though on a conveyer belt. In forests with fruit trees they may position themselves among the fallen fruit so that they have a ready supply of the small fruit flies *(Drosophila)* that infest them.

⊕ *The Bronze Mantella is widespread in lowland coastal regions of Madagascar.*

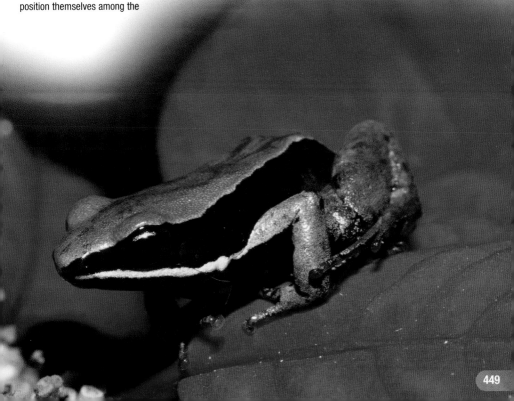

Yellow Mantella

Common name	Yellow Mantella
Scientific name	*Mantella crocea*
Family	Mantellidae
Size	0.71–0.94 in (18–24 mm).
Key features	A small but stocky mantella with a yellow or greenish back, sometimes with fine black speckles. The back half of each flank is the same color as the back, but the front halves merge to black, and the sides of the head are also black. There is not much variation apart from the intensity of the dorsal color.
Habits	Diurnal and terrestrial.
Breeding	Eggs laid in small pools or puddles.
Diet	Small invertebrates.
Habitat	Humid forests.
Distribution	Central Madagascar.
Status	Occurs only in a single locality of probably less than 200 sq. mi (500 sq. km) and is therefore listed by the IUCN as Endangered.
Similar species	The Green Mantella *(M. viridis)* is similar but lacks black on its flanks.

This species, which was described relatively recently, is not well known. It lives only in the moist forests around Andasibe on Madagascar, where several other rare frogs also occur. Like the Golden Mantella *(Mantella aurantiaca)*, it is bold. It lives on the forest floor, but males climb onto prominent perches to call throughout the wet season. Females lay about 50 brownish eggs in a damp place that is liable to flood, and the tadpoles take about 65 days to complete their development.

Several new species of mantellas were discovered in the 1990s as naturalists and scientists

⊕ *The largest mantella, at 1.4 inches (35 mm), is the Green Mantella* (Mantella viridis), *a close relative of* M. crocea.

began to explore Madagascar thoroughly. Another gem is *M. expectata*, from the south of the island, described in 1992. This species has a yellow back, black flanks, and bright blue limbs. All told, there are 15 species in the genus, of which six have been described since 1988. The most recent, *M. manery*, was described in 1999.

⤓ *Yellow Mantella on the forest floor, Madagascar.*

Green-backed Mantella

Common names	Green-backed Mantella, Climbing Mantella
Scientific name	*Mantella laevigata*
Family	Mantellidae
Size	0.94–1.18 in (24–30 mm).
Key features	The common name of this species is not helpful. Its back is yellow, not green, although sometimes it is greenish, apparently. The yellow coloration extends from the top of the head down the back but stops short of the vent. The lower back, flanks, and limbs are black with a few scattered blue spots. It has conspicuously expanded toe pads.
Habits	Diurnal and terrestrial.
Breeding	Eggs laid in tree holes.
Diet	Small invertebrates.
Habitat	Humid forests.
Distribution	Northeastern Madagascar.
Status	Locally common, but listed by the IUCN as Near Threatened because of a decline in the extent and quality of its habitat.
Similar species	Other species with a yellow or greenish back lack the large toe pads, and their markings are not as well defined.

The Green-backed Mantella and one other closely related species which does not yet have a name are the only *Mantella* species with sizeable toe pads. As this would suggest, they are arboreal, climbing up to 13 feet (4 m) from the ground.

The Green-backed Mantella has very different habits than the other species. It has been found hiding in water-filled tree holes in groups of two to six adults. When they are disturbed, they duck down under the water. In some places they also live inside broken bamboo stems that have collected water, and feed on small flies that are attracted to rotting bamboo litter.

Egg-laying takes place inside the bamboo tubes or in tree holes, and the frogs attach their eggs singly just above the water level. Although some of them dry out and some disappear, each occupied hole contains one tadpole or, if there is more than one, the tadpoles are of different ages.

The tadpoles have a horny beak, similar to that of some tree frogs that eat frogs' eggs. This feature has given rise to the theory that the female visits the tadpoles regularly and lays an egg for them to eat, as in the poison dart frogs belonging to the *Dendrobates pumilio* group—although this has not been confirmed.

⊙ *Unusual among the mantellas for being a climber, the Green-backed Mantella has expanded toe pads. This one was photographed on a tree trunk at Nosy Mangabe, Madagascar.*

Painted Mantella

Common names	Painted Mantella, Madagascan Mantella
Scientific name	*Mantella madagascariensis*
Family	Mantellidae
Size	0.87–1.22 in (22–31 mm).
Key features	A black frog with large patches of yellow around the bases of the limbs. The lower parts of the hind legs are orange, with varying amounts of black stippling.
Habits	Diurnal and terrestrial.
Breeding	Eggs laid in leaf litter.
Diet	Small invertebrates.
Habitat	Humid forests.
Distribution	Central and E Madagascar.
Status	Locally common, but listed by the IUCN as Near Threatened because of the decline in the extent and quality of its fragmented habitat.
Similar species	Several.

The Painted Mantella belongs to the *variegata* group of mantellas, a collection of highly variable species that have often been confused with each other in the past. They are all colorful. Cowan's Mantella *(Mantella cowani)*, for example, is black with orange patches around the base of its limbs; while Baron's Mantella *(M. baronii)* is black with patches of green, yellow, or orange on its flanks and limbs. The similarity between these and the Painted Mantella, and possibly other as yet undescribed species, has baffled scientists.

The skin of Baron's Mantella is known to contain alkaloid derivatives similar to those of the American poison dart frogs (Dendrobatidae), and therefore the coloration is said to be aposematic (warning). So the similarities between all these species may be the result of Batesian or Müllerian mimicry, a defensive strategy in which one species mimics the appearance of another to benefit from its poisonous qualities. Until more work is done on their skin secretions, there is no way of knowing whether all the species of similar appearance are toxic (in which case they will be Müllerian mimics) or whether one or more harmless species mimics one or more poisonous ones (in which case they will be Batesian mimics). Where two species in this group occur together they tend to be very similar, but when one occurs away from the others it can be variable and not always resemble other populations.

⊖ *Included in the* variegata *group is the Splendid Mantella (Mantella pulchra). It has metallic colors on its back and flanks.*

⊕ *The highly colorful Painted Mantella has many "lookalikes."*

Sainte Marie Pandanus Frog

Common name	Sainte Marie Pandanus Frog
Scientific name	*Mantidactylus bicalcaratus*
Family	Mantellidae
Size	0.87–1.02 in (22–26 mm).
Key features	A small frog with a triangular head, long limbs, and obviously expanded tips to its toes. Very like a tree frog in general appearance. Pale brown, yellowish, or green in color, and translucent. Its back is covered with fine speckles of a paler color.
Habits	Crepuscular and semiarboreal.
Breeding	Eggs laid in leaf axils.
Diet	Small invertebrates.
Habitat	*Pandanus* forests.
Distribution	Eastern Madagascar.
Status	Locally common.
Similar species	The Tsarafidy Pandanus Frog *(M. pulcher)* is slightly larger and more boldly marked.

These lively little frogs live only on large screw pines *(Pandanus)* and a few closely related plants, all of which are large, rosette-forming shrubs with stiff, toothed leaves. Each large plant is the entire world to a colony of frogs, which never leave it (except, presumably, when the plant dies). They hide away deep in the leaf axils and are invisible for most of the day. They begin to emerge in late afternoon and hop around from leaf to leaf, never descending to the ground, even when the plant is low.

The male's call is unknown, but females lay small clusters of eggs on the leaves of the plants. Atmospheric humidity prevents them from drying out. The eggs hatch after three to 12 days, and the tadpoles, which are flattened in shape and have a long whiplike tail, wriggle down the leaves and into the small pools of water that collect at their bases. If the pool dries out, the tadpoles are thought to be capable of wriggling up or down through other leaves until they find a more suitable place.

⊙ *This Sainte Marie Pandanus Frog was observed on a leaf at Maroantsetra, Madagascar.*

Boulenger's Madagascar Frog

Common name	Boulenger's Madagascar Frog
Scientific name	*Mantidactylus boulengeri*
Family	Mantellidae
Size	0.98–1.18 in (25–30 mm).
Key features	A small brownish frog that is variable in its color and markings. There is often a light yellow line down the back, and the skin is dry and granular, like that of a toad. The fingers are not webbed at all, and the toes are only slightly webbed. The irises are coppery.
Habits	Active by day and night, and mainly terrestrial.
Breeding	Eggs laid among leaf litter.
Diet	Small invertebrates.
Habitat	Primary forests.
Distribution	Madagascar.
Status	Locally common.
Similar species	Other brown *Mantidactylus* species. However, most have longer legs and different calls.

A frog of the forest floor, Boulenger's Madagascar Frog lives in dry and wet forests and has even moved into plantations of introduced eucalyptus trees. It appears to have no affinity with water, and males call from the ground during the day. Females lay small clutches of eight to 10 relatively large eggs, and the tadpoles have not been found—given the preferred habitat, it is likely that this species undergoes direct development without a free-swimming tadpole stage.

Observations on closely related species have proved that direct development is widespread in this group. The eggs are typically large—up to 0.4 inches (10 mm) including the jelly in some species—and the clutches are small. They are laid among wet dead leaves. Two to three weeks after laying, the hind legs appear; a few days later they are joined by the front ones. The tadpoles are moving about inside the egg capsule by this time. They break out a day or two later and have just the remnants of a

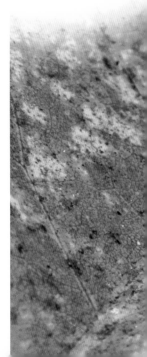

tail, which is totally absorbed after another day. Complete development, from egg-laying to hatching, therefore takes about three weeks.

⤵ *Boulenger's Madagascar Frog, Andasibe, Madagascar.*

Central Madagascar Frog

Common name	Central Madagascar Frog
Scientific name	*Mantidactylus opiparis*
Family	Mantellidae
Size	1.18–1.57 in (30–40 mm).
Key features	A medium-sized brown frog with a pointed snout and a fold of skin down each side of its back. Between the folds the back is brown or tan, and outside them the flanks are black. There is a white line along the lower jaw, reaching to the base of the front legs. The hind feet have some webbing, but the front feet are unwebbed.
Habits	Diurnal and terrestrial.
Breeding	Eggs laid on the ground, near streams.
Diet	Small invertebrates.
Habitat	Alongside streams that run through forests.
Distribution	Madagascar.
Status	Locally common and widespread.
Similar species	Other brown *Mantidactylus* species, such as *M. brevipalmatus*, but the black flanks and contrasting white line along the lower jaw are helpful in identifying *M. opiparis*.

The group of *Mantidactylus* frogs to which the Central Madagascar Frog belongs is characterized by the shape and habits of its tadpoles. The adults live on the forest floor and rarely climb. The males call from not more than 10 feet (3 m) from the banks of streams. Females lay their relatively large eggs in leaf litter at the edges of the stream.

When the tadpoles hatch, rain or floodwater washes them into the water. They live in the quieter stretches, where dead leaves collect. They are funnel-feeders, which means that their mouth has no teeth or scraping apparatus. Instead, it is surrounded by a rim of flaps that form a funnel, directed upward. They feed by hanging from the surface film and engulfing small particles of plant and animal food that collect there. They grow to 2 inches (50 mm) long, and the newly metamorphosed froglets are 0.5 inches (13 mm) long. Funnel-feeders are not unique to the Mantellidae—some Asian horned frogs *(Megophrys)* and New World leaf frogs *(Phyllomedusa)* also have tadpoles of this type.

⬆ *The Central Madagascan Frog is a ground-dweller that lives alongside forest streams.*

➡ Mantidactylus brevipalmatus *is similar to the Central Madagascar Frog, but its flanks are lighter.*

Tsarafidy Pandanus Frog

Common name	Tsarafidy Madagascar Frog
Scientific name	*Mantidactylus pulcher*
Family	Mantellidae
Size	0.87–1.1 in (22–28 mm).
Key features	A small translucent green frog with scattered dark markings over its back and flanks. A dark line runs from the tip of its snout, through the eyes and onto the flanks. The hands are not webbed, and the feet only moderately so. The fingers and toes end in large toe pads.
Habits	Active in the evening and early morning on *Pandanus* plants.
Breeding	Eggs laid on leaves.
Diet	Small invertebrates.
Habitat	Only on *Pandanus* plants.
Distribution	Eastern Madagascar.
Status	Localized.
Similar species	Other green *Mantidactylus* frogs that live in *Pandanus* plants are less brightly colored and lack the dark line through the eye.

Like the Sainte Marie Pandanus Frog *(Mantidactylus bicalcaratus),* this species is never found away from the plant that forms the center of its colony. In the forests where *Pandanus* forms the understory these frogs can be found hopping along the leaves early in the morning and late in the afternoon. If they are disturbed they do not leap away haphazardly as other frogs might do, but hop from leaf to leaf, working their way back to the center of the plant, where they hide in the crevices at the base of the leaves.

This species breeds by laying its eggs on the leaves. The tadpoles wriggle down into small pools of water that collect in the leaf axils. When they metamorphose, they join the colony. A sizeable *Pandanus* plant can provide a home for 20 to 30 individuals of varying ages, and more than one species of pandanus frogs can be found in a single plant. The species presumably spreads when individuals are driven out through lack of territory or when a plant dies. If plants are moved—to an ornamental garden, for instance—the colony of little frogs moves with them.

⊕ *Tsarafidy Pandanus Frog, Andasibe, Madagascar.*

Other Mantellids

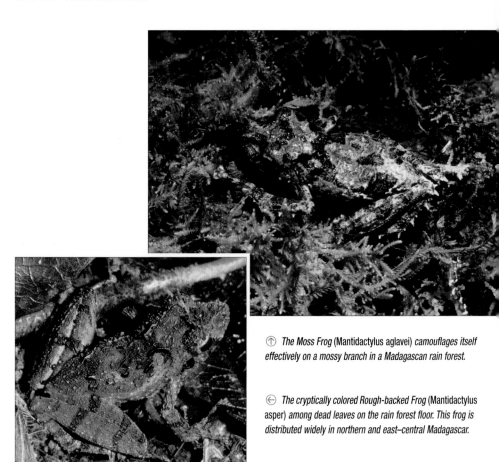

⊕ The Moss Frog (Mantidactylus aglavei) camouflages itself effectively on a mossy branch in a Madagascan rain forest.

⊖ The cryptically colored Rough-backed Frog (Mantidactylus asper) among dead leaves on the rain forest floor. This frog is distributed widely in northern and east–central Madagascar.

⊕ The highly variable Blue-legged Mantella (Mantella expectata) lives alongside streams running through baobab forests in the dry regions of southwestern Madagascar.

Other Mantellids

↑ *The White Mantidactylus* (Mantidactylus luteus) *lives on the ground and in trees in pristine rain forest.*

→ *Known only from a few localities on Madagascar, the White-fronted Mantidactylus* (Mantidactylus albofrenatus) *was seen here on a leaf on Nosy Mangabe.*

Namaqua Rain Frog

Common name	Namaqua Rain Frog
Scientific name	*Breviceps namaquensis*
Family	Microhylidae
Size	1.77 in (45 mm).
Key features	A dumpy frog with an almost globular body and short, flattened snout. Its limbs are very short and its hind feet have hard flanges for burrowing. Dark brown above with lighter patches, fading to white on the flanks.
Habits	Nocturnal and burrowing.
Breeding	Underground.
Diet	Small invertebrates.
Habitat	Dry, scrub-covered mountainsides and hillsides.
Distribution	South Africa (Namaqualand and Western Cape).
Status	Very rarely seen.
Similar species	The other 15 species of rain frogs all have similar body shapes, but the coloration and distribution are usually enough to differentiate them from each other.

Rain frogs are remarkable little frogs that live out their lives under extreme conditions. They have parallels in other parts of the world, notably the Sandhill Frog *(Arenophryne rotunda)* from Western Australia. The Namaqua Rain Frog lives in a desert habitat consisting of dry, rocky slopes and dry riverbeds. It also occurs in the Cederberg Mountains farther south, in similar situations. It spends the greater part of each year beneath the surface, having burrowed down into the sand or soil using the "spades" on its hind feet. As it descends, the alternating movements of its two back feet cause it to spin around as it goes.

Breeding takes place in response to heavy rain, at which time the frogs burrow back up to the surface and emerge to search for mates. Males have a whistling call, the source of which is hard to locate (but not for the female frogs, presumably). Conventional amplexus for a species with such a rounded body and short limbs is not an option, so the frogs secrete a milky white substance that temporarily glues the male to the female's back. At this point they burrow back down into the soil together and create an underground chamber in which the small clutch of eggs is laid. The eggs become coated with sand, and the female may stay with them. There is no free-living tadpole stage, and the newly emerged froglets leave the nest as soon as they hatch.

⊖ *The Namaqua Rain Frog, seen here in Clanwilliam, South Africa, is a burrowing species that lives in predominantly sandy, dry areas.*

Tomato Frog

Common name	Tomato Frog
Scientific name	*Dyscophus antongili*
Family	Microhylidae
Size	Males to 2.56 in (65 mm). Females to 4.13 in (105 mm).
Key features	A large red frog with a wide body, narrow head, and a bluntly tapering snout. Its eyes are large and prominent and seem to give it a permanently surprised expression. Its skin is smooth except for a pair of fleshy ridges running along either side of its back. There are sometimes small black markings on its flanks and hind limbs.
Habits	Terrestrial and nocturnal.
Breeding	In permanent and temporary pools.
Diet	Invertebrates.
Habitat	Forest clearings and sparsely wooded scrub.
Distribution	Madagascar; found only in the northeast, around the Bay of Antongil.
Status	Rare. Because of its limited range and its appeal to collectors, it is listed by the IUCN as Near Threatened.
Similar species	There are two other species of *Dyscophus*, but they are not likely to be confused with the bright red Tomato Frog.

The large, bright red Tomato Frog is one of the more celebrated species from an island packed with unusual frogs and other animals, but it is unlikely to be confused with any other species. The Tomato Frog occurs only in a very limited area, around the Bay of Antongil in the northeast of the country. There it lives in varied situations, but its natural habitat is probably the seasonally dry open forests of the region. The town of Maroantsetra and other smaller villages have grown up right in the middle of its small range and, at least on the face of it, the frog seems to have adapted reasonably well to the disturbance, living in gardens, smallholdings, plantations, and even at the rural airport.

It is mostly active at night, although it may sometimes be seen early in the morning and late in the evening, sitting at the entrance to its burrow, waiting for a meal.

After rain, the male calls from shallow water in swamps, ditches, and temporary pools. He has no nuptial pad, which makes grasping the larger female difficult. Therefore, although typical amplexus is axillary, the male often slips down to a lower position during mating.

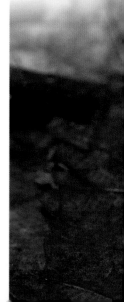

The female lays in excess of 1,000 small black eggs that form a slick on the surface. The tadpoles are filter feeders, with their mouth at the very front of their head. Their eyes are situated on the sides of the head, and their body is flattened from top to bottom. Assuming their pools do not dry out, they metamorphose in about 45 days. The juveniles do not have the bright red coloration of the adults, being dull yellow on their back and darker on their flanks.

The red color of the Tomato Frog and of the closely related False Tomato Frog (*Dyscophus guineti*) is a warning coloration. These frogs inflate their body and secrete a white, slimy secretion from the skin if they are handled. This can produce a rash in humans and is probably distasteful or toxic to predators.

⊖ *Habitat loss means that the Tomato Frog is under threat. However, the species has been bred widely in captivity.*

Tomato Frog (cont'd.)

→ *Tomato Frogs exhibit an extreme example of sexual dimorphism. The females are almost twice as big as the males.*

Brown Tomato Frog

Common name	Brown Tomato Frog
Scientific name	*Dyscophus insularis*
Family	Microhylidae
Size	1.57–1.97 in (40–50 mm).
Key features	A medium-sized frog with a triangular head and body when seen from above. Its limbs are short and there is no webbing between the fingers. In males the toes are partially webbed, less so in females. Usually brown, sometimes reddish brown in color, with two indistinct paler stripes on the edges of the back.
Habits	Nocturnal and burrowing.
Breeding	In temporary pools.
Diet	Invertebrates.
Habitat	Dry forests.
Distribution	Madagascar, mainly along the west coast.
Status	Very rarely seen.
Similar species	The other two tomato frogs are more brightly colored.

This tomato frog is less colorful than its two relatives *(Dyscophus antongili* and *D. guineti)* and lives in western Madagascar, where conditions are drier. It is not as well known as the two other species, and some details of its breeding habits are unrecorded. Its tadpoles live in temporary pools, exposed to the sun. Like many microhyliid tadpoles they are filter feeders, eating microscopic freshwater organisms. They catch them by engulfing mouthfuls of water, which they filter before expelling it through their gills. All the while, their

long tail flickers backward and forward to maintain a steady current of water toward their mouth.

Although the Brown Tomato Frog has tadpoles that are of the typical microhylid type, the breeding habits of other Madagascan microhylids are a little more unusual. Some are more like the more familiar ranid-type tadpoles, others lay their eggs in tree holes, and some have direct development. One species, *Stumpffia pygmaea*, produces foam nests, the only microhylid to do so. Finally, the males of some species remain with their eggs until they hatch.

⬇ *Brown Tomato Frog, Madagascar.*

Great Plains Narrow-mouthed Toad

Common name	Great Plains Narrow-mouthed Toad
Scientific name	*Gastrophryne olivacea*
Family	Microhylidae
Size	0.98–1.26 in (25–32 mm).
Key features	From above, this small toad is teardrop shaped, with a rounded body tapering toward a pointed head. There is a distinctive fold of skin behind the head, and its limbs are short. It is gray or olive-green in color, without markings, or with a few small scattered dark spots.
Habits	Secretive, nocturnal, and terrestrial.
Breeding	In flooded fields, ruts, and small pools.
Diet	Small invertebrates, especially ants.
Habitat	Grasslands, open woods, and deserts.
Distribution	North America, from Nebraska south to the Gulf Coast and across to Arizona, then into the lowlands of N Mexico.
Status	Common.
Similar species	The Eastern Narrow-mouthed toad (*Gastrophryne carolinensis*) has a more easterly distribution, although the two species overlap in parts of Texas and adjacent states. It is brown rather than gray and has a strongly patterned back.

This small toad is easily overlooked by anyone who is not in the habit of peering under flat rocks or boards, where it often crouches in the day or during short spells of dry weather. It may also go deeper underground, retreating into the cracks in drying mud or entering the burrows of rodents or reptiles.

Nest holes belonging to the tarantula *Dugesiella hentzi* are especially favored, and an unusual relationship has evolved between the two species. At several times the size of the toad, the spider could easily kill and eat it, but it tolerates (and may even encourage) the toad's presence in its burrow. If a predator such as a snake enters, the toad hides under the tarantula, and the tarantula defends them both. For its part, the toad does not eat the young tarantulas when they hatch, even though they are a similar size to the toad's main prey—ants. In return for the spider's protection, the toad eats its most destructive enemies (also ants) which enter the burrow in search of eggs or spiderlings. The toad's diet of ants causes it to accumulate toxins in its body and secrete distasteful substances if molested. These substances can cause a burning sensation in humans if they come into contact with mucous membranes in the lips, tongue, or eyes.

Male Great Plains Narrow-mouthed toads call, making a short buzzing sound, from flooded fields, swamps, and temporary pools and puddles after rain; cattle tanks are also used. At times they may use deeper, more permanent bodies of water if they are

⬆ *The Great Plains Narrow-mouthed Toad is a terrestrial frog. It uses a running or hopping movement to avoid danger.*

choked with plants. The eggs are very small, black and white, and form a film on the surface. The tadpoles are small and have no horny beak or rasping teeth. They metamorphose after 30 to 50 days, and the small toads measure about 0.5 inches (13 mm).

➡ *The closely related Eastern Narrow-mouthed Toad* (Gastrophryne carolinensis), *seen here in Texas.*

Rufous-sided Sticky Frog

Common name	Rufous-sided Sticky Frog
Scientific name	*Kalophrynus pleurostigma*
Family	Microhylidae
Size	1.38–2.24 in (35–57 mm).
Key features	A small frog with a triangular head and body and a sharply pointed snout. The head looks especially angular owing to the contrasting coloration: light brown on the back and darker on the side, with a well-defined line where the two colors meet. The hind feet have traces of webbing but there is none on the front feet.
Habits	Nocturnal and terrestrial.
Breeding	In small temporary pools.
Diet	Invertebrates, especially ants.
Habitat	Lowland forests.
Distribution	Southeast Asia (Malaysian Peninsula, Sumatra, Borneo, and the Philippines).
Status	Secretive and hard to find.
Similar species	Several other *Kalophrynus* species are similar but *K. pleurostigma* is the largest.

Cryptic in shape and coloration, this secretive frog dwells on the forest floor and easily escapes notice. Its coloring is a form of counter-shading—dark below and light above—and it provides excellent camouflage when it is crouching on dead leaves. Add to this the fact that the Rufous-sided Sticky Frog does not migrate to water to breed, and that it does not congregate in large numbers, and it is clear why its natural history is not well known—even though it has a wide range and is probably quite numerous in suitable places. If it is noticed, its main defensive mechanism is to exude a sticky mucus from glands in its skin, which is offputting to a potential predator.

Males make a short chirping call from a breeding site that consists of a small temporary pool in the ground, or a water-filled rot hole in a fallen tree trunk. Clutches of eggs are small, as are the tadpoles, and they appear to grow, develop, and metamorphose without feeding, subsisting entirely on their yolk. Juveniles and adults feed on ants and will often wait at the side of an ant trail, picking off the insects one by one as they walk by. More than 100 ants may be eaten in a single sitting.

⊖ *Giving it the appearance of a dead leaf when seen from above, the triangular shape and brown-red or grayish green coloring of the Rufous-sided Sticky Frog help it stay hidden. This frog was found at Gombak, Peninsular Malaysia.*

Asian Bullfrog

Common names	Asian Bullfrog, Banded Bullfrog, Ox Frog
Scientific name	*Kaloula pulchra*
Family	Microhylidae
Size	2.13–2.95 in (54–75 mm).
Key features	A rounded frog with a short, blunt snout and short limbs. The hind feet have a bony flange and the toes are webbed. The toes of the front feet are not webbed but are expanded into small pads. The center of the back is dark brown, bordered by a pair of wide, putty-colored stripes that extend onto the snout.
Habits	Nocturnal and semiburrowing.
Breeding	In temporary pools.
Diet	Invertebrates.
Habitat	Disturbed forests, fields, villages, and towns.
Distribution	Tropical Asia (India to China and south to Malaysia, Sumatra, Sulawesi, and Borneo).
Status	Very common.
Similar species	Unlikely to be confused with anything else, although there are several other species of *Kaloula* in the region.

This frog is probably more naturally at home in forest clearings and grasslands, but it has adapted well to changes made by human activity. Throughout most of Asia it is often seen in and around towns and villages, living among garbage, under houses, and in drains, culverts, and roadside ditches. In dry weather it remains in hiding but emerges as soon as rain starts, especially in the late afternoon and evening.

Despite its relatively large size, it eats small prey items, predominantly ants. Its call is a loud groan, similar to the lowing of cattle, and a chorus of males creates an unforgettable symphony. Breeding sites include flooded fields and gardens, puddles in roads, and drainage ditches. The males float on the surface of the water and puff themselves up to a huge extent when they call. The eggs form a film on the water's surface, and the small black tadpoles disperse over wide areas of shallow puddles and floods.

⬇ *The closely related Painted Asian Bullfrog (Kaloula picta). These frogs inflate themselves to twice their usual size when calling or when feeling threatened.*

480

→ Sometimes nicknamed the "chubby frog" by pet owners, the Asian Bullfrog is quite distinctive.

Malaysian Tree Hole Frog

Common name	Malaysian Tree Hole Frog
Scientific name	*Metaphrynella pollicaris*
Family	Microhylidae
Size	1.14–1.57 in (29–40 mm).
Key features	Small, with a teardrop-shaped body and warty skin. Its fingers and toes are partially webbed, and they have well-developed pads at their tips. Grayish green in color, with faint brown markings that are changeable and can turn dark on occasion.
Habits	Nocturnal and semiarboreal.
Breeding	In tree holes.
Diet	Small invertebrates.
Habitat	Highland forests.
Distribution	Malaysian Peninsula.
Status	Secretive and hard to find.
Similar species	Plenty of other small microhylids are similar, but the warty back and partially webbed feet are usually enough to identify this one.

The Malaysian Tree Hole Frog is found only in primary forests above 1,800 feet (550 m), which means it has a broken distribution on a number of isolated mountain ranges down the peninsula. The distribution probably became discontinuous as a result of climatic changes thousands of generations ago. Being small and dull colored, it is a difficult species to find, and it does not appear to occur in great densities. Males and females are partially arboreal, clambering about in trees and bushes at night in search of small insect prey. Their toe pads are very effective, and they also have pads on the palms of their hands and feet.

During the rainy season males set up home in a small tree hole that contains a few inches of water. These may be from 4 to 30 feet (1.2–9 m) above the ground. They probably also use the broken hollow stems of bamboo, but this has not been confirmed. They definitely use artificial sites such as rusted and holed metal roadside posts, however.

Having established a suitable "nest," they call with a single repetitive piping note, which may be amplified by the opening in which they are sitting. Ripe females make their way up to a calling male, using the pads on their toes to help them climb. The eggs are laid in the hole, and the tadpoles live and develop in the water it contains. It is not known if the tadpoles feed, but it seems unlikely.

⊖ *The Malaysian Tree Hole Frog at Bukit Fraser, Perak, Malaysia. The well-developed toe pads are clearly visible here.*

Borneo Tree Hole Frog

Common name	Borneo Tree Hole Frog
Scientific name	*Metaphrynella sundana*
Family	Microhylidae
Size	0.75–0.98 in (19–25 mm).
Key features	A small, plump frog with a squat body, warty skin, and bulging eyes. The toes are half webbed with well-developed pads at the tip and additional fleshy pads at the base. It is light grayish brown with a large dark marking in the center of its back and yellow patches on the hidden surfaces of its hind legs. These patches are sometimes present also on the upper surfaces of its front legs.
Habits	Nocturnal and semiarboreal.
Breeding	In tree holes.
Diet	Small invertebrates.
Habitat	Lowland forests.
Distribution	Borneo.
Status	Very common.
Similar species	The squat body and warty back separate this species from others in the region.

This species is the lowland counterpart of the Malaysian Tree Hole Frog *(Metaphrynella pollicaris)*, and they are the only two members of the genus. Whereas the Malaysian species is restricted to elevations above 1,800 feet (550 m), the Bornean version is restricted to elevations below 2,300 feet (700 m). Within this elevation range, however, it is one of the most common and ubiquitous species in Borneo. Its calls can be heard almost every night, but they are more insistent during or after rain.

Males and females move about on the forest floor to forage for small insects, and they also climb up into bushes and shrubs. Breeding, however, takes place in substantial trees with holes in their trunks. These may be as low as 24 inches (61 cm) from the ground. Holes may sometimes contain two males, so these frogs do not appear to be territorial.

Some scientists have suggested that the tone of their call varies according to the size, and therefore the acoustic qualities, of the hole from which they are

calling. There is some logic to this idea, since females would then be able to judge the size and suitability of each hole before approaching a male, but this has yet to be confirmed. Given its abundance, it is surprising that the tadpoles of this species are unknown.

⊕ *Borneo Tree Hole Frog, Sukau River, Sabah, Borneo.*

Berdmore's Narrow-mouthed Frog

Common names	Berdmore's Narrow-mouthed Frog, Large Pygmy Frog
Scientific name	*Microhyla berdmorei*
Family	Microhylidae
Size	0.94–1.26 in (24–32 mm).
Key features	A small, round-bodied frog with a warty back and very long hind limbs. The toes on its hind feet are also long and are webbed. The toes have expanded pads. Light brown or tan with a large dark mark on its back and dark bars on its hind legs.
Habits	Nocturnal and terrestrial.
Breeding	In temporary pools.
Diet	Small invertebrates, especially ants.
Habitat	Primary and secondary lowland forests.
Distribution	Thailand, Malaysia, Sumatra, and Borneo.
Status	Common.
Similar species	There are several similar microhylids, and close examination is necessary to identify them.

This is a species of primary lowland forests, although it may also be found in regrown forests and is common in clearings such as those alongside large roads. Its brown coloration, however, makes it difficult to spot against the dead leaves and debris on which it lives. Several other species—the exact ones depend on which part of the range is being considered—are similar in coloring and behavior. Like most microhylids, Berdmore's Narrow-mouthed Frogs are secretive and skulking, specializing in the art of not being noticed. Many are potential prey for a variety of snakes and larger frogs. If they are discovered, their long hind legs take them skittering away, and they are hard to catch.

Males call from the edges of shallow pools in clearings, mostly temporary and formed after heavy rain—tire ruts, animal wallows, and even hoof prints are used. These frogs' calls are insectlike and the frogs are very hard to locate, often calling from the base of a clump of grass or from among dead leaves.

The eggs are small and float on the surface, where the oxygen supply is greatest. The tadpoles are small, numerous, and black, and they metamorphose at a small size.

→ *Berdmore's Narrow-mouthed Frog, Peninsular Malaysia.*

Red Narrow-mouthed Frog

Common names	Red Narrow-mouthed Frog, Guangdong Rice Frog
Scientific name	*Microhyla rubra*
Family	Microhylidae
Size	1.5 in (38 mm).
Key features	A small, plump frog with short limbs and no webbing on its hands. Its body is teardrop shaped, and its snout comes to a point. Its back and the tops of its limbs are pale reddish brown; its flanks and the sides of its head are grayish and mottled.
Habits	Nocturnal and terrestrial.
Breeding	In temporary pools.
Diet	Small invertebrates, especially ants.
Habitat	Forests and cultivated land.
Distribution	Bangladesh, India, Myanmar, Sri Lanka.
Status	Common.
Similar species	Other microhylids. The reddish back of this species is distinctive.

This is a frog of the forest floor and from disturbed habitats such as plantations and gardens, where it lives among the leaf litter and is rarely seen. It is most abundant in dry, open places and less common in dense rain forests with a closed canopy. It hides during the day beneath rocks and logs and emerges at night to forage for small insects, especially ants and termites. Although it is mainly terrestrial, it sometimes climbs up into low bushes.

It starts to breed at the beginning of the

rainy season, and males congregate around shallow pools—densities of more than 20 frogs per square yard have been recorded. Pairs in amplexus move into deeper water and may be completely submerged. The eggs are laid in large rafts that float on the surface. The tadpoles are very small and filter microscopic particles from the water. The froglets are also very small at metamorphosis.

This Red Narrow-mouthed Toad was photographed in Puttalam, a dry-zone district near the west coast of Sri Lanka.

Sri Lankan Rice Paddy Frog

Common name	Sri Lankan Rice Paddy Frog
Scientific name	*Microhyla zeylanica*
Family	Microhylidae
Size	About 0.98 in (25 mm).
Key features	A small frog with an elongated and rounded body and a short head. Its hind limbs are long and its toes are webbed but do not have expanded pads. It is smooth-skinned, and dark grayish brown in color, with a pair of wide paler lines that start on the snout and run down either side of the body.
Habits	Nocturnal and terrestrial.
Breeding	In temporary pools.
Diet	Small invertebrates, especially ants.
Habitat	Primary montane forests.
Distribution	Sri Lanka.
Status	Listed by the IUCN as Endangered because of a decline in the extent and quality of its fragmented and restricted habitat.
Similar species	None in the region.

This tiny frog has a very limited range in the highland forests of Sri Lanka, where conditions are cool and humid nearly all the time. Its natural history is poorly known, but it breeds in small bodies of temporary water and lives among leaf litter.

Clearance of the forest in the central highlands of Sri Lanka, notably for the planting of tea but also for other crops such as cardamom, has resulted in a reduction of habitat for this and other species. It has also resulted in a noticeable drying out of the land—

rainfall has decreased in recent years, and some amphibians and reptiles that used to be common have become scarce. At the same time, scientists have been reevaluating the frog fauna of Sri Lanka as a whole, and in recent years the number of species has risen by more than 100 new species. These were overlooked frogs, mostly from rain forests, and their discovery has increased the pressure from conservationists to protect what little remains of the original forests.

The Sri Lankan Rice Paddy Frog, Nuwara Eliya, Sri Lanka.

Red-banded Rubber Frog

Common names	Red-banded Rubber Frog, Banded Rubber Frog
Scientific name	*Phrynomantis bifasciatus*
Family	Microhylidae
Size	2.09–2.56 in (53–65 mm).
Key features	Smooth-skinned with a shiny, rubbery texture. The head is flattened and the body widest just in front of the hind legs. The fingers and toes have small pads but little or no webbing. Spectacularly colored, with a pair of pink stripes running down either side of an otherwise jet black back. The limbs have round pink spots.
Habits	Nocturnal and mainly terrestrial.
Breeding	In temporary pools.
Diet	Small invertebrates, mostly ants and termites.
Habitat	Moist grasslands.
Distribution	East and southern Africa.
Status	Common but secretive.
Similar species	The Spotted Rubber Frog (*P. affinis*) and the Marbled Rubber Frog (*P. annectans*). Although the colors of these species are similar to those of the Banded Rubber Frog, the patterns are different, as their names suggest. Two other species occur farther north.

This frog's bright colors warn that its skin contains toxins. It inflates its body to make itself appear bigger if threatened. It also tucks in its head and raises itself on all four legs, while arching its body. The skin toxins contain irritants that can cause painful swelling if the frog is handled by a person with scratches on his or her skin. This can be followed by difficulty in breathing, headache, and nausea. Despite their toxicity, a type of heron, the hammerkop, eats these frogs.

The Red-banded Rubber Frog breeds in shallow temporary pools, including those formed in the footprints of large animals, such as elephants. They are explosive breeders in response to summer rains. The female lays 300 to 1,500 eggs, and the tadpoles are small and almost transparent, with pigment only along the midline. Their tail is thin and whiplike. The tadpoles often shoal together and remain motionless just below the surface of the water, filtering small single-celled algae and diatoms from the water. They take up to three months to complete their development.

⊕ *Red-banded Rubber Frog, South Africa.*

Rot-hole Tree Frog

Common names	Rot-hole Tree Frog, Boulenger's Giant Tree Frog
Scientific name	*Platypelis grandis*
Family	Microhylidae
Size	1.69–3.46 in (43–88 mm).
Key features	A large tree frog with prominent eyes, a warty back, and very conspicuous triangular pads on the tips of its toes. Dark brown with indistinct lighter markings and a darker bar across the head, between the eyes.
Habits	Nocturnal and arboreal.
Breeding	In water-filled tree holes.
Diet	Invertebrates, mostly ants.
Habitat	Mature forests.
Distribution	Eastern Madagascar.
Status	Rarely seen.
Similar species	This is the largest of the *Platypelis* species, and its warty back combined with large toe pads separate it from frogs in other genera.

This very large tree frog is restricted to mature forests where large trees grow because it depends on holes in their trunks for breeding. Males call from water-filled holes, and females climb the tree to join them, in much the same manner as the Asian tree hole frogs *(Metaphrynella)*.

Males protect their hole from other males by inflating their body to block the entrance, by making a grumbling call, or by physically fighting off the intruder. After the female has laid her 100 or so eggs she leaves the hole, but the male remains with them and later with the tadpoles. The eggs are laid individually and they float on the surface of the pool. The tadpoles do not feed (in common with those of several other microhylid frogs) and they take about four to five weeks to complete their development. In experiments with eggs laid in captivity, the tadpoles died if the male was removed, although it is not known how his presence benefits them.

Despite their large size these frogs appear to feed mainly on ants. If they are handled roughly they produce a white, sticky substance from glands in their skin and, in this way, they resemble the Milky Tree Frog *(Phrynohyas venulosa)* from South America.

⊖ *Looking just like a blotch of lichen, this Rot-hole Tree Frog was spotted resting on a tree in a Madagascan rain forest.*

Tiny Digging Frog

Common name	Tiny Digging Frog
Scientific name	*Plethodontohyla minuta*
Family	Microhylidae
Size	To 0.87 in (22 mm).
Key features	A very small frog with a plump body, powerful hind legs, and fingers and toes that lack both webbing and expanded toe pads. The skin of its back is slightly granular. It is light brown or tan, with darker squiggles in an irregular pattern.
Habits	Nocturnal and arboreal.
Breeding	Unknown; related species lay their eggs in leaf litter.
Diet	Invertebrates, mostly ants.
Habitat	Mature forests.
Distribution	Northeastern Madagascar.
Status	Rarely seen.
Similar species	Other *Plethodontohyla* species.

Sometimes seen in the late afternoon, this tiny frog hops around in leaf litter mainly at night. Much of its life cycle is unknown, but males call from the forest floor at night, especially during heavy rain. Their call is a short whistling note repeated several times quickly, then a pause before another series of notes. Although the eggs and tadpoles of this frog are

unknown, those of a similar species, *Plethodontohyla tuberata*, are laid in a jelly mass in small depressions in leaf litter. The jelly liquefies, and the tadpoles develop in the resulting fluid but do not feed.

The genus *Plethodontohyla* contains at least 11 small or very small leaf-litter frogs from the humid forests on the eastern side of Madagascar. Two species breed in tree holes, and the others are thought to breed on the forest floor. The generic name comes from Greek: *plethodont* means "full of teeth," and "*hyla*" is a mythical creature of the forest.

⬅ *The Tiny Digging Frog, seen here on Nosy Mangabe, Madagascar, measures less than 1 inch (2.54 cm) from snout to vent.*

Rainbow Burrowing Frog

Common name	Rainbow Burrowing Frog
Scientific name	*Scaphiophryne gottlebei*
Family	Microhylidae
Size	1.5 in (38 mm).
Key features	A plump frog with distinctive coloration. Its back is mostly red or pink with thick black borders. Within and around the red areas are patches of lime green, also bordered by black. The rest of the body and the limbs are white with black markings. Its hind feet are webbed and its fingers, but not its toes, end in large pads.
Habits	Nocturnal; burrowing and climbing.
Breeding	In pools.
Diet	Invertebrates, mostly ants.
Habitat	Canyons in rocky places.
Distribution	South-central Madagascar.
Status	Perhaps abundant, but limited to a single small area of less than 40 sq. mi (100 sq. km) and therefore classified by the IUCN as Critically Endangered.
Similar species	None.

This extremely interesting frog was described only in 1992. It comes from a single locality in one of the more remote parts of Madagascar, the Valley des Singes in the Isalo National Park, a region of strange weathered limestone formations. The frogs live in cool, deep, narrow gorges where the sun rarely penetrates, so avoiding the intense dry heat that central Madagascar experiences. It can also burrow down into the sandy soil to escape very dry weather.

Not only is it a specialized burrowing species, it is also a good climber. The pads on its front feet help it climb up the sheer canyon walls, and it has been found many feet above the ground at night. It can access small holes and crevices in the rock face, where it can hide protected from the heat and from the flash floods that rush through the canyons following heavy rain.

It breeds in the rock pools that are left behind after the floods have receded. Details of the eggs in this species are lacking, but the tadpoles are known to be unique. They have anatomical peculiarities that separate them from any other known species. They also have the unusual habit of resting during the day with their head buried in the sandy substrate and their body sticking out at an angle of about 45 degrees,

while feeding on particles trapped in the sand. At night they swim freely in the water.

Shortly after its discovery, the Rainbow Burrowing Frog was collected in large numbers for the pet trade, and there were concerns for its future. For this reason it was given total protection. But its secretive lifestyle and

⊕ *The Rainbow Burrowing Frog burrows to escape the searing heat and dry winds of south–central Madagascar.*

seasonal abundance now lead scientists to believe that collecting is probably not as great a threat to its survival as the mining activities that take place in the area.

Marbled Burrowing Frog

Common name	Marbled Burrowing Frog
Scientific name	*Scaphiophryne marmorata*
Family	Microhylidae
Size	1.38–1.97 in (35–50 mm).
Key features	A very rotund species with a globular body and small, pointed head. Its eyes are fairly small but prominent and its back is covered with large and small warts. Its back is olive green with irregular patches of light green and brown.
Habits	Nocturnal; burrowing.
Breeding	In quiet forest pools.
Diet	Invertebrates, mostly ants.
Habitat	Primary forests.
Distribution	Eastern Madagascar.
Status	Locally common, but secretive. Listed by the IUCN as Vulnerable because of a decline in the extent and quality of its fragmented habitat.
Similar species	The combination of toe pads on the front feet and green coloration separates this species from other Madagascan frogs.

This is a burrowing frog with bony flanges on its hind feet (*Scaphiophryne* means "spade toad"), with which it burrows backward into loose soil or leaf litter. Like the Rainbow Frog *(S. gottlebei),* it has adhesive pads on the toes of its front feet and presumably climbs into trees, although this has not been confirmed. The Marbled Burrowing Frog is a forest species that is hardly ever seen outside the breeding season, which takes place when heavy rains inundate the forests in which it lives. Males call day and night in small temporary forest pools.

This "species" is now thought to consist of three very similar species: *S. marmorata, S. spinosa,* and *S. boribory* (the last described as recently as 2003).

They are all similar in coloration but differ from each other in the extent of the tubercles on their back— *S. spinosa* having pointed, thorny warts, *S. boribory* having almost no warts at all, and *S. marmorata* being intermediate. This goes to show that the island of Madagascar is still not well known from a herpetological perspective, and many more species are undoubtedly waiting to be discovered.

⊕ *Marbled Burrowing Frog, central Madagascar.*

Marbled Balloon Frog

Common name	Marbled Balloon Frog
Scientific name	*Uperodon systoma*
Family	Microhylidae
Size	2 in (51 mm).
Key features	A rotund, bloated frog with a short head and a prominent fold of skin between its eyes. Its front limbs are relatively long, and its hind limbs are short. Its back is brown with irregular lighter brown or tan markings.
Habits	Nocturnal; burrowing.
Breeding	In shallow water.
Diet	Invertebrates, mostly termites.
Habitat	Forests and grasslands.
Distribution	Pakistan, Bangladesh, India, and Sri Lanka.
Status	Probably common in places but rarely seen.
Similar species	None in the region.

This species can inflate its lungs to an enormous capacity, puffing itself up like a balloon. It is a specialized burrower and uses the bony ridges on its back feet to dig down backward into soft soil, with its head and eyes disappearing last. There are records of one frog that remained underground for 13 months without surfacing or, presumably, feeding. This frog was excavated from more than 3 feet (0.9 m) below the surface. At other times the Marbled Balloon Frogs retreat into termite nests, where they have a ready supply of food.

The monsoon rains instigate the frog's breeding season, and males call from the sides of torrents or rice paddy fields. The male's vocal sac is huge, almost as large as the rest of its body, and the call is said to be like that of a bleating goat. The Marbled Balloon Frog is a poor swimmer and floats at the surface. Like those of many other microhylids, the eggs float at the surface of still water, in a single layer. The filter-feeding tadpoles are black and have a long tail.

⊖ *Marbled Balloon Frog, Gampola, Sri Lanka.*

Other Microhylids

⤒ *The Green Burrowing Frog* (Scaphiophryne madagascariensis) *is restricted to the montane forests and savanna regions of central Madagascar.*

⤳ *With a wide distribution in Africa from Senegal to the Democratic Republic of the Congo, the Small-eyed Rubber Frog* (Phrynomantis microps) *inhabits both open grassy and wooded savanna.*

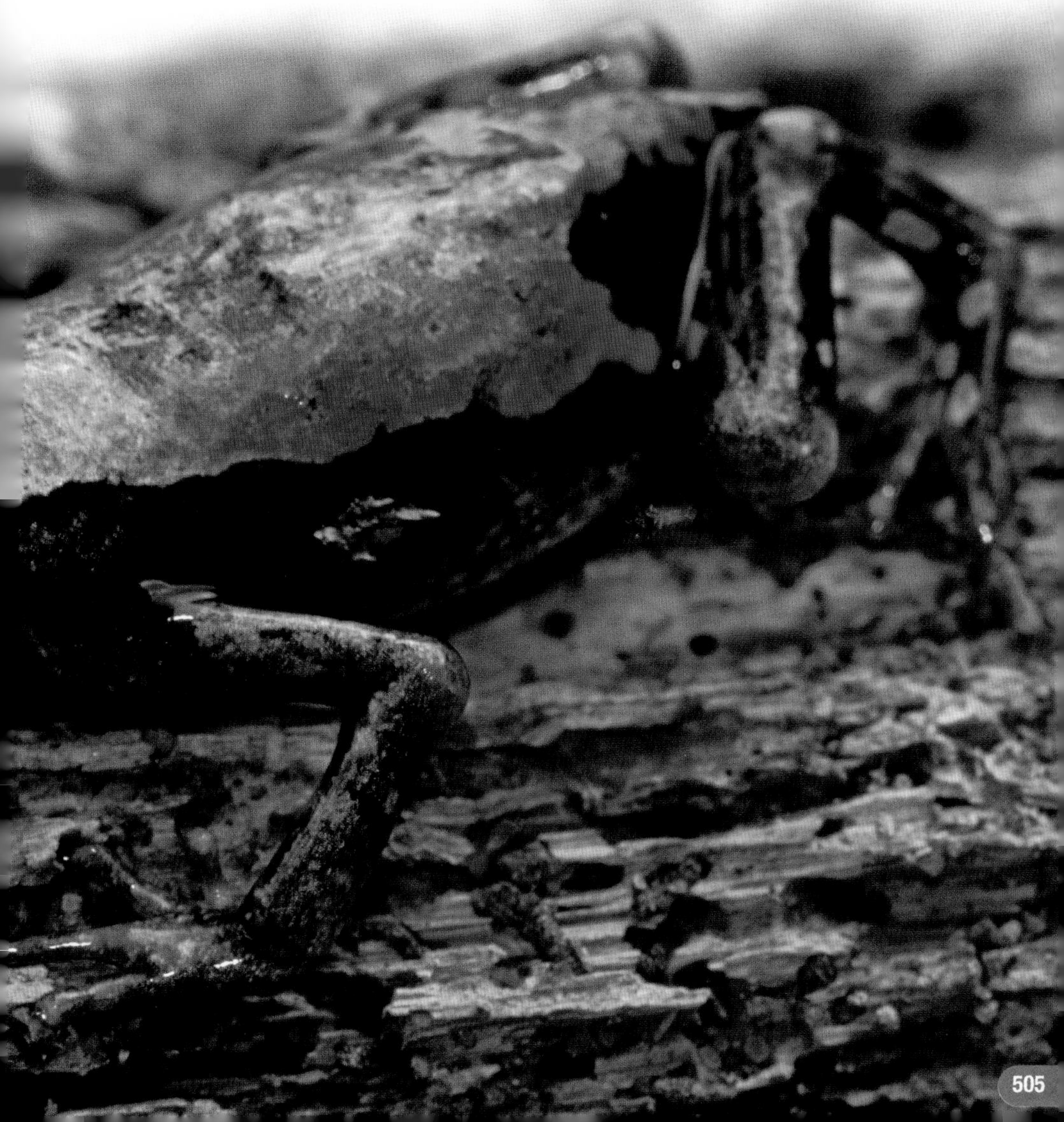

Other Microhylids

⤓ *The White-spotted Humming Frog* (Chiasmocleis albopunctata) *comes from Brazil, Paraguay, and Bolivia and lives and breeds in temporary waterbodies and flooded areas.*

⊕ *This is* Barygenys flavigularis, *a microhylid from the montane rain forests of New Guinea.*

Other Microhylids

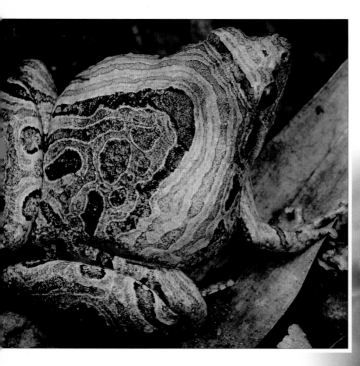

⊙ *Known from Argentina, Paraguay, Brazil, and Bolivia, Mueller's Narrow-mouthed Frog* (Dermatonotus muelleri) *breeds explosively in temporary pools.*

⊙ *The Beautiful Pygmy Frog* (Microhyla pulchra) *from China, Thailand, Laos, Cambodia, and Vietnam is richly patterned in cryptic colors. It lives on the edges of forests, in grasslands, and cultivated areas such as fields and plantations.*

Seychelles Frogs

Common names	Gardiner's Frog, Palm Frog, Seychelles Frog, and Thomasett's Rock Frog
Scientific names	*Sooglossus gardineri, S. pipilodryas, S. sechellensis,* and *Nesomantis thomasetti*
Family	Sooglossidae
Size	0.43–1.57 in (11–40 mm).
Key features	Small, nondescript frogs. They have no webbing between any of their fingers or toes but have small, pointed toe pads. They have horizontal pupils and no external eardrums. They are mostly brown on the back, with darker flanks or irregular darker markings, making them difficult to see when resting among dead leaves on the forest floor.
Habits	Terrestrial. Apparently active by day and night.
Breeding	Direct development where known.
Diet	Small invertebrates.
Habitat	Moist forests, especially along ridges and among rocky outcrops where leaf litter accumulates.
Distribution	Mahé and Silhouette Islands, Seychelles.
Status	Gardiner's Frog is the most common and widespread species; the others are very uncommon and are listed as Vulnerable by the IUCN.
Similar species	There are no other small brown frogs on the Seychelles islands.

The larger islands of Mahé and Silhouette comprise the total extent of the distribution for Gardiner's Frog *(Sooglossus gardineri)*, Seychelles Frog *(S. sechellensis)*, and Thomasett's Rock Frog *(Nesomantis thomasetti)*, while the recently described Palm Frog, *(S. pipilodryas)* occurs only on Silhouette. These four species make up the entire family Sooglossidae, which is therefore endemic to the islands. One other native frog, *Tachycnemis seychellensis,* belongs to the family Hyperoliidae.

Male Gardiner's Frogs call from hidden sites on the forest floor, from leaf litter, and from the hollow stems of dead tree ferns. They call at night and during the day throughout the year, but more intensively during and immediately after rain. The call is a single high-pitched chirp that lasts only 0.14 seconds. Females are attracted, and amplexus is inguinal, with the male holding the female in front of her hind legs. She lays her eggs under leaves and stays with them for three to four weeks until they hatch directly into tiny frogs, each about the size of a grain of rice.

Male Seychelles Frogs also call from hidden sites, including rock crevices, but their calls are longer and more complex, lasting four times as long as that of Gardiner's Frog. Amplexus is also inguinal in the Seychelles Frogs, and the female stays with the eggs until they hatch into tadpoles, which takes about two to three weeks. The tadpoles then climb onto the female's back where they complete their development. (Some authorities report that it is the male that carries the tadpoles.)

Thomasett's Rock Frog is the largest species and also the rarest, restricted to moist forests at high altitude, where it calls from the highest peaks. This species sometimes calls from cliff faces, rock piles, or mossy tree trunks. Its subsequent courtship and breeding habitats are not known, but its eggs are large, suggesting that they develop directly.

⊕ Sooglossus gardineri *is found in high mountains on the Seychelles islands. It is one of the smaller endemic frogs, reaching about 0.6 inches (15 mm) in length.*

Glossary

Words in SMALL CAPITALS refer to other entries in the glossary.

Adaptation A characteristic shape, behavior, or physiological process that equips an organism (or group of related organisms) for its way of life and habitat.

Advanced Relatively recently evolved (opposite of PRIMITIVE).

Albino An animal that has no color pigment in its body and has red eyes.

Amplexus The position adopted during mating in most frogs and toads, in which the male clasps the female with one or both pairs of limbs. (See AXILLARY AMPLEXUS and INGUINAL AMPLEXUS.)

Anterior The front part or head and shoulders of an animal.

Aposematic coloration Bright coloration serving to warn a potential predator that an animal is distasteful or poisonous.

Aquatic Strictly living all the time in or near fresh water.

Arboreal Living in trees or shrubs.

Axillary amplexus Mating position in frogs, in which the male grasps the female behind her front limbs. (See INGUINAL AMPLEXUS.)

Barbel A small, elongated "feeler," or sensory process, on the head, usually of aquatic animals, e.g., some pipid frogs.

Bromeliad Member of a family of plants restricted to the New World. Many live attached to trees, including "urn plants" in which ARBOREAL frogs sometimes breed.

Call The sound made by male frogs or toads during the breeding season to attract a mate.

Cerrado The vast SAVANNA tropical grassland of Brazil.

Chromatophore A specialized cell containing pigment, usually located in the outer layers of the skin.

CITES An international conservation organization: Convention on International Trade in Endangered Species. (See IUCN.)

Class A taxonomic category ranking below PHYLUM, containing a number of ORDERS.

Cloaca Common chamber into which the urinary, digestive, and reproductive systems discharge their contents and which opens to the exterior.

Continuous breeder An animal that may breed at any time of year.

Critically Endangered A SPECIES that faces an extremely high risk of extinction in the immediate future.

Cryptic Having the ability to remain hidden, usually by means of camouflage, e.g., cryptic coloration.

Cutaneous respiration Breathing that takes place across the skin's surface, which is especially important in amphibians.

Dimorphism The existence of two distinct forms within a SPECIES, which is then said to be dimorphic. In species in which there are more than two forms, they are polymorphic. (See SEXUAL DIMORPHISM.)

Direct development Transition from egg to adult form without passing through a free-living larval stage.

Dorsal Relating to the back or upper surface of the body or one of its parts.

Endangered A SPECIES that is facing a very high risk of extinction in the near future.

Endemic SPECIES, GENERA, or FAMILIES that are restricted to a particular geographical region.

Epiphyte Plant growing on another plant but not a parasite. Includes many orchids and BROMELIADS and some mosses and ferns.

Estivation A state of inactivity during prolonged periods of drought or high temperature. During estivation the animal often buries itself in soil or mud. (See HIBERNATION.)

Explosive breeder A SPECIES in which the breeding season is very short, resulting in large numbers of animals mating at the same time.

External fertilization Fusing of eggs and sperm outside the female's body.

Extinct Term used when there is no reasonable doubt that the last individual of a SPECIES has died.

Family Taxonomic category ranking below ORDER, containing GENERA that are more closely related to one another than any other grouping of genera.

Fauna The animal life of a locality or region.

Fertilization Union of an egg and a sperm.

Genus (pl. genera) Taxonomic category ranking below FAMILY; a group of SPECIES more closely related to one another than to any other group of species.

Gill Respiratory structure in TADPOLES through which gas exchange takes place.

Gravid Carrying eggs or young.

Gular pouch Area of expandable skin in the throat region.

Hibernation A period of inactivity, often spent underground, to avoid extremes of cold. (See ESTIVATION.)

Inguinal Pertaining to the groin.

Inguinal amplexus A mating position in which a male frog clasps a female around the lower abdomen. (See AXILLARY AMPLEXUS.)

Introduced A SPECIES brought from lands where it occurs naturally to areas where it has not previously occurred.

Invertebrate Any animal that lacks a backbone.

IUCN International Union for the Conservation of Nature, responsible for assigning animals and plants to internationally agreed categories of rarity. (See CRITICALLY ENDANGERED, ENDANGERED, EXTINCT, LOWER RISK, VULNERABLE.)

Juvenile Young animal, not sexually mature.

Larva (pl. larvae) Early stage in the development of an amphibian after hatching from the egg.

Life cycle Complete life history of an animal from one stage to the recurrence of that stage, e.g., egg to egg.

Lifestyle General mode of life of an animal, e.g., nocturnal predator, aquatic herbivore, parasite.

Live-bearing Giving birth to young that have developed beyond the egg stage.

Lower Risk The status of a SPECIES that has been evaluated and does not satisfy the criteria for CRITICALLY ENDANGERED, ENDANGERED, or VULNERABLE.

Metamorphosis Transformation of an animal from one stage of its life history to another, e.g., from larva to adult.

Milt Sperm-containing fluid produced by a male frog during egg-laying to fertilize the eggs.

Mimic An animal that resembles an animal belonging to another SPECIES, usually a distasteful or poisonous one, or some inedible object.

Montane Pertaining to mountains or SPECIES that live in mountains.

Morph Form or phase of an animal.

Morphological Relating to the form and structure of a frog.

Neotropics The tropical part of the New World, including northern South America, Central America, part of Mexico, and the West Indies.

Nocturnal Active at night.

Nuptial pad An area of dark rough skin that develops in male amphibians on the hands, arms, or chest of some SPECIES prior to the breeding season. Its purpose is to allow the male to grip the female in AMPLEXUS.

Order Taxonomic category ranking below CLASS and above FAMILY.

Overwinter Survive the winter.

Ovum (pl. ova) Female germ cell or gamete; an egg cell or egg.

Parotid glands Pair of large glands on the shoulder, neck, or behind the eye in some toads.

Pigment A substance that gives color to part or all of a frog's body.

Primitive Evolved in more distant past (opposite of ADVANCED).

Satellite male A male frog that does not CALL but sits near a calling male and intercepts females attracted to it.

Savanna Open grasslands with scattered trees and bushes, usually in warm areas.

Semiaquatic Spending part of life in water.

Sexual dimorphism The existence of marked morphological differences between males and females.

Species Taxonomic category ranking below GENUS; a group of organisms with common attributes capable of interbreeding and producing healthy fertile offspring.

Subspecies A locally distinct group of animals that differ slightly from the normal appearance of the SPECIES; often called a race.

Substrate The solid material on which an organism lives, e.g., sand, mud, etc.

Tadpole Larval stage of a frog or toad.

Taxonomy The science of classification: the arrangement of animals and plants into groups based on their natural relationships.

Terrestrial Living on land.

Territorial Defending an area so as to exclude other members of the same SPECIES.

Territory An area that one or more animals defends against other members of the same SPECIES.

Toad Any stout-bodied, warty-skinned frog, especially one living away from water. The term has no taxonomic basis, although members of the FAMILY Bufonidae are often called toads.

Tympanum (pl. tympana) Eardrum.

Vent External opening of the CLOACA.

Ventral Describing the lower surface of the body or one of its parts.

Vulnerable A SPECIES that is facing a high risk of extinction in the medium-term future.

Web (or webbing) Folds of skin present between the toes of frogs and toads.

Xeric Adapted to life in an extremely dry habitat.

Yolk sac A large sac containing stored nutrients, present in the embryos of amphibians.

Further References

General

Arnold, E. N., *A Field Guide to the Reptiles and Amphibians of Britain and Europe*, Harper Collins, London, 2002.

Behler, J. L., and F. W. King, *The Audubon Society Field Guide to North American Reptiles and Amphibians*, Alfred A. Knopf, New York, 1979.

Berry, P. Y., *The Amphibian Fauna of Peninsular Malaysia*, Tropical Press, Kuala Lumpur, 1975.

Cei, J. M., *Amphibians of Argentina*, Monitore Zoologica Italiano (Italian Journal of Zoology), Monografia number 2, Florence, 1980.

Channing, A., *Amphibians of Central and Southern Africa*, Comstock Publishing Associates, Ithaca, NY, and London, 2001.

Cogger, H. G., *Reptiles and Amphibians of Australia*, 6th edn., Reed New Holland, Sydney, 2000.

Duellman, W., *The Hylid Frogs of Middle America*, Society for the Study of Amphibians and Reptiles, Ithaca, NY, 2001.

Duellman, W. E., and L. Trueb, *Biology of Amphibians*, Johns Hopkins University Press, Baltimore, MA, 1994.

Glaw, F., and M. Vences, *A Field Guide to the Reptiles and Amphibians of Madagascar*, 2nd edn., published by the authors, Bonn, 1994.

Grismer, L. L., *Amphibians and Reptiles of Baja California*, University of California Press, Berkeley, CA, 2002.

Halliday, T., and C. Adler (eds.), *The New Encyclopedia of Reptiles and Amphibians*, Firefly Books, New York and Toronto/Oxford University Press, Oxford, 2002.

Inger, R. F., and R. B. Stuebing, *A Field Guide to the Frogs of Borneo*, 2nd edn., Natural History Publications, Kota Kinabalu, 2005.

Koestler, A. *The Case of the Midwife Toad*, Random House, New York, 1971.

Mattison, C., *Frogs and Toads of the World*, Blandford Press, London, 1998.

McCranie, J. R., and L. D. Wilson, *The Amphibians of Honduras*, Society for the Study of Amphibians and Reptiles, Ithaca, NY, 2002.

Murphy, J. B., Adler, K., and J. T. Collins (eds.), *Captive Management and Conservation of Reptiles and Amphibians*, Society for the Study of Amphibians and Reptiles, Ithaca, NY, 1994.

Parsons, H., *The Nature of Frogs*, Greystone Books, Vancouver, Toronto, and New York, 2000.

Passmore, N. I., and V. C. Carruthers, *South African Frogs*, Southern Book Publishers and University of Witwatersrand Press, Johannesburg, 1995.

Rödel, M-O., *Herpetofauna of West Africa*, Vol. 1, "Amphibians of the West African Savanna," Edition Chimaira, Frankfurt am Main, 2000. (Contains a CD, Frog Voices of the West African Savanna by T. Ulmar Graf.)

Savage, J. M., *Amphibians and Reptiles of Costa Rica*, University of Chicago Press, Chicago, 2002.

Schiotz, A., *Treefrogs of Africa*, Edition Chimaira, Frankfurt am Mein, 1999.

Schleich, H. H., Kästle, W., and K. Kabisch, *Amphibians and Reptiles of North Africa*, Koeltz Scientific Books, Königstein, 1996.

Stebbins, R. C., and N W. Cohen, *A Natural History of Amphibians*, Princeton University Press, Princeton, NJ, 1995.

Tyler, M., *Australian Frogs: A Natural History*, Cornell University Press, Ithaca, NY, and London, 1994.

Zug, G. R., Vitt, L. J., and J. P. Caldwell, *Herpetology: An Introductory Biology of Reptiles and Amphibians*, 2nd edn., Academic Press, San Diego, 2001.

Web Sites

Frost, Darrel R. 2004. Amphibian Species of the World: an Online Reference. Version 3.0 (22 August, 2004). Electronic Database accessible at:
http://research.amnh.org/herpetology/amphibia/index.php American Museum of Natural History, New York.

Myers, P. 2001. "Vertebrata" (Online), Animal Diversity. Accessible at:
http://animaldiversity.ummz.umich.edu/site/accounts/information/Amphibia.html

http://elib.cs.berkeley.edu/aw/index.html
AmphibiaWeb, a site inspired by global amphibian declines, is an online system that allows free access to information on amphibian biology and conservation. Lists all known species of amphibians and gives species accounts, photographs, and distribution maps to some. New material is added constantly.

http://frogs.org.au/corroboree/
A Web site dedicated to the conservation of the Australian Corroboree Frog, which is one of Australia's most endangered species.

http://www.globalamphibians.org/index.html
The Global Amphibian Assessment (GAA) is the first ever comprehensive assessment of the conservation status of the world's known species of frogs, toads, salamanders, and caecilians. This Web site presents results of the assessments, including IUCN Red List threat category,

range map, ecology information, and other
data for every amphibian species.

http://www.herplit.com/

A listing of herpetological literature, including
older material.

http://www.kingsnake.com

Many pages about amphibians and reptiles, especially
their care in captivity, and links to other organizations.

http://www.livingunderworld.org/

A Web site giving information on a wide range of
amphibians, including their care in captivity.

http://www.open.ac.uk/daptf/index.htm

A Web site that records and documents information
concerning endangered frogs and toads and the
possible causes of their decline.

http://www.pipidae.net/

A Web site dedicated to the biology and the captive care
and breeding of pipid frogs (clawed frogs, Surinam toads,
and dwarf aquatic frogs). German and English versions.

http://www.redlist.org

IUCN Red List gives details of all threatened animals,
including amphibians.

http://research.amnh.org/herpetology/amphibia/index.html

"Amphibian Species of the World." A catalog of all
amphibian species with synonyms and additional
information, accessed with a good search engine.

http://www.si.edu/resource/faq/nmnh/zoology.htm#vz

General information about amphibians and reptiles
and links to many educational sites.

http://tolweb.org/tree?group=Living_Amphibians&contgroup=Terrestrial_Vertebrates

A collaborative Internet project produced by biologists
from around the world, containing information about
the diversity of organisms, their history, and characteristics.
All vertebrates are covered. The link given takes you
straight to amphibians.

Index

Picture Credits